RENÉ GIRARD, UNLIKELY APOLOGIST

RENÉ GIRARD, UNLIKELY APOLOGIST

Mimetic Theory and Fundamental Theology

GRANT KAPLAN

University of Notre Dame Press

Notre Dame, Indiana

University of Notre Dame Press
Notre Dame, Indiana 46556
undpress.nd.edu
Copyright © 2016 by the University of Notre Dame

Manufactured in the United States of America

Library of Congress Cataloging-in-Publication Data
Names: Kaplan, Grant, author.
Title: René Girard, unlikely apologist : mimetic theory
and fundamental theology / Grant Kaplan.
Description: Notre Dame : University of Notre Dame Press,
2016. | Includes bibliographical references and index.
Identifiers: LCCN 2016028705 (print) | LCCN 2016032538 (ebook) |
ISBN 9780268100858 (hardcover : alk. paper) |
ISBN 0268100853 (hardcover : alk. paper) | ISBN 9780268100872 (pdf) |
ISBN 9780268100889 (epub)
Subjects: LCSH: Girard, René, 1923–2015. | Desire (Philosophy) |
Desire—Religious aspects—Christianity. | Apologetics. |
Philosophical theology. | Christianity—Philosophy.
Classification: LCC B2430.G494 K37 2016 (print) |
LCC B2430.G494 (ebook) | DDC 194—dc23
LC record available at https://lccn.loc.gov/2016028705

∞ This paper meets the requirements of ANSI/NISO Z39.48-1992
(Permanence of Paper).

This book is dedicated to Emily and to the fruits of our love,

Maximilian and Augustine

CONTENTS

ACKNOWLEDGMENTS

My impressionistic understanding of mimetic theory got its first real boost when the late Stephen J. Duffy, a colleague's colleague, encouraged me to include René Girard and Sebastian Moore in a course syllabus on original sin. In this period of gestation, I was browsing the book tables at a conference and noticed that Moore had endorsed James Alison's *On Being Liked*. This endorsement was enough to persuade me to purchase Alison's book. Those three authors—Girard, Moore, and Alison—were writing about what I wanted to think more about, questions at the heart of the Christian experience.

In the fall of 2007, I began an appointment at Saint Louis University. There I had the good fortune of gaining the friendship of Brian Robinette, who helped me understand mimetic theory more deeply, both through his written work and through our many conversations. His book *Grammars of Resurrection* and the positive reception it received convinced me of the viability of the project that has now come to fruition.

Around that time I had contacted Girard, and he agreed to meet with me in Palo Alto, California. We had lunch together and talked for most of an afternoon at his home. He also consented to an interview conducted a few months later. Our conversations reinforced my hunch that Girard was a Christian apologist, and with that the book project came into focus.

I have been giving papers on mimetic theory since 2009. I wish to thank the following venues for allowing me to articulate earlier parts of this project: the Mater Dei Institute, the Lonergan Workshop, the Saint Louis Society of Catholic Theologians, the Catholic Studies Program at Loyola University, Maryland, the Catholic Theological Society of America, the College Theology Society, and the Colloquium on Violence & Religion

(COV&R). In less formal settings, the Campion Society of Saint Louis University and Bethel Lutheran Church in University City gave me forums for talking about how mimetic theory goes right to the heart of Christianity's most central claims. Of particular note was the 2013 COV&R meeting, where Martha Reineke proposed that James Alison respond to the papers by John Edwards and me. This generous arrangement and James's insightful response encouraged me to push through to the end.

Various academic outfits have also supported me. I thank SLU's Department of Theological Studies and the university's Mellon Fund for travel funding and also for giving me a summer stipend in 2008. I am also thankful to the Peter Thiel Foundation for making me an Imitatio Fellow in 2012, and for fostering collaboration between scholars.

Kevin Vander Schel, Chelsea King, Ryan Duns, and Jordan Wood gave insightful comments on the entire manuscript. I also benefited greatly from the extensive comments and critique offered by the blind reviewers. All of these people made the work a much better one.

I have benefited greatly from an informal writing group within my department. James Voiss, Mary Dunn, Randy Rosenberg, and Bill O'Brien offered helpful and generous feedback on some very rough drafts. In particular, Randy Rosenberg merits many thanks for helping me think through the fundamental and systematic points of contact between mimetic theory and theology. His *Concrete Subjectivity and the Human Desire to See God*, in print with the University of Toronto Press, will be of major import for mimetic theory.

I would also like to thank the many colleagues in the Department of Theological Studies who have encouraged me during the writing of this book. I am particularly thankful for the support of my department chair, Peter Martens. Other members of the SLU community, especially Jennifer Rust, Eleonore Stump, and Paul Lynch, have provided lively and memorable conversation in and outside the halls of our common humanities building. And I do not know how the project would have come to fruition without Benjamin de Foy, the incarnation of the scientist one dreams of having as a colleague when imagining life at a Catholic university.

Along the way I have been equipped with excellent research assistants. They have also taught me a thing or two about being a scholar and a writer. They include Jonathan King, Erick Moser, Robert Munshaw, Yvonne Angieri, James Lee, and Joshua Schendel. Thanks are also due to the participants in the Fall 2014 seminar on mimetic theory, in particular for their many good questions and high-level discussions. I am also grateful for the work that Friederike Ockert has done in helping me through the final stages of indexing the book.

Through COV&R and Imitatio I have benefited from many conversations with both emerging and established scholars. In particular, I owe thanks to Jeremiah Alberg, Ann Astell, Scott Cowdell, John Edwards, Stephen Gardner, Joel Hodge, Mathias Moosbrugger, Wolfgang Palaver, Nikolas Wandinger, and James Williams. I am especially indebted to James Alison and Andrew McKenna. I began pestering James about his work a decade ago. Any prudent person would have run in the opposite direction. Lucky me. James's generosity exceeds his prudence. Andrew, likewise, has treated me like a family member, as he has done for so many other Girardians.

In the world of academic theology one is fortunate to find first-rate theologians committed to a common ecclesial mission, even while pursuing vastly different projects. I continue to be sustained by friendships with Beth Beshear Toft, John Betz, Ulrich Lehner, Anna Bonta Moreland, Trent Pomplun, Christopher Ruddy, and Jeremy Wilkins. I hope that my contribution might enrich them as much as their writings and words of wisdom enrich me.

The time between the book's infancy and completion has been marked by numerous births, deaths, and transformations. My partner, Emily, has patiently endured, and even enthusiastically promoted, a project that began around the time we fell in love. Her employment as a teacher at a single-sex school, additionally, has provided a steady stream of mimetic anecdotes. The gestation period of this book encompasses not only our wedding but also the birth of our two sons: Maximilian Rafter and Augustine Otto. Two deaths must be mentioned. John Jones, who served as the acquisitions editor at Crossroad/Herder, was the salesperson when I bought my first book by James Alison. The purchase sparked a conversation that led to a powerful friendship. It is a rarity for an editor (or anyone) to listen in the way that John listened to me. Being a friend of John's meant being welcomed into a listening presence that derived from a profound spirituality. He believed in me as a theologian and encouraged me in my work. One fruit of that belief was his decision to include my dissertation in an informal "series" devoted to young theologians at Crossroad/Herder. I think he loved me, and I know that I miss him.

René Girard passed away when the book was on the way to publication. In 2008 he gave me a copy of *Achever Clausewitz*, and his inscription gave blessing to my project. I dearly wish I could have shown it to him.

An earlier version of chapter 6 appeared as "Widening the Dialectic: Secularity and Christianity in Conversation," in *New Voices in Catholic Theology*, ed. Anna Bonta Moreland and Joseph Curran (New York: Crossroad/Herder, 2012), 23–51. I thank Crossroad Publishing for permission to reproduce an amended version of the earlier chapter.

INTRODUCTION

In the 1960s and 1970s, a French intellectual produced a series of books and articles that, if nothing else, presented an affront to the very notion of disciplinary division. Trained as a historian, this intellectual's first major book offered a theory of the novel. He then developed a grand hypothesis of cultural origins without doing any fieldwork or having any training in anthropology and ethnology. He continued writing literary criticism until 1978, when he co-authored a book about, among other things, Christianity and religious theory. The part on Christianity included commentary on numerous biblical verses, despite the author having no training in biblical studies or theology. One might be surprised that these books received much acclaim at all, but they did. But surely, by now, whatever reception the books might have been given, the fad inspired by this author would have passed.

The writer referenced here, of course, is the recently deceased René Girard (1923–2015), perhaps the most atypical member in the ultra-elite Académie française, into which Girard was inducted in 2005. From the 1970s to the late 2000s, Girard continued to write, reflect, dialogue, and reassess. To the surprise of many, some of his most fruitful dialogues have come with theologians and scholars of religion. This engagement has spurred Girard to review, reconsider, and even revise his opinions about Christianity, the Bible, and the nature of sacrifice. Yet nearly four decades after Raymund Schwager's epochal application of Girard's thought,

Must There Be Scapegoats? (1978), theologians continue to engage Girard and the mode of thinking labeled "mimetic theory." By any measure, both the number of "Girardians" attempting to apply mimetic theory to theological questions and those theologians willing to engage, incorporate, or caution against such applications seems to be growing. The years 2013–2014 witnessed two major monographs on Girard and theology and the first dissertation written on a Girardian theologian (James Alison).[1] The biannual *Bulletin of the Colloquium on Violence & Religion* (cited simply as *Bulletin* throughout the book), which is dedicated to mimetic theory, confirms this growth of Girardians and their work in the bibliography it publishes each issue.[2]

One can also measure Girard's relevance through the encounter of major theologians with his corpus. Leading contemporary theologians who have critically engaged mimetic theory in their written work include John Milbank, Sarah Coakley, Rowan Williams, Miroslav Volf, David Bentley Hart, Robert Doran, and Neil Ormerod. This engagement is not new. Already in 1980, Hans Urs von Balthasar, on any short list of the most important twentieth-century theologians, asserted the relevance of mimetic theory for theology, especially soteriology. In volume 3 of his *Theodramatik* (vol. 4 in the English translation), Balthasar declared, "Girard's is surely the most dramatic project to be undertaken today in the field of soteriology and in theology generally."[3] Balthasar went on to outline what he considered to be serious shortcomings, including Girard's failure, at least up to that point, to delineate an account of the Passion that properly understood the place of divine initiative in these salvific events. Girard (and Raymund Schwager), surmised Balthasar, "have brought us to the final elements of the drama of reconciliation, yet without offering a satisfying conclusion."[4] Balthasar reached this judgment by determining that "Girard's synthesis is a closed system, since it wants to be 'purely scientific,' and that Girard's project repeats the same mistaken dialectic as Karl Barth's."[5]

Balthasar's judgments affected, perhaps more than those of any other theologian, the reception of Girard in Christianity. For our sake, it is important to note, even if only anecdotally, how Balthasar's analysis has been received in recent literature. Through his archival research, Mathias Moosbrugger has given a more layered picture of Balthasar's relationship to Girard. Moosbrugger discovered a lively correspondence, from 1977 until Balthasar's death in 1988, between Balthasar and Schwager, two Swiss Jesuits.[6] Their correspondence reveals that, by December 1981, Balthasar had already been convinced, as he wrote to Schwager, that "Girard's insight" [*die Wahrheit Girards*] could be integrated into his project for a theology of the cross.[7]

It is not only Girardians who have made claims for the ongoing possibility of bringing Girard into conversation with Balthasar's dramatic theology. In 2012, Kevin Mongrain, the author of *The Systematic Thought of Hans Urs von Balthasar*,[8] published an article on Girard and Balthasar that revisits Balthasar's conclusions about Girard's project in light of Girard's post-1978 work.[9] Here Mongrain argues that, by utilizing a "Balthasarian lens," one can discern how "Girard is in the genus of Christian theologians who put the processes of spiritual transformation at the center of their soteriologies." Mongrain also shows overlap between Girard and Balthasar regarding their resistance of "false gnosis" and their seeking "to protect a distinctly biblical theology of spiritual transformation."[10]

Two key points can be drawn from Mongrain's essay. First and most obviously, Mongrain extends the conversation between Balthasar and Girard. Mongrain notes that Girard had read Balthasar's analysis of mimetic theory.[11] Mongrain also acknowledges Girard's post-1978 alterations, in partial response to Balthasar's analysis: "The revisions Girard has made to his thought seem to be attempts to answer it from within a shared [with Balthasar] anti-Satanic and apocalyptic framework. . . . Read through the Balthasarian lens, we can see this revision and others like them as Girard's attempt to make his thought more immune to Gnostic re-writing and, consequently, more capable of offering effective resistance to the speculative theologies of false gnosis."[12] Mongrain notes the evolution in Girard's thought on issues ranging from the understanding of sacrifice to the assessment of nonbiblical religions, and he offers this evolution as evidence for Girard's inclusion in the theological community. Second, Mongrain argues that Girard's work be read as theology: "Girard's theory is not theological in the narrow academic and highly specialized and atomized sense of *disputatio* in the scholastic tradition and *Wissenschaft* in the modern research university."[13] Mongrain points out that such a definition might disqualify any number of theologians, noting, "Girard writes theology like someone who respects the Biblical narrative in all its messy imprecision as the source of truth about God and history."[14]

Theologians, according to Mongrain, have not successfully integrated Girard into Christian theology. To make this happen, he implores "a new approach to reading Girard theologically." Rather than taking Girard at his word that he is not doing theology, Mongrain suggests: "It is best to treat [Girard] as a theologian from the start, and then map him into a pre-existing theological world of which he is more or less already a citizen."[15] Paired with Moosbrugger's work, Mongrain's argument demonstrates that efforts to relate mimetic theory to theology continue apace.

Although largely sympathetic to Mongrain's imperative both to read Girard through a certain hermeneutical lens and to interpret him as a certain type of spiritual-mystical theologian, I aim to do something slightly different from what Mongrain suggests. This book takes up the relation between Girard and theology in several keys. In one key, it understands mimetic theory as a heuristic. By heuristic I mean a model that allows theological narratives and positions to become more intelligible. In this key, mimetic theory, like phenomenology, different social theories, or, to go back several centuries, Aristotelian science or Neoplatonic metaphysics, helps theology to understand what it is and to explain what it means. Within the realm of apologetic or fundamental theology, mimetic theory makes theology intelligible, and, by so doing, makes it more persuasive. Yet it would be extremely shortsighted to conceive the relationship between mimetic theory and theology as merely heuristic. Girard himself gave voice to these concerns when he wrote, "Theologians should refrain from making use of the mimetic reading for parochially ecclesiastical interests. . . . [If mimetic theory] is perceived as a mere servant of this or that theology, *ancilla theologiae*, its effectiveness is nullified."[16] Girard thought his insights had such import for the social sciences that he did not want his writings circumscribed by faith claims. In chapter 2, I take up this question in greater detail. For now it suffices to say I agree with Mongrain that theologians have been thrown off Girard's theological scent by Girard's emphatic avowal, further problematized by

Girard's contradictory statements that his conclusions originated from legitimate and purely scientific enquiry.

In another key, I show how mimetic theory, when put in dialogue with particular theologians, can advance theological discussion in areas where mimetic theory has been "applied" less regularly. On this level, I present a dialogue with theology that recalls earlier theological efforts. There has developed something of a "canon" of books that bring Girard into dialogue with various theological themes. Such books are not merely introductions to the theological implications of mimetic theory, but they are also attempts to apply Girard's insights to particular questions and thus advance the *status quaestionis*. Vintage examples include Schwager's *Must There Be Scapegoats?* and *Jesus in the Drama of Salvation: Toward a Biblical Doctrine of Redemption*, and James Alison's *The Joy of Being Wrong: Original Sin through Easter Eyes*. In the past decade, one could add Mark Heim's *Saved from Sacrifice: A Theology of the Cross* (2006), Brian Robinette's *Grammars of Resurrection* (2009), and Robert Doran's *The Trinity in History: A Theology of Divine Missions* (2012).[17] In comparison to Alison and Schwager, these theologians are not Girardians *sensu stricto*—they do not begin their theological explorations from Girardian presuppositions. It would be more accurate to say that they want to bring Girard into conversation with both classical Christian theology and with other contemporary theologians.[18]

I toggle between the efforts of Schwager and Alison, on the one side, and Heim, Robinette, and Doran, on the other. Like the latter group (and one could say the same of Schwager), I had already done the work necessary to "join the theological guild" before discovering Girard. My training in the subdiscipline of fundamental theology yielded a sense, as I delved deeper into Girard's work, that mimetic theory could bring something important to bear in questions of fundamental theology. This training also enabled the process of showing those who have entered theology through the Girardian door that Girard's corpus, however groundbreaking it may be, works in concert with the efforts of other leading theologians. After chapter 1, in which I outline Girard's intellectual project, each subsequent chapter not only discusses Girard's contribution to a given topic but also aligns it with other efforts by leading theologians from this and the previous century.

In this sense, *René Girard, Unlikely Apologist: Mimetic Theory and Fundamental Theology* advances on Michael Kirwan's *Girard and Theology*, both by exploring topics omitted by Kirwan and by offering a more extended conversation on these topics.[19]

Besides explaining the keys in which Girard's work engages theology, it behooves me to provide the reader with some clarification of the area of theology in which this engagement takes place. To speak in the most general terms, Christian theology performs two basic operations. The first operation attempts to "make reasonable" revealed objects of faith, like different creedal or biblical claims, through appeals to authority, tradition, and other theological doctrines. When done well, this kind of theology gives its readers and hearers a deeper appreciation for Christianity's mysteries and a greater awareness of the logical connections between various articles of faith.

The second operation borrows from other discourses—often philosophical—in order to give greater rationality to the tenets of faith, or to lend persuasive power to its worldview or its fundamental assumptions. Various theologians, most famously Aquinas, have applied Aristotle's theories of human action in order to understand more deeply how human beings become habituated into the virtues that make a person holy. Analogously, John Paul II's theology of the body used phenomenology, among other resources, to explain more persuasively the Church's sexual teaching. Liberation theologians, likewise, have used Marxist and critical social theory to reshape Christology and moral theology.

Making explicit these two theological operations helps to locate the place of fundamental theology within Christian theology proper. Beginners learn Anselm's definition that theology is *faith seeking understanding*. In this framework, one begins with faith and moves toward understanding. Theology thus comes in the form of explanations about the nature of belief itself, or about the understanding of different doctrines. If, for instance, one is animated by an incipient belief in God's saving love or the redemptive element of Jesus' death, theology aims to deepen this belief by giving accounts of the Trinity, or the Incarnation, or by showing the reasons behind the morality that follows from these beliefs, or their basis in biblical texts. Church communities hope that such forms of theological reflection on belief and on specific doctrines or creedal points will not merely provide a kind of intellectual superstructure to safeguard faith, but that they will deepen the belief of those who engage in theology.

Fundamental Theology

Not all, however, begin their theological explanations from a stable position of faith. The content or form of belief is itself shaky or confused. *Fundamental* theology steps into this aporia. Unlike theology proper, fundamental theology asks questions about the very nature of belief and about the anthropological claims underlying this belief. The conditions of modernity demand that theologians not only assist in the deepening and broadening of already existing faith, but that, in addition, theologians must address the unbeliever and engage the reasons and the framework in which unbelief and even hostility toward the Christian message have become viable alternatives to believing. Here fundamental theology operates as a border discipline, attempting to speak theologically, not so much as *faith seeking understanding* but rather *unbelief seeking belief*. It forestalls questions about scripture's authority in relation to tradition, and it attends to questions of whether or not humans have the capacity to hear the word of God and record it. It also explores theological presuppositions about the relationship between scripture and tradition, faith and reason, Christianity and other religions, the nature and process of divine revelation, and the authority of the scriptures. The underlying premise is that fundamental theology investigates the fundament or foundation of theology prior to more traditional theological reflection, that is, the distinct theological spheres of questions included under such topics as soteriology, pneumatology, ecclesiology, Trinitarian theology, and so on.

"Apologetics" is the more familiar term for at least part of that to which fundamental theology lays claim. At least since Paul preached in Athens (Acts 17), Christians have been doing "apologetic" theology. Apologetics, however, does not always understand itself as a properly theological discipline. One can be a perfectly good apologist as a philosopher, or a natural scientist, or a scholar of religion. Although such famous modern apologists as G. K. Chesterton and C. S. Lewis were believing

Christians, they did not begin, at least in their famous treatises, from a *theological* starting point. Apologetics argues to faith or against unbelief, but it does not aim to understand the basis and principle of belief from within a self-consciously theological discourse. As a branch of theology, fundamental theology does not exclude taking a position of faith that seeks understanding. Yet unlike other disciplines, the central aim of fundamental theology involves exploring the edges of faith: dialogue with nonbelievers, presuppositions for believing, religious epistemology. Fundamental theology certainly covers terrain similar to that of apologetics but does so from a different orientation. One can understand this orientation from within a theology that explicates the difference between sin and grace; another is through the category of conversion. Before turning to such explications, it will be helpful to linger with fundamental theology and to filter our preliminary understanding through a few memorable theological expressions.

The great Jesuit theologian Karl Rahner wrote about the relationship between fundamental theology and apologetics in his *Dictionary of Theology*. Rahner's distinction helps to locate mimetic theory in this discussion. For Rahner, fundamental theology concerns itself both with providing a defense against those who deny Christianity's revelation and with "clarifying *fundamental* questions for Christian theology's self-understanding."[20] Rahner insists that fundamental theology's apologetic task does not relegate it to the pre-theological realm. Fundamental theology occupies a place within theology "proper," which encompasses systematic and dogmatic theology.[21] It concerns the formal element of theology rather than its content (*das Was*). Fundamental theology's parameters cover, according to Rahner, the loss of belief, the relationship between theology and philosophy (faith and reason), and the believability of faith in light of the relationship between theory and practice.[22] *René Girard, Unlikely Apologist*, therefore, lies within the parameters of theology as outlined by no less an authority than Rahner.

The religious insight of Blaise Pascal helps deepen the Rahnerian grooves of this claim. Pascal's most relevant claims about apologetics come in the first aphorism (no. 555) of section 8 of the *Pensées*, "The Fundamentals of the Christian Religion."[23] Here Pascal presents Christianity not simply as a set of truths, but as a salvific religion—one can only know God if one also knows oneself as in need of redemption. Belief in Christ molds these two components into one: Christ is the Son of God who redeems us. Pascal writes, "We cannot know Jesus Christ without knowing at the same time both God and our own wretchedness." By wretchedness, Pascal means a state from which we cannot save ourselves. Any knowledge of God unrelated to the need to be redeemed becomes pointless. Such a position undergirds Pascal's negative opinion of deism. Since deism has no soteriology, Pascal regards it as "almost as far removed from the Christian religion as atheism."[24] The *essence* of Christianity consists in the indissoluble nature of two truths: the knowledge of God and the fallen state of humanity. Pascal writes, "The knowledge of only one of these points gives rise either to the pride of the philosophers, who have known God, and not their own wretchedness, or to the despair of atheists, who know their own wretchedness, but not the Redeemer." Neither group has knowledge of God as the Redeemer.

According to the same aphorism, religious knowledge outside the framework of the need to be converted is useless and barren. When Pascal speaks of those who seek God "without Christ," he means those who seek without the desire to be saved by the God whom they seek. Natural theology left to its own devices falls "either into atheism, or into deism, two things which the Christian religion abhors almost equally." The God of Jesus Christ, like the God of Abraham, Isaac, and Jacob, does not want to be known for the sake of being known. This God "is a God of love and of comfort, a God who fills the soul and heart of those whom He possesses, a God who makes them conscious of their inward wretchedness, and His infinite mercy, who unites Himself to their inmost soul, who fills it with humility and joy, with confidence and love."

For Pascal, the nature of salvific knowledge has consequences for how it is received. One cannot simply be told these truths—only when one begins to see oneself as complicit in the actions that put Jesus on the cross does the knowledge of redemption through Jesus' blood become real. Here, as alluded to above, the theological move to relate the sinful condition to the need for grace bubbles to the surface. If apologetics aims to convert unbelievers or to save believers from unbelief, Pascal implies that apologetics must speak of this movement as graced. Such a movement does not remove rational reflection from the theological project or

jettison reasons for believing. Rather, it positions all rational justifica-
tions as secondary to the prior movement of grace by the God who loved
us first (1 John 4:19).

Pascal ends this "section" of the *Pensées* by referring to the paradox
that Christianity is rationally compelling, but this fact does not lead one
to believe: "Our religion is wise and foolish. Wise, because it is the most
learned, and the most founded on miracles, prophecies, etc. Foolish, because it is not at all this which makes us belong to it. . . . It is the cross
that makes them believe . . . And so Saint Paul, who came with wisdom
and signs, says that he has come neither with wisdom nor with signs;
for he came to convert [*convertir*]. But those who come only to convince [*convaincre*], can say that they come with wisdom and with signs"
(no. 587). One can be convinced of Christianity's truth but still un-
moved by it. Pascal here implies that arguments meant to overwhelm do
not matter as much as a witness that compels.[25] One finds a similar shape
to Girard's apologetics, and the rest of this book offers a mimetic fundamental theology in a Pascalian key.

This mode of proceeding can be supplemented with a remark by
Avery Dulles about the apologetic task in Rahner's mature theology. For
Dulles, Rahner asserts that human reason, in the mind of the believer,
is elevated supernaturally toward the Christian faith. This conviction
alters the apologist's task:

> To awaken explicit faith, the apologist must present the contents of Chris-
> tian revelation not as an extraneous element foreign to the hearers' per-
> sonal experience but rather as an interpretation of what they have already
> encountered through the inner workings of grace in the depths of their
> consciousness. The primary task of the apologist, then, is to exhibit how
> the whole system of Christian teaching is the one complete answer to the
> primordial question that man is to himself.[26]

This passage captures how the apologetic task elicits the question of grace.
Before I return to Girard, it will be helpful to say more about grace. Such
an explicitly theological category as grace would seem to present a problem for Girard, who has maintained that mimetic theory is not a faith-
based theory, and that the argument for the scapegoat mechanism does

not require Christian conviction as a presupposition for acceptance. The subsequent chapters in this book do more than operate in a set of keys or modes. They also argue—sometimes as the most fundamental point in a given chapter, other times as a secondary matter—that Girard's mimetic theory is not merely an explanatory tool for theology but also an apology for Christianity. By locating this apologetic feature of mimetic theology against the background of a theology of grace, it will stand out more strikingly.

It is difficult to read mimetic theory theologically without intuiting its implications for the doctrine of original sin. Girard's forceful rejection of "romanticism" makes for a seamless transition to the framework of sin and grace (sin–grace, rather than nature–grace, is more often than not the apt binary for mimetic theory). Wolfgang Palaver, one of the leading theological expositors of mimetic theory, succinctly states how the mimetic insight increases consciousness of one's own culpability: "Where false pride persuades humans to believe they are consummate and free of flaw, their inevitable fall leads to overwhelming self-accusations that most often must be shifted onto others."[27] Unlike Tobin Siebers, who argued that "mimetic theory was incompatible with grace," Palaver insists that "Girard's primary objective exists much more in an anthropological apologetics of biblical thought, or rather in displaying the plausibility of biblical revelation without having to revert to any rash theological presuppositions."[28] Girard, according to Palaver, thinks he has a scientific basis for describing *post lapsum* humanity as he does. A description of humanity in the thrall of escalating violence creates an aporia that makes God's redemptive revelation necessary.

Palaver illuminates how grace works in Girard's thought by contrasting it with Kant's *Religion within the Limits of Mere Reason*. Like Girard, Kant's *Religion* begins by talking about "radical evil." Palaver describes this as "the presence of evil in humanity," to which Kant "offers a kind of anthropological apologetics that contains only irreligious, indirectly theological analysis."[29] Kant's theology of grace is undeniably Pelagian. Kant locates the solution for the radically evil situation of humanity within humanity's own powers.[30] Palaver concludes, "Kant's 'moral religion' remains within the limits of reason and allows no room for the influence of grace."[31] By contrast, Girard shows human culture, on its own, as a "closed system." Humanity cannot free itself by itself; it needs divine intervention: "Only with the help of the grace of God, thus, can humanity free itself from the dungeon of scapegoat logic."[32]

For his part, Girard has also written about the need for grace, especially as his work has become more openly engaged with theology. In *I See Satan Fall Like Lightning*, to give just one example, he remarks, "To break the power of mimetic unanimity, we must postulate a power superior to violent contagion. . . . [The Resurrection] is the spectacular sign of the entrance into the world of a power superior to violent contagion."[33] Such passages as this one, which occur frequently in Girard's later works, have not gone unnoticed. Mongrain concludes: "Girard's thought has also become more and more concerned with expressing the paradoxical unity of gratuitous grace and human free will."[34] Mongrain cites an interview where Girard responds to a question about positive mimetic desire. Girard notes: "Wherever you have that desire, I would say, that really active, positive desire for the other, there is some kind of divine grace present. This is what Christianity unquestionably tells us."[35] Mongrain feels justified in calling Girard a "theologian of spiritual transformation" because of the central place of conversion in Girard's work. Only through the process of conversion does the mimetic capacity return to the original goodness for which it was intended.

Whereas Mongrain seeks to connect Girard to Balthasar and John Cassian, Palaver aims to connect Girard to Augustine, the *doctor gratiae*.[36] Girard himself noted, "Three quarters of what I say is in Augustine."[37] Palaver highlights the centrality of grace in Augustine, especially in the anti-Pelagian works: "For Augustine, complete self-empowerment is not possible on one's own; he argues expressly that there must be an external impetus—the gift of grace—to bring about positive mimesis."[38] Palaver's intuition on this point overlaps with my attempt to connect James Alison's work to more traditional theology. Like Girard, Alison is best understood as an heir of the Augustinian tradition, at least in terms of grace.[39] This connection yields a helpful metaphor for the role of grace in the mimetic constellation. Grace, writes Palaver, is "the outer boundary of [Girard's] anthropological apologetics."[40] Girard's narration of the Passion places saving grace as a central motif. Palaver continues, "In contrast to Kant, the mimetic theory transcends the realm of mere reason and incorporates the mystery of grace that led to the reversal of the disciples' point of view."[41] The concavity of a world without grace, which Girard equates with the cultural dominance of the archaic sacred and the psychological dominance of rivalrous desire, enables Girard to illustrate how grace transforms the sinful shape of things when it enters into the story.

The tension between sin and grace lies at the heart of any explication of the relationship between mimetic theory and theology, and it underlies the apologetic power of Girard's thought, which comes out in the rest of the book. The theological element in mimetic theory enables a theology of conversion. According to Girard, mimetic theory itself has a distinctly Christian shape. He opens his final major work, *Battling to the End*, by stating: "Since the beginning of the 'novelistic conversion' in *Deceit, Desire, and the Novel*, all of my books have been more or less explicit apologies of Christianity."[42] This statement flew in the face of previous statements by Girard, and it seemed to belie the evidence: Girard's first two books make almost no reference to the gospel. Yet within the framework of sin and grace, Girard's later utterance gains intelligibility.

Beyond offering heuristic devices to help make Christian dogmatic claims intelligible, mimetic theory lays bare processes of religious conversion.[43] It describes the kind of interpersonal knowledge that leads adherents to reorder the fundamental questions undergirding their moral judgment and performance. Its descriptive claims enter into the normative and existential realms. Girard himself has highlighted the connection between mimetic theory and conversion: "The knowledge of mimesis is really tied to conversion."[44] Mimetic theory, at least as Girard imagines it, does not simply offer a neutral, a-theological mode of discourse that theologians can, if they so wish, apply to theology; rather, it already works within the horizon of conversion, or grace. Elsewhere Girard notes, "To become Christian is, fundamentally, to perceive that it isn't just others who have scapegoats."[45] Girard here points to the experience of what he calls, in his first major work, *novelistic* conversion. In this experience, the person comes to understand himself as afflicted by the sinful condition. Girard considers this experience normative for the Christian believer. Girard's judgment, however, begs a question: Is mimetic theory a mode of discourse for the *already* converted, in order to help them make explicit their faith commitments, or is it a mode of discourse that aims to bring about conversion? This question drives the work at hand, and in each chapter I either help answer it or rely on a previously suggested answer in order to make my argument.

To date, no monograph on Girard has attempted to read mimetic theory as apologetic or to interpret Girard as a fundamental theologian. Some of my following chapters betray an obvious overlap with Kirwan's *Girard and Theology* and Scott Cowdell's *René Girard and Secular Modernity*. Neither of these books, however, discusses at length the topics in fundamental theology treated herein. My own work supplements these contributions by demonstrating how Girard's thought, though not strictly theological, operates within a horizon of religious conversion that enables it to enrich contemporary theology in ways that have not yet been teased out.

Chapter 1, "Mimetic Theory as Heuristic," offers an introduction to mimetic theory by focusing on the anthropological claims and breakthroughs that Girard articulated in his early works. This chapter produces an account of the human person as *homo imitator*, and it unpacks the cultural and religious consequences that result from this anthropological claim. Like previous introductions to mimetic theory, I begin with mimetic desire, and I then transition to claims about human origins, most centrally the scapegoat mechanism. Next, I treat Girard's interpretation of the religious system produced by archaic cultures that relied on scapegoating. I end with a brief nod toward Christianity, leaving an evaluation of the relationship between Christianity and archaic religion for chapter 4. Chapter 2, "Mimetic Theory and Rational Faith," begins the engagement of mimetic theory and fundamental theology by analyzing how Girard conceives the relationship between faith and reason. This chapter reviews some of the confusion alluded to above, namely, that Girard seemed both to deny and then confess the influence of Christianity on the development of his theory. I also examine some of Girard's autobiographical remarks in order to reconcile these seemingly contradictory claims and to answer some of Girard's critics on this topic.

Chapters 3 and 4 come closest to providing a constructive theological project. Chapter 3, "Mimetic Theory and the Theology of Revelation," examines the doctrine of revelation, a central topic for fundamental theology over the past fifty years. It begins by outlining a problematic way of understanding how revelation works, as represented in Avery Dulles and René Latourelle. I then pivot to the hermeneutical philosophy of Martin Heidegger, Hans-Georg Gadamer, and Walter Ong in order to show how philosophically unsettling the standard approach to revelation can be. Only then do I take up Girard, with the aim of demonstrating how he exemplifies a hermeneutic approach to revelation that Heidegger, Gadamer, and Ong all seem to require. Chapter 4, "Realizing a Mimetic Theology of Religion," covers the relationship between Christianity and religion. I question approaches that view the category of religion on a flat line, and I argue, with the help of Wilfred Cantwell Smith and William Cavanaugh, that *religion* is a modern, Western construct. When liberated from such a construct, it becomes feasible to understand Christianity less as a religion and more as a critique of religion. Such a conclusion conforms to Girard's own statements about Christianity's relationship to religion. In addition, it makes it possible to conceive how a mimetic interpretation of Christianity also permits a generous reading of other post-Axial religions, which Girard repeatedly attempted to do in his later works.

Chapter 5, "Imagining a Mimetic Ecclesiology," treats the subject of the Church from the perspective of mimetic theory. The chapter brings mimetic theory into conversation with traditional apologetic arguments concerning the Church. Since Girard's own discussions of ecclesiology are so thin, I take a pause from Girard's corpus in order to engage with James Alison. Alison's disparate writings on the Church, organized for the first time in this chapter, yield what I call a "mimetic fundamental ecclesiology." They also bring this ecclesiology into conversation with the image of the Church provided by Pope Francis and the "ecclesiology of friendship" sketched by John Dadosky.

Chapters 6 and 7 treat the relationship between mimetic theory and (1) modernity and secularism, and (2) atheism. Chapter 6, "Trajectories of Modernity: Girard and Taylor in Conversation," argues that mimetic theory makes it possible to construct a theology of modernity or secularism. Girard's theology of the secular shares a great deal in common with Charles Taylor's, the main interlocutor in this chapter. Girard's more compelling account of "essential" Christianity, according to the argument made here, lends Girard a more perspicacious reading of modernity than even the acclaimed reading of Taylor. Finally, chapter 7, "Mimetic Theory and Atheism," concerns Girard's reading of atheism, and of modernity's most compelling anti-Christian, Friedrich Nietzsche. In the chapter I set Girard's interpretation of atheism alongside Michael Buckley's noteworthy genealogy of atheism. I then align Girard's interpretation of Nietzsche with that of David Bentley Hart's. Both of these chapters exemplify, perhaps more clearly than earlier chapters, the performative element of the book. In some cases it is best to demonstrate the ongoing relevance of Girard for Christian theology by examples (in contrast, say, to the method of categorization).

René Girard, Unlikely Apologist concludes by recalling the positive and negative assessment of mimetic theory by leading theologians over the last forty-five years. The capacity of mimetic theory to gain the attention of such a collection of leading theologians speaks to its promise, but the pattern of dissatisfaction that these authors have with Girard indicates some of the challenges to Girard's interpretation. My epilogue revisits the introduction's claim about Girard's ongoing relevance for twenty-first-century theology.

CHAPTER ONE

MIMETIC THEORY AS HEURISTIC

Mimetic Anthropology

The foundation and driving force behind mimetic theory derives from Girard's thesis about the shape of human desire. According to Girard's own testimony, this thesis, or discovery, did not generate from his own genius. One finds the same insight already in Aristotle: "The instinct of imitation is implanted in man from childhood, one difference between him and other animals being that he is the most imitative of living creatures, and through imitation learns his earliest lesson; and no less universal is the pleasure felt in things imitated."[1] Mimetic theory cannot even claim to have discovered this forgotten insight from antiquity. Erich Auerbach produced a famous study on literary theory—*Mimesis*—in the 1950s, which predated Girard's earliest efforts.[2] What is unique to Girard, and to mimetic theory, however, is the attempt to plant this insight in the ground, to water it, and to attend to its growth. Girard's importance, especially for theology, derives from his exploration of the implications of mimetic desire for different fields of study, especially anthropology and religion.

Desire, according to mimetic theory, is most primarily mediated through another person rather than generated from the individual subject. Mimetic desire is what most clearly distinguishes human beings from other primates. Girard makes this point quite forcefully in the opening section of *Things Hidden*: "There is nothing, or next to nothing,

in human behaviour that is not learned, and all learning is based on imitation. If human beings suddenly ceased imitating, all forms of culture
would vanish . . . To develop a science of man it is necessary to compare human imitation with animal mimicry, and to specify the properly
human modalities of mimetic behaviour, if they indeed exist."[3] Girard's
claim for the centrality of mimesis in human behavior has been confirmed by recent neuroscience.[4] In 1996, a group of Italian scientists in
Parma discovered "mirror" neurons. According to Scott Garrels, "Mirror
neurons are brain cells that are activated regardless of whether the individual is performing a particular motor movement or observing the same
movement being made by another person."[5] In other words, these neurons *mirror* observed action. If one person sees another enjoying a hot-
fudge sundae, the former's neurons respond similarly to how they would
if their subject were the one enjoying the sundae.

Although this discovery focused on a study of macaque monkeys,
scientific experiment indicates that the human brain has "many more,
and more widely distributed, mirror neurons than monkeys, and that
these are fired off from birth onwards."[6] In addition to imitating adult
actions, infants distinguish between adult intentions and the completed
act, evidencing even more clearly how infant brains seek to imitate the intention, not the action itself. From this data, Garrels concludes: "Human
infants are thought to be immersed in a rich social matrix of self–other
reciprocity and intersubjective experience from the very beginnings of
life."[7] Humans do not learn to imitate as an act of departure from an earlier, more spontaneous autonomy; imitating itself is innate to human nature, as Girard had argued before this groundbreaking research.

The discovery of mirror neurons has important consequences both
for the discipline of anthropology and for any theology seeking overlap
with natural science. The motor and problem-solving skills of a three-
year-old child will be no more advanced than that of many primates,
but the former will know far more words than even the most verbose
chimpanzee.[8] But what does this say about human particularity? Garrels summarizes: "So foundational is our capacity to imitate, that many
researchers believe it to be the linchpin that contributed to a wide-
scale neural reorganization of the brain, allowing for the coevolution of
more complex, social, cultural, and representational abilities from earlier

primates to humans."[9] The imitative capacity enables humans to experience a mutuality that is more neurologically connected than that between other mammals. Humans can "lock into" other humans to a degree not achieved by other species. James Alison concludes, "Humans are exceptionally finely prepared imitating bodies for whom imitation, at which we can indeed improve, is the normal conduit through which we acquire language, gesture, memory and empathy, and so receive ourselves as ourselves."[10] Reflection on mirror neurons points to the same conclusion as Girard's mimetic theory: we learn our accents, our preferred colors, and our notion of beauty from our communities, which give us a sense of who we are by telling us what we want.

Mimetic theory, of course, undermines one of modernity's most fiercely defended dogmas: the sovereignty and goodness of individual choice. One is free, we learn from a thousand advertisements and grand narratives, to determine one's own tastes, preference, likes, and dislikes. Although mimetic theory prioritizes the social over the individual, it does not eliminate individual sovereignty or choice. Girard on several occasions has rejected determinism or reductionism.[11] Girard upholds some measure of human freedom, however truncated, and maintains that human behavior cannot be reduced to biological or neurological predictors. The biological basis of imitation does not remove the capacity to moderate the object of imitation. Nevertheless, Girard's notion of mimetic desire, which he calls "the real 'unconscious,'" challenges our default mode of thinking about human agency.[12]

Girard applies the term "Romanticism" to the movement that clings most tightly to the notion of our desire's autonomy.[13] Romanticism bases authenticity and individuality on the strength and spontaneity—love at *first* sight—of one's desires; hence, a mimetic desirer is an inferior desirer. Girard notes: "Romantic and modern ideologies have always promoted either a 'true love' or, nowadays, a 'real desire' that provides us with a badge of spontaneity. Intensity and authenticity are supposed to go hand in hand. Mimetic desire is regarded as weak on the ground that it is merely a copy and that copies never come up to the level of the original."[14] Girard's first major work, *Deceit, Desire, and the Novel*, which appeared in French in 1961 under the title *Mensonge romantique et vérité romanesque*, undercuts the Romantic presumption. This title, playing off

the homophony between "romantic" and "novelistic," translates more accurately to "Romantic deceit and novelistic truth." The book's central
concern is to show how certain novelists overcome the Romantic position held earlier in their lives. Girard explains in the opening pages:

> The great novelists reveal the imitative nature of desire. In our days its
> nature is hard to perceive because the most fervent imitation is the most
> vigorously denied. . . . The romantic *vaniteux* does not want to be any-
> one's disciple. He convinces himself that he is thoroughly *original*. In the
> nineteenth century spontaneity becomes a universal dogma, succeeding
> imitation. . . . Romantic revulsion, hatred of society, nostalgia for the
> desert, just as gregariousness, usually conceals a morbid concern for the
> Other.[15]

Girard's work in literary theory argues that some of Western history's
great novelists—Cervantes, Proust, Flaubert, Stendhal, Dostoevsky—
and its greatest modern playwright—Shakespeare—understood the mimetic kernel of desire and the consequences that such desire has for
human relationships and for social cohesion. Rather than portray heroes
as Romantic souls unaffected by society, these authors reveal how the
truly authentic "hero" humbly admits the derivative nature of his desires,
and therefore whatever liberation the hero achieves takes a different hue.
Near the conclusion, Girard writes, "This time it is not a false but a genuine conversion. The hero triumphs in defeat; he triumphs because he is at
the end of his resources: for the first time he has to look his despair and
his nothingness in the face. But this look, which he has dreaded, which
is the defeat of his pride, is his salvation."[16] Girard's analysis of desire offers a stern challenge to the illusion that Romantic authenticity rescues
its representatives from the great mass of imitators.

    Being hardwired for imitation means living in the paradox that one's
sense of identity remains enmeshed within and is received from another.
Mimetic hardwiring makes possible not only language acquisition but
also any kind of education. It also precipitates conflict, competition, and
violent escalation. Girard notes, "Imitation does not merely draw people
together, it pulls them apart. Paradoxically, it can do these two things
simultaneously."[17] One observes this especially in the teenage years, when

friends can experience severe fallouts just a few short months after an intense bond. Without mimetic theory, most people find themselves at a loss to explain this falling out, or if they do explain it, they do so through the language of difference: *they just grew apart*. For mimetic theory it is similarity carelessly managed, rather than difference, that explains both individual and social conflict.

Mimetic theory offers an insight into the late-modern solution to the problem of conflict. Capitalism promises to quell competition over objects by creating a surplus of goods so great that everyone's desires could be met. Yet what fun is it to possess an object universally and cheaply attainable? The allure of both the nightclub and the Ivy League remains rooted in a shared exclusivity.[18] Scarcity persists, therefore, since certain objects of desire—especially lovers—cannot be multiplied, let alone mass-produced. Girard notes: "Eros cannot be shared in the same manner as a book, a bottle of wine, a piece of music, a beautiful landscape."[19] Friendship based on a common love of music or of a certain style of clothing receives a stiff challenge when the two friends fall in love with the same person; or it struggles to bear the weight of a third friend who disrupts the balance of mediated desire. If desire is mediated through another, it follows, almost inevitably, that unchecked mimetic desire will result in conflict. Further, on account of mimetic hardwiring, reciprocity quickly escalates conflict.

Mimetic Theory and the Foundation of Culture

Mimetic theory asks its readers to imagine a primal scene of mimetic desire gone awry: two children play peacefully until one child suddenly notices a toy long ignored by the second child, who owns the toy. Although she, the owner, has not wanted to play with this toy for weeks, she suddenly needs to have the toy held by her friend. Her playmate enlivens her desire for the object, but the focus is on the object—the toy—instead of the subject—the playmate, that is, the real initiator of desire. This confusion about the source of desire reflects what Hegelian social theory calls "false consciousness." Such a primal scene, where one could foresee a violent eruption absent parental oversight, also applies to adults.

The possibility of escalating reciprocity does not simply disappear upon reaching the age of reason, or adulthood. Adults learn to mask their desires more deftly, but they do not cease desiring mimetically. On this point Girard argues, "An equivalent situation rarely occurs among adults. That does not mean that mimetic rivalry no longer exists among them; perhaps it exists more than ever, but adults, like the apes, have learned to fear and repress rivalry, at least in its crudest, most obvious, and most immediately recognizable forms."[20] Between children and adults there lies a continuity, not a break, in the pattern of desire. Adulthood does not correspond with the cessation of mimetic desire.

Just as watchful parents prevent destructive escalation among children, so too do various social mechanisms prevent adult conflict, including impartial judiciaries, police oversight, and strongly enforced social mores. In his attempt to extend the anthropological reach of his nascent literary theory, Girard wondered how the earliest humans dealt with this problem. If mimetic desire explained the existence of so many modern structures, how did the earliest human societies manage this desire? In his second major book, *Violence and the Sacred*, Girard sought to examine early human cultures in light of his mimetic hunch.[21] For more than a decade, Girard familiarized himself with the major works of cultural anthropology and with ethnological studies. *Violence and the Sacred* extended mimetic theory into these fields.

Among the dozens of anthropological, ethnological, and ancient texts he consulted, Girard found mounds of evidence that pointed toward mimetic escalation and different forms of resolution. Yet no theorists of the earliest human communities connected the dots—they lacked the key insight into *homo imitator*, an insight that allowed Girard to order the evidence and discover *scapegoating* as the founding mechanism of ancient culture. Before exploring this insight, it merits lingering a little while on the difference between humans and animals.

Unlike in the mind of other animals, the imitative quality of the human mind easily entangles humans in patterns of reciprocal escalation. Before the discovery of mirror neurons, Girard noted, "Today we know that animals possess individual braking mechanisms to insure that combats between them seldom result in the actual death of the vanquished."[22] In one lecture, Girard commented on a sight familiar to those who have driven California's Central Coast during winter months.[23] Here the great elephant seals rest on a stretch of beach, determining dominance and caring for their young. Yet despite the tussles that erupt every few minutes, the stronger seals do not kill the weaker ones, nor do the weaker ones gang up on the strongest. Paradoxically, it seems, in comparison to humans, the seals show both a greater inclination to violence and a more advanced capacity to curb it. Even at a nightclub, human behavior does not approximate the naked violence seen on the Central Coast. Yet when conflict does arise, humans seem to possess a far less evolved breaking mechanism than advanced mammals, such as elephant seals.

Girard relates this difference to the mimetic capacity, which he observes already in mammals: "There must be a mimetic element in the intra-species fighting of many animals, since the absence of an object . . . does not always put an immediate end to the fighting. Eventually, however, the fighting comes to an end with a kind of submission of the vanquished to the victor."[24] Yet human intraspecies fighting, also based in a mimetic element, far outpaces even primates. Girard continues: "Unlike animals, men engaged in rivalry may go on fighting *to the finish* . . . An increased mimetic drive, corresponding to the enlarged human brain, must escalate mimetic rivalry beyond the point of no return . . . [It] must have caused, when it first appeared, the breakdown of societies based on dominance patterns."[25]

It is hard for us moderns to fathom this potential for destruction. Our advanced legal structures—possessing judiciaries unconnected to the crime—and sophisticated legal codes bottle up our reciprocal ferocity and channel it into the far less bloody realm of the online comment section. Primitive societies lacked any comparable breaking mechanisms. So how did humans come to learn how to live together in relative peace? This question, following Girard's recognition of modern cultural institutions, drove his further study.

In his theorizing about the beginnings of culture, Girard distinguishes between desire and appetite. Appetite is natural, whereas desire is learned or cultural.[26] Girard's speculation on primitive society does not concern itself with two subjects fighting over the last piece of food. At that level, precultural instinct, along with the scarcity of resources, explains violence. Girard is concerned with societies that have reached a surplus. When two people become locked into a mimetic relationship, they will enter a pattern in which the desire of one will be mediated to another. Unlike larger societies, where my desire for what a famous or powerful person wants can never interfere with their possession of this object (external mediation), in smaller groups such a threat dominates exchange (internal mediation). Girard describes it thus:

> I call this type of mimetic relationship *internal mediation*, and it is intrin-sically self-reinforcing. Due to the physical and psychological proximity of subject and model, the internal mediation tends to become more and more symmetrical . . . One is always moving toward more symmetry, and thus always towards more conflict, for symmetry cannot but produce *doubles*, as I call them at this moment of intense rivalry. . . . A mimetic crisis is always a crisis of undifferentiation that erupts when the roles of subject and model are reduced to that of rivals. . . . This crisis not only escalates between the contenders, but it becomes contagious with bystanders.[27]

When two members of a primitive society focus on the same object, they cannot be ultimately appeased by another object, for the focus of their desire is on the other person rather than the object. If they come to blows, they differ in no discernible way from other mammals. Recip-rocal violence only takes on a human shape when the two subjects con-ceive their own reaction as reciprocal rather than escalatory. This pattern reappears both on tranquil playgrounds and on violent streets, in do-mestic disputes and in the comment sections of blogs. Girard writes of this violent escalation: "Physical violence is the perfect accomplishment of the conflictual mimetic relationship, and it is completely reciprocal. Everyone imitates the other's violence and returns it 'with interest.' Un-involved spectators see this unmistakably. In order to understand it, we have only to view the relationship as Punch and Judy, bashing each other over the head."[28] The larger, mimetic human brain allows for advanced forms of flourishing but contains the possibility of increased, contagious violence. Could the first humans have gone through several waves of col-lapse before learning how to live together? Girard thinks so, and evidence continues to support him.

Not far from Saint Louis are the mounds of Cahokia, the largest sur-viving representation of the Mississippian "mound cultures."[29] Here was

located one of the largest pre-Columbian cities in North America, with
nearly twenty thousand inhabitants, who built the largest pre-Columbian
structure north of Mexico City—a mound where only a few of the
Cahokians lived. Yet before any Europeans arrived, the civilization collapsed for reasons unknown. Perhaps it was an ecological change, or too
much consumption of corn, or too rapid deforestation, or a disease. The
work of such historians as Jared Diamond, has made these natural explanations compelling.[30] Girard, of course, poses another possibility: "It is
possible to think that numerous human communities have disintegrated
under the pressure of a violence that never led to the mechanism I have
just described. But the observation of religious systems forces us to conclude that the mimetic crisis always occurs."[31] Visitors to Cahokia pass
through the museum without hearing about Mound 72, where hundreds
of skeletons were found. Most of these people in this pit had been mur-
dered, some with their heads and hands cut off, others buried alive. One
man was found buried on a bed of twenty thousand beads in the shape
of a falcon, indicating a conflation of his death and divine forces. Might
Cahokia's demise have resulted from mimetic contagion? Might the religious structure of Cahokia have collapsed under its own weight, unable
to find a permanent solution to the problems that stem from mimetic violence? Although Cahokia is not one of the earliest human civilizations,
it is of interest for the evidence it leaves: a massive sacrificial system, and
a collapse suffered from within, rather than from an invading army. According to mimetic theory, human instability derives from mimetic desire
and the constellation of emotions and consequences that orbit it: envy,
reciprocity, jealousy, escalation, repetition, and contagion. In *Battling to
the End*, his last major work, Girard spells out some of these dangers:

> Humans are different from animals, for the latter succeed in containing
> their violence in what ethnologists call networks of dominance. Humans
> cannot control reciprocity because they imitate one another too much and
> their resemblance to one another increases and accelerates.
>
> We have to imagine that *for these very reasons* the first human groups
> self-destructed.[32]

In the context of considering the potential for collapse due to mimetic
violence, Girard set out to examine primitive cultures and to see what

could explain how humans learned to avoid self-destruction. From this beginning, Girard eventually came to understand the functional role of religion for social survival.

Archaic Religion

At least since the Enlightenment, Western intellectuals have questioned the purpose of primitive religion. A look at any number of religious texts and practices uncovers two seemingly irrational features: taboos and (often bloody) ritual. For modern critics like Voltaire and Nietzsche, religion constitutes a conspiracy by priests to take advantage of natural institutions, like agriculture, that produce surplus for a society.[33] For other critics it results from prescientific and therefore prerational thinking. Only unenlightened people would create elaborate taboos about physical contact, or believe in the evil eye, or suppose that blood sacrifice could be efficacious. Girard summarizes this viewpoint: "The Enlightenment viewpoint [says that] religion is superstition and if ritual is everywhere it's because cunning and avid priests impose their abracadabras on good people."[34] Girard thinks such a claim fails to understand the mimetic nature of humanity. Only with the right anthropology can one interpret archaic religion properly.

According to mimetic theory, taboos and rituals arise to prevent mimetic conflagration and to quench or contain it once it takes place. Taboos exist to prevent mimetic contagion. Girard explains: "Religion instructs men as to what they must and must not do to prevent a recurrence of destructive violence. When they neglect rites and violate prohibitions they call down upon themselves transcendent violence."[35] Practitioners of archaic religion may be mistaken, but they are not irrational.

In his 2008 article "Vengeance Is Ours," Jared Diamond tells the story of warring clans in the New Guinea highlands.[36] In this governmentless society, clans have elaborate and delicate ways to control reciprocity should violence erupt. Diamond writes about Daniel Wemp of the Handa clan, who sought to revenge the violence done to his uncle by a member of the Ombal clan. Diamond's focus on Papua New Guinea leads him to posit the *universal* desire for vengeance. Diamond comments, "As I eventually came to realize, Daniel's thirst for vengeance and his hostility to rival clans are really not so far from our own habits of mind as we would like to think."[37] He ends by talking about his father-in-law's remorse for not exacting revenge on those responsible for murdering his Jewish family members in 1940s Poland.

From the perspective of mimetic theory, Diamond's story shows how a culture without a clearly defined third-party judiciary deals with conflict. The dispute began with the destruction wrought by a pig. According to Diamond, "The Ombal man became angry, demanded compensation, and assaulted the Handa pig owner when he refused. Relatives of both parties then joined in the dispute, and soon the entire membership of both clans—between four and six thousand people—was dragged into a war that had now raged for longer than Daniel could remember."[38] Wemp, Diamond's former taxi driver, felt responsible for avenging the death of his uncle, who had been brought into the skirmish despite having no part in the original dispute. Over a long and violent period of escalation, the clans did not destroy one another. The precise rules of engagement, and the value placed on life (roughly eighty pigs), helped prevent further escalation. The clandestine nature of the battles made it difficult to determine who had killed whom; the overly aggressive inclination of one person was held in check by the clan, which would suffer collectively from reprisal. From within the framework of mimetic theory, the patterns of human behavior rooted in the *homo imitator*—reciprocity, doubling, escalation—seemed entirely predictable.

Diamond concludes that stateless societies have difficulty moving from war to peace because they lack a central, impartial judiciary. In an exchange with Diamond, Wemp seems to admit this: "The Western way, of letting the government settle disputes by means of the legal system, is a better way. But we could never have arrived at it by ourselves: we were trapped in our endless cycles of revenge killings."[39] As any adept student of political science knows, despite eradicating honor killings and mob violence, nation-states generally mirror the very same patterns of reciprocal violence, but on a much larger scale, in their wars with other states. Despite Wemp's confession, the clans were not trapped in an endless cycle. In their response to Diamond, Paul Sillitoe and Mako John Kuwimb claim that "the casual observer errs in thinking that revenge is an expression of uncontrolled emotions and savagery, whereas ironically it is an effective safeguard against such chaos and lawlessness."[40] Sillitoe, an anthropologist, and Kuwimb, a native of the New Guinea highlands, show how a rudimentary justice system has helped temper reciprocal violence and minimize skirmishes.[41] They conclude that the culturally normative revenge ethic, especially given its strict parameters, has paradoxically sustained an egalitarian tribal order.

Examples from the Cahokia Native Americans and the New Guinea highlanders do not prove mimetic theory, but they offer hints about how premodern civilizations dealt with conflict: one by massive killings, the other by carefully reciprocated violence. For Girard, the mimetic thesis enables one to *untangle* the rationality from actions that might have seemed counterintuitive or befuddling at first glance—indiscriminate disposal of human life, never-ending war between primitive tribes. Girard applies the same hermeneutical enterprise to primitive religious rules and taboos. Although they may appear absurd, such taboos have a rational function. Girard notes, "A good example of an apparently absurd prohibition is one that in many societies prohibits imitative behavior. One must not copy the gesture of another member of the community or repeat his words. The same concern can no doubt be seen in the prohibition of the use of proper names, or in the fear of mirrors, which are often associated with the devil in traditional societies."[42] Other examples of taboos include touching a corpse, or blood, or even coming into contact with a woman during her menstrual cycle.[43] The seeming irrationality of such taboos is rooted in real fears about the contagious capacity of violence. Many primitive societies kill one or both of a set of twins out of fear that their presence could lead to greater reciprocal violence.[44] All of these fears become intelligible within a mimetic hermeneutic. Within the bounds of sound reason, societies implement measures that anticipate and contain violent loci.

Girard's hermeneutic involves not only interpreting these phenomena but also explaining the failure of ethnologists and anthropologists to read the evidence correctly. Girard argues: "The simple illogicality of the prohibition [against mirrors] confirms rather than weakens our thesis, for in the light of mimetic conflict one can very well understand why certain absurd prohibitions should exist."[45] Yet before (and after) mimetic theory, anthropologists struggled to account for the development of these taboos. Girard continues, "Until now thinkers have always centered religious systems on the effects of external threats and natural catastrophes, or in the explanation of natural and cosmic phenomena. In my opinion, mimetic violence is at the heart of the system."[46] The prohibitions and taboos that religious systems enforce begin to make sense in light of mimetic theory. Yet, because modern ethnologists share the biases of modern thought, they rely on outdated accounts that never convincingly explain the ubiquity of religion: "Ethnologists should long since have drawn on their cumulative evidence to explain the function of these prohibitions and even to discover their origins. . . . Modern philosophers invariably choose as representative the most 'irrational' and bizarre (at any rate to modern eyes) aspects of religious prohibitions. Thus they manage to convince themselves that religion has no connection with reality."[47] Girard felt that mimetic theory unlocked the pattern of human relations, including the relations that develop and lie behind the emergence of religion. Taboos and prohibitions form important data for reconstructing archaic society. Ritual, however, helped Girard unlock humanity's darkest secret.

Ritual and the Scapegoating Mechanism

Whereas taboos prevent mimetic escalation, ritual expels mimetic violence once unleashed. The foundation of ritual is the scapegoat mechanism. Girard often describes the crisis that leads to scapegoating in mechanistic or deterministic language: "Since the power of mimetic attraction multiplies with the number of the polarized, it is inevitable that at one moment the entire community will find itself unified against a single individual."[48] From such statements, which are dispersed throughout Girard's corpus, commentators seamlessly transition from antagonistic mimesis to the scapegoat mechanism.[49] Despite having grounds for making such a transition, it seems more plausible to explain the emergence of ritual and the presence of taboos as two strands or themes that arise from antagonistic mimesis. Such an explanation also avoids an overly deterministic account of religious "stages." Girard himself has clarified the antideterministic quality of his theory of the scapegoat: "I have never said that the mimetic mechanism is deterministic. We can hypothetically assume that several prehistoric groups did not survive precisely because they didn't find a way to cope with the mimetic crisis."[50] Humans are not programmed to scapegoat, but scapegoating arises consistently and pervasively as one available option for addressing mimetic conflagration.

The nature of scapegoating is clear enough: the scapegoat functions as a release and allows the community to abandon what Girard calls "the endless cycle of vengeance." It interrupts the process of repetitive and escalating violence. Girard notes: "But suddenly the opposition of everyone against everyone is replaced by the opposition of all against one. . . . There is now the simplicity of a single conflict: the entire community on one side, and on the other, the victim."[51] Scapegoating enables societies to release their need for revenge and reciprocation while forestalling further reciprocation. Girard explains, "Society is seeking to deflect upon a relatively indifferent victim, a 'sacrificeable' victim, the violence that would otherwise be vented on its own members."[52]

There is an undeniable echo of Girard's description in contemporary experience. We can hardly make it through the day without relying on scapegoating to consolidate group identity. It happens on the playground and in the department meeting. Once we understand the pervasiveness of scapegoating, and see its function in matters large and small, we can intuit the utility of scapegoating for societies that needed it far more urgently than middle school students or university professors do. Yet there also seems to be an unbridgeable difference—we do not murder our boss or stone the unpopular kid in middle school. It seems that contemporary escalation has its limits.

Examining a recent incident will help clarify the analogy between ancient and modern scapegoating. In the 2003 Major League Baseball playoffs, an avid Chicago Cubs fan reached for a foul ball near the stands down the left-field line. In so interfering with the play, he prevented the Cubs' left fielder, Moises Alou, from making the catch that would have brought the Cubs closer to an elusive World Series appearance. The Cubs went on to lose the game, for a variety of reasons, but what followed became one of the most curious sports stories in recent memory. Steve Bartman, the infamous fan who interfered with Alou, became a scapegoat: the city of Chicago unleashed its venom on him.[53]

Perhaps no professional franchise has endured a longer streak of bad luck than the Chicago Cubs. Since 1908, the team has failed to win a World Series. Yet in 2003, things were supposed to be different. The team boasted three talented pitchers and seemed poised to make it to the World Series. Its opponent, the undecorated Florida Marlins, had been in existence for less than twenty years. Chicago led the series 3 to 2, and its best pitcher, Mark Pryor, had tossed seven magnificent innings without allowing a run. The Cubs led 2–0 in Game Six, just five outs away from their first World Series appearance since 1945.

Alou was a notoriously bad outfielder, neither fast nor especially reliable with the glove. Left field, after all, is reserved for the worst outfielder. Alou, whose bat more than made up for his shoddy fielding, missed a chance to extend the Cubs' lead in the previous inning. He struck out with two runners on base. Perhaps Alou was still processing this failure when, upon failing to catch the foul ball, he jumped up and down and shouted expletives in the direction of Bartman. As the Cubs collectively unraveled in the eighth inning, giving up seven runs and making numerous errors, Cubs' fans quickly turned on Bartman. Before long the crowd began chanting "asshole" at Bartman. He received an escort by a cadre of policemen, not before being assaulted by more fans, who both cursed and threw beer at him. The Cubs lost the deciding game a day later, as another Chicago pitcher failed to protect a lead. The Marlins went on to win the World Series against the vaunted Yankees. The Cubs made the playoffs in 2007 and 2008, but they did not win another playoff game until 2015.

There are parallels between a sporting event and a religious ceremony. One attends the former as a spectator, but spectators can affect what happens on the field. Most teams play better in front of a friendly audience. Loud fans can affect the opposing team's concentration. A well-located, verbally willing fan can distract a player. Bartman interfered with the game, just as any fan does by cheering, or simply showing up, and as dozens of fans do each day by speaking to and even interacting with players during a live game—the tempestuous Joey Belle (with the Cleveland Indians at the time) once drilled a fan in the chest with a ball after the fan invited Belle, a recovering alcoholic, to a keg party. Fan interaction happens at the front row of every basketball game, or each time a player reaches into the stands for a live ball.

Powerful forces converged that night in Chicago. It was a crucial moment in the game. The team had long been cursed.[54] The player responded vehemently. The television crews focused their cameras on Bartman His appearance made him worthy of scorn. The uproar continued after his departure from the stadium. Within hours, his home telephone number was available to Cubs fans on a popular Internet message board, resulting in dozens of death threats against Bartman. Police officers were called on to protect his residence. How close was Bartman from being lynched? How serious was the mob aligned against him? What if it had been Game Seven of the World Series? What if he had been a White Sox fan? It is not hard to see in the case of Bartman all of the elements of a classic scapegoat, a convenient fall guy upon whom the crowd's fury is unleashed. When examining the Bartman incident, it would be a mistake to see only similarity between ancient and modern scapegoating. Powerful people, including the commissioner of Major League Baseball and the owners of the Cubs, came to Bartman's defense. Key Chicago players did the same, and his friends provided a ring of protection. Bartman was not lynched. Although many would have done violence to him, and a stadium of 40,000 avid fans rained down boos on him, most people came quickly to their senses and realized that one man was shouldering blame that deserved to be shared.

Alex Gibney, director of the documentary about the Bartman incident, pointed out that when things go wrong, humans tend to focus the blame on one person. We know and recognize the "scapegoat phenomenon." In a discussion with a sports journalist, Gibney asked, "Why did we need to seek out one person to blame it all on?"[55] He also has indicated that the real question is not, "When will Cubs fans forgive Steve Bartman?" but, "When will Steve Bartman forgive Cubs fans?" According to Girard, being modern means recognizing the scapegoat mechanism for what it is. It only works effectively if we remain unconscious of what we are doing. Of course, we still scapegoat, and in these instances we remain unaware, but it is now almost impossible to scapegoat with the same lack of awareness as did primitive societies.

At this point one might ask: What is the scientific basis for Girard's belief in the scapegoat mechanism? The scapegoat mechanism works more as a lens or presupposition through which to interpret the traces left by primitive religion. Since we lack video archives from the founding of Rome or the mounds of Cahokia, Girard begins from the evidence that we do have: (1) myths of origin and (2) cultural rites, rituals, and institutions—marriage, kingship, trade, religious ceremony, domestication of animals, sacrificial substitution, and so on. Positing the scapegoat mechanism explains the emergence of these rites and myths according to a single principle. And by studying these rites and myths, the scapegoat mechanism becomes more and more plausible. Before Girard, most scholars of religion began either with ritual or myth, and they explained the latter through the former, or the former through the latter. Girard thinks the scapegoat mechanism allows the study of religion to move beyond this impasse: "It is no longer a question of relating ritual to myth or even myth to ritual. Such procedures invariably produced a circular train of argument, from which the only means of escape seemed to lie in designating some arbitrary point of departure. It is good that this futile mode of thought has been abandoned."[56]

Girard's insight into the nature of ritual sheds light on how mimetic theory explains cultural origins. In *Violence and the Sacred*, perhaps Girard's most thoroughly researched book, he references Greek dramas, especially the Oedipus myth, in addition to many non-Western studies, and refers to fifty-three different monographs on ancient cultures. From this data, he posits: "The extraordinary number of commemorative rites that have to do with killing leads us to imagine that the original event must have been a murder. . . . And the remarkable similarities among the sacrificial rites of various localities suggest that the murder was always of the same general type."[57] In the same chapter, Girard turns his attention to a study of the Dinka, who still practice sacrifice.[58] Girard's summary of Dinkan animal sacrifice is helpful:

> The insistent rhythm of choral incantations gradually captures the attention of a crowd of bystanders who at first appeared scattered and self-absorbed. Participants begin to brandish weapons in mock warfare. A few isolated individuals strike out at others, but without any real hostility. . . . From time to time somebody detaches himself from the group to beat the cow or calf that has been tied to a nearby stake, or to hurl insults at it. There is nothing static or stilted about the performance; it succeeds

in giving shape to a collective impulse that gradually triumphs over the forces of dispersion and discord by bringing corporate violence to bear on a ritual victim.[59]

The ritual hints at a real murder in the past. Through language (choral incantations) the individual members gather into a collective. They become the "same" mob that killed a scapegoat, from which their sense of community derived. Girard continues: "In this rite the metamorphosis of reciprocal violence into unilateral violence is explicitly and dramatically reenacted. And it seems to me that the same can be seen to hold true for an infinite number of rites if one keeps a sharp eye out for signs (often, admittedly, fragmentary and elusive) that reveal the functioning of this particular metamorphosis."[60] Those performing the ritual are not "at play." They recall an earlier, foundational murder by reenacting the original event. Girard connects the manner in which Dinkas ritually sacrifice cows with the treatment of the *pharmakos* in classical Greek literature: "The actual execution sometimes consists of a veritable stampede of the entire group directed against the victim. In this case, it is the victim's genitals that are singled out. The same is true of the *pharmakos* who is whipped on his sexual organs with herbaceous plants. There is thus some reason to believe that the animal victim is a stand-in for an original victim accused, like Oedipus, of patricide, incest, or of some other sexual transgression."[61] Girard's analysis of ancient Greek rituals, the role of the *pharmakos*, and primitive cultures from around the world, yielded a remarkable symmetry. Dinkas used cows, and ancient Athenians used humans, but both rituals gain their intelligibility against the backdrop of an earlier incident. Girard explains, "The rite [surrounding the *pharmakos*] is therefore a repetition of the original, spontaneous 'lynching' that restored order in the community by reestablishing, around the figure of the surrogate victim, that sentiment of social accord that had been destroyed in the onslaught of reciprocal violence."[62]

Girard goes on to note strange continuity between the way different societies treat not only outcasts but also kings or queens. The latter are singled out as the cause for both unity and discord. On the basis of their mysterious power, one should not physically touch royalty. Traces of this taboo still exist in modern England, where one may touch the queen only lightly.[63] Girard points out that coronation ceremonies operate analogously to sacrificial rituals. The psychic distance between the coronation and the original murder determines the fate of the king, who, like the *pharmakos*, was preserved for the purpose of quelling a future mimetic crisis. Kings, argues Girard, became kings by learning how to transform their precarious status into real power during the *interregnum*. At some point, a community ceased to sacrifice the king and replaced him with a suitable substitute. Girard explains, "Since sacrifice is always a question of substitution, it is always possible to make a new substitution and henceforth to sacrifice only a substitute of the substitute."[64] In peaceful coronation rituals, just like in animal sacrifice, Girard discerns traces of early, more violent rituals. Yet most ethnologists, no matter how great the similarities, seem unwilling to draw any parallel between enthronement rituals that mirror collective violence and scapegoating rituals.[65] Girard extends his analysis to other rites and cultural institutions, including marriage, burial ceremonies, rites of passage, the domestication of animals, and the emergence of agriculture.

Although Girard's work follows a theoretical arc, he came to it through a strongly rational method. Only a scapegoat mechanism that brought about peace could explain the function of so many different kinds of ritual. And only through an attempt to see the rationale behind these rituals did Girard arrive at the scapegoat mechanism. His reading can be caricatured as monistic, a critique Girard addressed in an early work: "Any thesis that maintains that ritual is the imitation and reenactment of spontaneous, unanimous violence may well seem fanciful, even fantastic, as long as one considers a few isolated rites. But when one widens the scope of the inquiry, supporting evidence appears at every turn."[66] The real question for Girard is whether another explanation is more plausible. Girard's two foundational texts on sacred violence—*Violence and the Sacred* and *Things Hidden Since the Foundation of the World*—not only argue for the scapegoat mechanism, but they also show the shortcomings of other theorists, whether they be structuralists, Marxists, Freudians, or Cambridge ritualists. After describing rites of African monarchies, the cannibalistic rites of the Tupinamba, and the sacrificial ceremonies of the Aztecs, Girard asserts, "Everything changes once we begin to realize that the various 'scapegoat' phenomena are not the reflection of some ill-articulated guilt complex, but rather the very basis of cultural unification, the source of all rituals and religion. Seen in this light, the differences between these three ritual institutions do not appear so great; . . . The differences are due to the three different ways in which three societies look at the same process: the loss and subsequent recovery of social unity."[67] Stronger than the differences between rites, notes Girard, are the similarities between them. The modern tendency to laud difference *as such* has prevented earlier scholars from seeing the overarching commonality between such rites and their common origin in the scapegoat mechanism. Although we will never recover evidence from 753 BCE Rome to find out just what happened between Romulus and Remus, Girard considers his own investigation to be scientific.[68] The question of the scapegoat mechanism as an originating force of culture rests or falls on real evidence:

> Our theory should be approached, then, as one approaches any scientific hypothesis. The reader must ask himself whether it actually takes into account all the items it claims to cover; whether it enables him to assign to primitive institutions an origin, function, and structure that cohere to one another as well as to their overall context; whether it allows him to organize and assess the vast accumulation of ethnological data, and to do so in a truly economical manner, without recourse to "exceptions" and "aberrations." Above all, he must ask himself whether this theory applies not in single, isolated instances but in every conceivable situation. Can he see the surrogate victim as that stone initially rejected by the builders, only to become the cornerstone of a whole mythic and ritualistic edifice?[69]

Girard posed this question in 1972. Over the past forty years subsequent data has only strengthened his thesis. The scapegoat mechanism has become more, not less, plausible.

Mythic Concealment

In addition to taboos and rites, the scapegoat mechanism generates myths. Like rites, myths of origin show traces of an earlier scapegoat. Mythic texts reference but do not prove the founding murder. They provide data as effect to cause. Akin to modern tests that find gunpowder traces in the fingers of potential homicide culprits, Girard locates a violent trace in myths linked to earlier violence.

Cultures that come to the cusp of a mimetic catastrophe only to restore order through the scapegoat mechanism experience the victim as both the cause and resolution of mimetic escalation. Just as a ritual can only be effective if the participants are not aware of its true function, so the storytelling that commemorates the event must be unconscious about its concealing effect. The original victims referenced in these myths often develop supernatural powers to preserve peace after their death: they become gods who both threaten and protect. The myths that recall these gods both conceal and reveal the real history that lies behind them. Girard states: "I intend to show that all myths must have their roots in real acts of violence against real victims."[70]

Several things happen when cultures resolve a mimetic crisis through scapegoating. On the cusp of a crisis, where the differentiation upon which the society had relied becomes blurred, the group identifies and subsequently kills a victim. Myths point to this violence, but their authors remain largely unaware of what these concealing myths leave revealed, just as those who direct all of their rage at another do not realize how much such gestures reveal of themselves. Can it be that so many mythic stories have no real connection to any past events, let alone a murder? Girard thinks it unlikely. Take, for instance, the birth of Zeus. Various versions of this tale reference Zeus receiving "protection" from Kronos, which involved a circling dance around the child.[71] In the version Girard cites, the Curetes charged with protecting the baby "clash their weapons and behave in as noisy and threatening a way as possible."[72] Reading with a Girardian lens, we can see that collective murder lies behind the myth: danger looms; the child is part god; he is encircled by what seems like a mob, members of which brandish weapons. In an earlier, less refined version of the myth, the violence might have been more overt; in a later version, perhaps they might not behave in so threatening a manner. The distance from the founding murder conditions the concealment of the original violence.[73] But a real murder lies behind the mythic retelling.

In *The Scapegoat*, Girard set out to defend himself against critics who claimed that in *Violence and the Sacred* and *Things Hidden* Girard himself did violence to the texts from ancient and foreign cultures. To this end, Girard interprets a medieval text by Guillaume de Machaut.[74] Written at the time of the Black Death (1340s), Machaut charges Jews with poisoning the water, which caused the death of "ten times one hundred thousand." In response to such destruction, "every Jew was destroyed, some hanged others burned; some were drowned, others beheaded with an ax or sword."[75] Girard recalls this medieval text of persecution to raise the point that every modern person "does violence" to this text by imposing an external structure on it. We know that many people died from the plague, but that the cause was a disease transmitted by rats through the water supply—the cause was not Jews. We also know that the real violence done to the Jews derived from imagined acts of Jewish transgression. We understand the dynamics of Jewish persecution too well to read the text in any other way. Every "enlightened" person distinguishes the real from the imaginary in such texts. Girard makes the same division between true and false in his interpretation of myths: Oedipus did not cause the plague in Thebes by sleeping with his mother and killing his father. Yet the Thebans responded to the plague with the same attitude as the medieval residents of Navarre: by scapegoating a likely culprit—in the case of Oedipus, an outsider with a limp.

The violence done to Oedipus and to the Jews of Navarre are not myths of origin proper, like the story of the founding of Rome. Nor do they solve a crisis that began with mimetic violence. The towns of Thebes and Navarre suffered from disease. Yet the attempt to scapegoat an outsider in order to avert further misfortune echoes an earlier problem-solving pattern. According to Girard, both stories qualify as mythic because they take the perspective of the persecuting mob.

Before turning to the divinization of the victim, a brief recapitulation of Girard's position is in order. By presupposing a real victim behind the mythic tales, Girard is able to realign the various elements in myths that have been hitherto lacking coherent explanation. Girard argues that positing a real victim "allows us to understand why disorder prevails at the beginning of the myth; why the victim, at the moment of being driven out of the community, is considered guilty of having committed a crime that poses an immediate or long-term threat to the community. It allows us to understand why the lynching of this victim appears to be a just and good act."[76] Although myths tell their story from the perspective of the persecutors, one can still see the victim behind the text: "The face of the victim shows through the mask in the texts of historical persecutions. . . . In mythology the mask is still intact; it covers the whole face so well that we have no idea it is a mask."[77] In other words, the reader has no idea from the story itself that the victim is innocent, not guilty. To presume the victim's innocence requires carrying out a demythologization à la Girard.

Let us return to the scene in Chicago after the Cubs' infamous defeat. The people who might have done violence to Steve Bartman believed, at least for a few precious moments, in his total guilt. Belief in the victim's culpability orients the scapegoating process. When viewed from afar, people regard as tragically farcical the attitude of Germans toward Jews, Hutus toward Tutsis, and Greeks toward Turks. Yet the same people regard their own hatred of their enemies as justified. Girard decorates this condition with penal imagery: "Imprisonment in this system allows us to speak of an unconscious persecutor, and the proof of his existence lies in the fact that those in our day who are the most proficient in discovering other people's scapegoats, and God knows we are past masters at this, are never able to recognize their own. Almost no one is aware of his own shortcoming. . . . We only have legitimate enmities. And yet the entire universe swarms with scapegoats."[78] A mythic portrayal of the victim requires an author unaware of the differences the third-party reader of a persecution text recognizes: between the real and the imagined. Of Guillaume de Machaut, Girard writes, "The details that are so revealing in his text are not revealing for him, evidently, but only for those who understand their real significance."[79] The text of persecution lacks awareness. Only those sufficiently removed from the text, yet aware enough of the universality of persecution, can distinguish the mythic causality from the real victim behind the myth and the real events referenced. This dynamic explains how texts can reveal what the author had intended to conceal, much as a bully can reveal his own fear and low self-esteem.

The previous sections of this introduction to mimetic theory have covered the constellation of archaic religion—taboos, rituals, scapegoats, myths of origin—yet it has said almost nothing about God. Girard's etiology of religion attains intelligibility without any appeal to the supernatural or the divine. Indeed, Girard offers a wholly anthropocentric account of the divine. Humans project gods in the process of reflecting on the peace made possible by the victim. Myths tell stories in which gods resemble victims, and victims resemble gods. The gods bring order and chaos, comfort and fear, to communities unaware of how order disintegrates and peace returns. Yet approximate to these divinities lies the corpse of a victim; the story of Zeus's birth bears a discernible trace to an infanticidal ritual. According to Girard, "The victims are transfigured into all-powerful manipulators of disorder and order, founding ancestors, or divinities. . . . The divinized victims become models of ritual performance and countermodels of prohibition. This is how religion and culture originate."[80] Continued belief in the gods derives from the efficaciousness of this belief and the practices that engender it.

Archaic religion has both a negative and a positive function. From a utilitarian, anthropocentric standpoint, archaic religion is a good. The high priest in the Gospel of John, Caiaphas, articulated this *religious* logic: "Better one man die for the people than that the whole nation perish" (John 11:50). Archaic religion allows societies to attain a peace and stability upon which every human culture is built. It would be foolish to dismiss archaic religion out of hand, as the Enlightenment did. Girard's interpretation explains why our archaic forefathers crafted gods out of mere human projections. These gods, and the corresponding ceremonies and rites devoted to them, did not indicate a departure from rational existence but instead constituted an ode to the events that enabled humanity to survive the repercussions of its evolving intelligence.

Evangelical Revelation

Girard admits that when he first turned to the Judeo-Christian scriptures, he had expected to find the same pattern in comparative mythology and ethnology. Although infused with similar levels of violence, the structure of the Old Testament differed fundamentally from that of myths. Instead of finding myths that covered up the founding violence, Girard discovered tales that revealed this violence. Consequently, Girard attributed to Judaism and Christianity a set of insights he described as revelatory: that God has nothing to do with violence and that God sides with the victim. In the New Testament, God not only sides with the victim, but God *is* the victim. This is the evangelical truth "hidden since the foundations of the world" (Matt. 13:35). The gospel undoes myth by revealing what these myths tried to conceal. Michael Kirwan helpfully lays out this contrast: "The Gospel revelation is one that uncovers even more radically the truth which myth seeks to conceal, that is, the murderous interaction of human desires in order to preserve or protect a social order in time of crisis."[81]

The scriptural witnesses provide the insight necessary to demystify not only religion but also the entire human web of desire and reciprocation that entangles so many people with such regularity. Girard writes, "The Bible has given us the privileged tool of demystification."[82] This citation comes from Girard's book on Job, which begins as a typical scapegoat tale. Job stands out for his excellence—symbolized through his wealth and fortune. When Job loses everything, his friends, who represent the crowd or the mob, tell him that God must be punishing him. If it were a myth, there would be little difference between Job and Oedipus. Instead of a mythic text that conceals, the book of Job is a revelatory text that unveils. For Girard, the book of Job stops being a myth when Job gets to tell his side of the story.

The alignment of God with the victim, first expressed in Judeo-Christianity, marks a profound shift in religious consciousness. Unlike mythic victims, Job gets to proclaim his innocence: "The victim has the last word in the Bible."[83] This change in perspective radically undermines the cultural institutions generated by societies that developed from the perspective of the persecutors. Here Girard's insight converges with Nietzsche's: Christianity revalues good and evil. Although Nietzsche correctly assessed Christianity's impact, he misjudged its claims.[84] Christianity extends the Hebraic revelation and thus unleashes a demythologizing (anti)potency into the world. Because of Christianity, modern observers discern the falsity in so many texts of persecution. Girard declares, "No one is deceived any longer by the accusations of incest or infanticide made against the Jews during the Black Death in order to 'convince' them that they were the cause of the plague."[85] Indeed, we are able to take the side of the victim to such a degree that in some instances, being a victim is almost profitable, that is, in the politics of self-victimization.

From within Girard's paradigm, the look of a fleshed-out mimetic theology quickly takes shape: baptism means belonging to a community that inculcates a different pattern of belonging, a community built on a different order from that of the city of man. Jesus is the incarnate Word of God, who reveals the meaning of creation, the nature of our alienation from God (original sin), and our ultimate destiny (eschatology). The Holy Spirit, or *paraclete* ("defense attorney"), grants believers the power to know the innocence of the victim (pneumatology), whom Satan, the accuser, calls guilty. The Father, Son, and Holy Spirit give one another into being in such a way that the difference between relation and identity breaks down so that "three in one" and "one in three" becomes newly intelligible (Trinitarian theology). Their gift of creation intends to simulate the same pattern of peaceful difference (protology). God creates human beings, the image and likeness of God, for the sake of this communion (theological anthropology). This creative, divine initiative also explains why God becomes one of us (incarnational theology), so that humans understand the peaceful difference between themselves and God (theology of prayer), and themselves and others (theological ethics). The shape and order of Christian theology are easily intelligible from within the Girardian horizon and have been explicated by theologians following mimetic theory, and by Girard himself.

This chapter has introduced mimetic theory in a way that makes it easy to see how it can function as a general heuristic for Christian theology, both in terms of the way theology makes sense to itself and how theology argues for the plausibility of Christian truths to those outside the fold. Subsequent chapters both concentrate the mimetic heuristic and perform a mimetic interdiction into key theological questions. Chapter 2 begins by analyzing the way nature and grace meet in locating the place afforded to faith and rationality within Christian theology.

MIMETIC THEORY
AND RATIONAL FAITH

Framing the Problem: Girard and His Critics

Perhaps no topic lies closer to the heart of fundamental theology and apologetics than the relation between faith and reason. Mainstream Christian theology, especially the Catholic variety, has maintained the compatibility between the revealed truths of faith and reason. The truth that Christian faith proclaims cannot contradict philosophical and scientific truth.[1] The benevolence of God's creation does not contradict any scientific truth about the world's coming to be. The doctrine of original sin does not contradict what the truths discovered by modern genetics tell us about DNA and the genes shared between parents and their offspring. Traditional Christian theology also affirms the intelligibility of its faith claims. Indeed, the very task of theology is to make faith claims intelligible. Theology brings an ordered sensibility into the doctrines and fundamentals of the faith. A belief in this possibility implies, of course, a certain trust in logic and the power of rationality itself.

The claims of the preceding paragraph, however uncontroversial they may sound, have always met resistance, and for good reason. For the gift of faith takes a supernatural shape—a god not part of creation enters that creation in the form of a man; angels speak, supernatural powers intervene, and believers experience, often in dramatic and miraculous ways,

43

the healing grace that seems to interrupt so many patterns of human experience. As early as Paul's First Letter to the Corinthians, Christianity
declared the message of Christ crucified "foolishness" to the Gentiles
(1 Cor. 1:25). Loyal to this sentiment, theologians throughout Christian history, most prominent among them Tertullian, Luther, Pascal, and
Kierkegaard, have insisted that these supernatural truths had nothing to
do with the "wisdom of the world," be it philosophical, scientific, or any
other "respectable" source of truth. Tertullian declared, "I believe because
it is absurd," and he asked the rhetorical questions: "What has Athens to
do with Jerusalem? What concord is there between the Academy and the
Church?"[2] Luther called reason "the devil's whore."[3] Pascal, as my introduction chronicled, imagined an infinite distance between the god of the
philosophers and the god of religious experience. And Kierkegaard distinguished faith from other kinds of knowing by describing it as a leap
beyond reason. More relevant than the witness of these major figures is
the sentiment among ordinary believers that philosophy and science, especially cosmology and evolutionary biology, stand in permanent contrast to the truths of faith. Whence such insistence on incompatibility?

Mapping the relationship between faith and reason inevitably brings
a theology of grace to the surface. Both the introduction and chapter 5
describe the dynamic movement of grace. In this dynamic, the believer,
as forgiven, comes to realize the shape of this grace as more of an entry
into something bigger than a conceptual grasping of something to be
known discursively. This apparently elusive distinction has precedent in
classical theology. In the *Summa Theologiae*, Aquinas famously stated a
medieval axiom: "Grace builds upon nature; it does not destroy nature,
but perfects it."[4] Yet the relation between nature and grace is not simply
between two orders, one logically following another, like too much alco-
hol and a hangover. Rather, the graced, or supernatural, is better understood as wildly disproportionate rather than as consequent to the natural
order of things.[5] This disproportion, according to a broad reception of
the debate, does not set the supernatural against the natural, but it does
preclude its naturalization. The supernatural gift of faith makes possible
the understanding that constitutes the discipline of theology. On account of the nature of the life-giving truth promised to those who believe, many important Christian thinkers have insisted on this specific

difference, and they have found in thinkers like Tertullian a satisfying expression of this difference.

Theological reflection on the relation between faith and reason, therefore, has the task not only of showing compatibility between the two terms but also of showing the theological priority of faith. Anselm gave a noteworthy expression to this priority: "For I do not seek to understand that I may believe, but I believe in order to understand . . . Unless I believe, I would not understand."[6] Girard echoed this dictum when he explained, "The process [of conversion] is therefore perfectly rational, but it stems from a higher reason than ours. In my view, we have here [in mimetic theory] a new illustration of a very great traditional idea, faith and reason upholding each other. *Fides quaerens intellectum* and vice versa."[7] Knowledge of God requires the already-having-been-converted disposition in order to understand the object of faith's deepest mysteries. Premodern, or classical, theology, in part due to a notion of reason as participatory rather than autonomous, was able to hold faith and reason together in a fruitful tension.

This tension, maintained through the creation of certain distinctions in the medieval period, began to unravel in modernity. As modern accounts and norms for responsible knowing took shape, faith-based accounts, which had long been considered more reliable, became marginalized because of what was considered a hopelessly subjective or emotional standpoint. Modernity replaced premodern accounts of knowing with ones that privileged objectivity and lack of presupposition. Formerly queen of the sciences, theology had to settle for a much lower position on the scientific totem pole.[8] How could theology be considered equal to other sciences if, for instance, it gave such a large emphasis to arguments from authority?

In reaction to changing notions of knowledge and reason, theologians in the modern period increasingly devoted their attention to explaining how faith could once again build a bridge to reason. Many theologians refused to accept modern understandings of human reason uncritically, especially those that presumed a conflict between human rationality and religious belief. Theologians reconceived the priority of faith and also aimed to provide a theology of science and of human rationality. Nowhere was this push stronger than in the Catholic Church, which at the First Vatican Council (1870) insisted—with the fullest magisterial weight—on the possibility of knowing God through the light of natural reason.[9]

Much recent and current theological hand-wringing about reason and revelation, or the rationality of faith, derives from the tension that results from holding together two nonnegotiables: the donated or graced shape of Christian faith, and the rational structure of theological inquiry. Against the backdrop of this tension it is easier to explain the diverse but unrelenting dissatisfaction with Girard's method. Critics have accused Girard of being both too Christian and not Christian enough. Is René Girard a social scientist, whose own understanding of science does not rely on any prior belief or faith commitment, and who just happens to be a confessing Christian? Or is Girard a Christian apologist *sub rosa*, whose Christian commitments undergird his unique approach to questions in cultural anthropology? Girard himself has added to this confusion, complain critics, by contradicting himself about the relationship between his Christian faith and his purported scientific method. The ongoing debate about mimetic theory's relationship to theology forms a key vector in the wider argument that I am taking up in these pages. On this basis, an overview of some key critiques of Girard seems necessary.

A recent shot across the bow came from Sarah Coakley. In her inaugural lecture as Norris-Hulse Professor of Divinity at the University of Cambridge, Coakley bemoaned Girard's influence on Christian theology. Coakley called the continued influence of Girard's theory of sacrifice "astounding," and she evaluated its theological application to be "uncritical."[10] The lecture also determined Girard's irredeemably violent understanding of sacrifice to be the shadow side of a conception of Christianity stripped of its rightful rationality. Coakley's cursory remarks recall an older yet persistent misreading of Girard. Although Coakley qualifies her claims by pointing to the modification of Girard's thought since the 1970s, the basic criticism still stands.[11]

One purpose of this chapter is to exonerate Girard from two kinds of accusations: (1) his work excludes the theological; (2) his theological commitments reveal an insufficiently scientific approach by one claiming to do social science. From this analysis, the subtle nature of Girard's claims will become more apparent. Critics have too often assumed that because Girard says one thing, another must necessarily follow. In terms of the topic at hand, many commentators have failed—understandably considering Girard's own equivocations—to grasp the specifically Christian mode of Girard's argumentation. Michael Kirwan confirms this judgment when he writes, "Discussions about the 'scientific' status of Girard's theory have, on the whole, produced more heat than light. Critics will speak of Girard's discovery as a revisable hypothesis of science or a revealed truth of theology, or some combination of the two."[12] It is feasible, however, that Girard's affirmation of Christian rationality does not exclude his affirmation that faith and conversion are required components for any authentic insight into Christian truth.

Next to Hans Urs von Balthasar, no theologian has affected the discussion of mimetic theory more than John Milbank, the leading English theologian and inspiring force behind "radical orthodoxy." In his magnum opus, *Theology and Social Theory*, he states that theology must tread carefully around modern social theory, because "'scientific' social theories are themselves theologies or anti-theologies in disguise."[13] Even worse, these antitheologies rest on faith claims that directly contradict Christianity. Such fields as political science, anthropology, and sociology transport their hidden assumptions into pseudotheological discourses. In a masterful exercise in "archaeology," Milbank shows how deviant forms of theology, such as late medieval nominalism, made possible the creation of the spheres of secularity and autonomy on which so many modern discourses, such as those on rights, sovereignty, and private property, are based. He also shows how postmodern theorists, especially Nietzsche, root their critiques in a violent or agonistic ontology. Such an ontology bases itself on a theological presupposition that replaces Christianity's peaceful ontology with an agonistic one.

One might have surmised that Milbank's critique of modernity would find an ally in mimetic theory, both on account of Girard's contrast between Heraclitus and the Gospel of John and on account of his clear delineation between Christianity and religion.[14] Yet Milbank considers Girard's theory to echo a pre-Christian, agonistic metaphysics.[15] By eschewing a peaceful ontology, Girard's method, like modern social science, denies itself the chance to meld a scientific study of religion with the truth of Christianity. After noting Girard's recuperation of

Augustine's two cities (of God and of man), Milbank complains, "Girard stands fully within the positivist tradition . . . Religion can be 'explained' in social terms."[16] For Milbank, Girard's theory accepts the presupposition that modernity can objectively understand religion. Like Claude Levi-Strauss, Milbank's Girard unfairly criticizes ancient hierarchy: "It follows that Girard's entire attempt to 'explain' religion also privileges this same [modern] liberal culture."[17] Despite Girard's affirmation of Augustine's theoretical framework of the two cities, Milbank concludes that Girard differs fundamentally from Augustine on this point, in that Girard gives too strong of an ontological priority to the city of man.

It is not the task of the current chapter to correct Milbank's reading of Girard.[18] Milbank's argument, it can be said, represents a common critique of Girard's social scientific methodology. One first needs a social *theory*—mimetic desire—in order to arrive at a theological truth or set of truths—in this case the gospel. Such approaches, even by professed Christians or theologians, accept the modern displacement of theology, the shortcomings of which Milbank has highlighted so powerfully. Girard's method was mere grist for Milbank's mill. The question remains, a quarter century after Milbank's *Theology and Social Theory* appeared: What explanatory function does mimetic theory claim to give Christian theology?

For most anthropologists, on the other hand, mimetic theory remains radioactive. Anthropologists who encounter mimetic theory deem it unscientific because of its relationship to Christianity. In an age when popular anthropology and analysis of religion is almost a cottage industry, recent works in these genres either dismiss Girard with a wave of the hand or ignore him entirely.[19] There is a general suspicion that Girard operates as an apologist *manqué*.[20] By reading biblical revelation as a Rosetta Stone for interpreting the origins of culture, Girard's methodology exceeds the boundaries of modern social science. Since he is doing theology, argue modern anthropologists, there is no reason to reckon with it as anthropology. Robert North, Hayden White, and Markwart Herzog condemn mimetic theory for being insufficiently scientific. North argues that Girard's use of evidence fails to be falsifiable: "Whatever we *can* know that *fits* the theory is triumphantly adduced as proof of it. Whatever we can point to as *contradicting* his theory is equally acclaimed as a proof of the built-in unawareness, and thus as a justification of his system as a whole. Heads I win, tails you lose summarizes Girard's reading of the violent traces in mythology."[21] Similarly, Herzog and White consider Girard's approach to fall short of scientific standards.[22] Whereas Girard was too much of a social scientist for Milbank, he was not nearly enough of one for these critics.

Charles Bellinger's treatment of Girard splits the difference between the above critiques. After noting that Girard does not write as a theologian, Bellinger affirms that Girard "is clearly a religious thinker" who aims to "interpret human behavior using the Bible as his epistemological starting point."[23] Such a statement would seem to place Bellinger's subsequent critique in the former, scientific camp. Yet Bellinger, himself writing as a Christian, lauds faith-driven approaches to understanding violence, and he judges Girard's approach by this standard. Bellinger makes a recommendation: "Girard ought to drop the pretense of adhering to the methodological atheism of social science . . . He ought to write straightforwardly as a Christian apologist and argue that a theological mode of knowing is required for real insight into human behavior."[24] While affirming Girard's biblical starting-point, Bellinger laments Girard's scientific pose, which makes assent to the Christian faith seem superfluous to mimetic theory.

The ambiguity of Girard's position on the scientific, yet faith-based, nature of mimetic theory has also elicited questions from his interviewers. In *Battling to the End*, Benoît Chantre notes, "You do not speak of the pope in your books, and yet you are deeply Catholic, which is something that always bothers the scientific community and people of faith."[25] Echoing the comments recounted above, Chantre laments that Girard had managed to please nobody in this regard. Girard responded, "I am a little tired of shuttling between those who believe in Heaven and those who do not, as if each had to remain in his corner and never talk with the other."[26] This citation indicates that Girard saw his role as that of a mediator between two opposed groups, and that he experienced fatigue from playing this role. Yet even his confession of frustration does not answer whether he is a social scientist who happens to be Christian or a crypto-theologian whose faith conditions his science.

Girard's own remarks have lent credibility to multiple positions. In a recent interview, Girard declared, "I am fundamentally an anthropologist and a rationalist." Mimetic theory, Girard continued, does not require any prior faith commitment to be understood or explained: "This phenomenon as a scientific entity should be explained in purely anthropological terms. It takes no religious conviction to be understood."[27] Such a statement seems to verify Girard's insistence that mimetic theory can stand on its own *qua* theory. Girard made a similar claim in response to complaints about his pessimistic worldview: "I am first and foremost a researcher. I am not a French intellectual who proposes a certain way of looking at the new decade or the new millennium. I am a researcher, and what I have found seems to me to be true."[28] Such statements support Bellinger's hunch that Girard precludes any faith-based method in his research. Other statements, however, reveal a much more brazen faith-based approach. In *Battling to the End*, he admitted: "All of my books have been written from a Christian perspective."[29] *The Girard Reader* ends with this statement: "Mine is a search for the anthropology of the Cross, which turns out to rehabilitate orthodox theology."[30] Such claims, seemingly irreconcilable with the posture of scientific neutrality, problematize the attempt to articulate a coherent, Girardian account of the relationship between faith and reason.

It may be helpful at this point to deploy a metaphor from Bernard Lonergan. In *Insight*, he talks of an upper and lower blade. The upper blade yields generalities, whereas the lower blade produces empirical correlations.[31] Although I do not use the metaphor in the same way Lonergan does, the metaphor helps explain how one "blade" of Girard's theory, by itself, does not suffice without being in concert with the other blade. The blade metaphor is preferable to an optical metaphor because it conveys that no cutting takes place without both blades doing their part. Girard himself struggled to bring together the two blades in a conceptually satisfactory manner; instead, he would in one instant affirm the scientific character of his project, and in another instant declare that Christian faith commitments underpinned his entire intellectual project. The metaphor works, I think, because the two blades are not incompatible; rather, they constitute two distinct operations, and the absence of either one would render mimetic theory unable to cut. One must experience a kind of conversion to accept mimetic theory, but at the same time, the theory coheres from the perspective of scientific rationality.

The same hand-wringing and contrasting messaging that permeate modern theology also course through Girard's thought. The goal, then, is to organize these thoughts through a framework that will make them intelligible. Girard's attitude toward science seems to oscillate between an apology for the scientific nature of his own work and a brief against the bias in the science—anthropology—that he claims to do. Recapitulating Girard's attitude toward science will form the beginning of an answer to the critiques above. The answer will continue by recapitulating Girard's theology of reason, which he develops with the help of Pope Benedict XVI. Finally, the chapter takes up Girard's application of the Bible and Girard's autobiographical reflections on how his intellectual journey relates to his Christian faith. Here Girard utilizes more explicitly theological language, but it will be demonstrated how this usage is compatible with his earlier understanding of science and reason.

Science, Mimetic Theory, and the Problem of Bias

Girard's beginnings as a historian and then a literary critic make him an unlikely source for extended deliberations about scientific method. Since mimetic theory has come under such scrutiny, however, Girard found it necessary to explain the relation between mimetic theory and scientific method. Girard regards science as the process that lets us explain disparate facts by understanding their relationship to one another and bringing them into a pattern. One looks up at the sky, and there are only faraway lights, most of them stars. Science explains why they are only seen at certain times and in certain places, sometimes more clearly and sometimes less. This explanation requires not just observation but also induction, hypothesis, and theorizing. The heliocentric theory explains why certain planets are visible from certain locations; evolutionary theory explains why different animals share some of the same features, or why animals from the same species-family might have longer beaks, shorter necks, or dorsal fins. Yet neither theory arises from pure observation; it took geniuses like Copernicus and Darwin to challenge presuppositions and to discern patterns where none had previously been identified.

Girard maintains that mimetic theory performs the same kind of scientific deduction as Copernicus or Darwin performed in previous centuries. Mimetic theory and the theory of the scapegoat mechanism explain why religion exists in every culture, and why archaic religious practice was "red in tooth and claw." Girard notes, "Like all scientists, I am in search of the common factor, the pattern, rather than the difference."[32] Mimetic theory's ability to deduce a pattern from the disparate facts in early societies, argues Girard, makes it the most plausible account for how humans learned to survive. Like the theory of natural selection, it changes the way scientists look at the data. The similarity has led Michel Serres to call Girard the "Darwin of the human sciences."[33]

The emphasis on connecting the search for patterns with the shape of scientific inquiry is paramount for Girard. Patterns let one discern the intelligibility in the data, yet a pattern depends on the scientist's intuitive capacity, and it is not "just there." According to Girard, no scientist demonstrated this quality more perfectly than Charles Darwin. Each chapter in Girard's *Evolution and Conversion* begins with a quotation from Darwin—symbolizing Darwin's hitherto underrecognized impact on Girard.[34] Girard notes, "I believe there is something extremely powerful and admirable in his way of arguing, but I have always been fascinated by the way he thinks . . . I feel a strong kinship with [Darwin's] way of arguing: '*one long argument from the beginning to the end*.'"[35] Girard's admiration for and imitation of Darwin call into question those who accuse Girard of faith-based pseudoscience.

Girard has maintained that his own religious commitments did not prevent him from regarding mimetic theory as scientific. To gain greater clarity on how this could work, it will be helpful to recall another contested scientific theory. Almost all scientists before Copernicus thought that the sun revolved around the earth. Evidence was (and is) available for this theory every time they observed the sun *setting*. A heliocentrist cannot simply dismiss the evidence for geocentrism as faith-based or as antiempirical. Good science, however, requires more than observation; the eyes can deceive. Immanuel Kant made this very point in the second preface (1787) to his *Critique of Pure Reason*: "[Galileo, Torricelli, and Stahl] learned that reason has insight only into that which it produces *after a plan of its own*, and that it must not allow itself to be kept, as it were, in nature's leading-strings, but must itself show the way with principles of judgment based upon fixed laws."[36] Scientific progress requires the generation of laws or patterns (this is what Lonergan means by the upper blade), and the corresponding empirical confirmation. On their own, however, data (the lower blade) do not generate patterns. The geocentrists presupposed geocentrism, which a setting sun served to confirm. Yet awareness of more subtle movements of the stars and spheres, gained through technological advances, made the old geocentrism increasingly implausible. The invention of better telescopes did not cause but merely made possible the paradigm shift initiated by Copernicus. Analogously, Girard thinks he has come up with a theory to explain the confusing data that hovers about the question of how human culture began. Here it is worth citing Darwin: "Innumerable well observed facts were stored in the minds of naturalists ready to take their proper places as soon as any theory which would receive them was sufficiently explained."[37] Girard thinks the same situation applies to anthropology.

Girard's theory of the scapegoat mechanism has nonetheless engendered stiff opposition from social scientists. Some have pointed to Girard's lack of anthropological fieldwork, but the more trenchant complaint concerns the problematic relationship between mimetic "theory" and evidence.[38] As seen in chapter 1, such critics as Herzog and North complain that since mimetic theory cannot be proven false, it does not qualify as scientific. Karl Popper famously introduced the category of "falsifiability" to determine whether a field of study was scientific. Further evidence or a new interpretive framework could make the claims for heliocentrism false. According to Popper, the capacity to be disproven makes a scientific theory scientific. The Christian belief that God revealed Himself through Jesus of Nazareth, on the contrary, is not a *scientific* claim. It, along with belief in the existence of God, cannot be disproven. The Gospels may be demonstrated to be corrupted, the Church exposed as rotten, the moral character of Christian leaders vicious, but none of these can disprove the Christian claim about God, for such a claim is not *scientific*. The Christian faith makes *metaphysical and historical* claims not open to testing.

Girard's recent writings have clarified and qualified the scientific status of mimetic theory. In reflecting on his manner of argument in his earlier anthropological work, where he developed the theory of the scapegoat mechanism, Girard noted, "I think that the elements favourable to my thesis are too numerous and consistent to be disputed, but any of those taken by themselves cannot be regarded as a veritable proof. It is the multiplicity of consistent elements that constitutes proof."[39] In *Violence and the Sacred* and in *Things Hidden Since the Foundation of the World*, Girard enlisted facts about kingship, the domestication of animals, and various rituals that serve as evidence. Girard thinks that mimetic theory offers the best and clearest explanation of the different data.

For Girard, it is necessary to qualify somewhat the degree to which a field like anthropology can be scientific. Girard considers mimetic theory to be just as data-driven as other theories in cultural anthropology. Like many other social sciences, anthropology falls short of the certainty achieved in a laboratory. Still, mimetic theory has failed to win over many working anthropologists. Girard has reflected on this point: "I think the evidence in my theory is very strong, but possibly not well presented. It would perhaps be easier for someone with a background in logic."[40] In his later reflections, Girard seems vexed about how to communicate his theory in a way that would be more convincing.

Girard's reflections on the impact of mimetic theory explain his qualifications about the capacity for facts to change opinions. In *Evolution and Conversion*, he points to the hermeneutical problem that conditions the way a scientist receives different data. Because of this problem, he notes, "Everybody chooses to emphasize certain data more than others."[41] Once one knows where to look, Girard surmises, it becomes easier to find the pattern, much like patterns of natural selection were for Darwin: "When one is aware of the mimetic theory and finds examples such as this, one has a sense of recognition. This is the sort of evidence Hocart calls circumstantial . . . According to him, anthropological evidence is always indirect, circumstantial, like a clue in a detective story."[42] Girard here refers to the work of British anthropologist Arthur Maurice Hocart (1883–1939), who authored *Kings and Counselors*. Hocart's work pushed back against a naively objective approach to evidence.[43] The "science" of the origins of humanity is a science, but it cannot produce the level of repeatability that one finds in a lab, or pretend that facts alone drive the discipline.

The nature of anthropological research unsettles the ardor to use falsifiability as a gatekeeper for scientific legitimacy. When pressed on whether mimetic theory is falsifiable, Girard responded: "[Such a testing] would be of limited value. It would not be at the intellectual level of the theory as a whole, most of which cannot be subjected to empirical verification or falsification through empirical testing or the canons of contemporary science, especially the principle of falsifiability."[44] Such comments indicate how Girard's desire to argue for the scientific quality of his theory led him to question some of the boundaries that philosophers of science had erected. In *Evolution and Conversion*, he added, "The question of Popperian 'falsifiability' is a red herring since we aren't talking about a natural phenomenon that can be tested and debunked in laboratories. In the same way, Darwin's evolutionary theory can't be dismissed by the standard procedure of falsification. There are plenty of undoubtedly true things which are not verifiable or falsifiable in the Popperian sense."[45] Here it seems the case that Girard's questions about scientific legitimacy arose from a desire to describe reality rather than show the rationality of religious claims.

Girard thinks that many anthropologists eager to pass the Popperian threshold have, ironically, failed to be scientific. In the discipline there persists contempt for grand or universal theories. He laments, "If all universal notions are to be condemned as 'monolithic,' anthropology will never become a science, and its interest is quite limited."[46] Tepidity prevents modern anthropology from embracing mimetic theory. Yet an overly narrow view of science means that various norms of investigation fall outside of scientific purview. Girard includes mimetic theory in such a category: "Mimetic theory is not contemptuous of science; yet unlike the social sciences, it is not tempted to ape the methods of the natural sciences."[47] In *Evolution and Conversion*, Girard gives the example of witchcraft: How does a scientist determine whether the evil eye works? Or whether a person has control of supernatural forces that might make someone ill by sticking needles in a doll? Girard seems to conclude that the social sciences, and even evolutionary biology, make rational arguments based on evidence. Never *just there*, like a measurement, evidence gains force from the way it fits or contradicts earlier supposed evidence; it relies on presupposition. Because mimetic theory posits that myths attempt to conceal founding violence, mimetic theory has reason to believe that the evidence has already been tampered with. Many of the myths show only the barest trace of violence. Girard's claim that the data had been tampered with has not satisfied his critics. Still, his theorizing about the origin of cultures lies within the basic canons of reason and science.

Toward a Theology of Reason

Despite being accused of tainting the data through religious bias, Girard thinks accusations of bias apply just as easily to the field writ large. For Girard, bias prevents these disciplines from achieving a deeper understanding of cultural origins: "I do think that the approach to facts in the social sciences should be devoid of both religious and anti-religious assumptions."[48] Contemporary anthropology has been plagued by antireligious assumptions, and Girard traces these assumptions to the Enlightenment critique of religion. Girard argues, in short, that if anthropologists were more rational, they would be more receptive to religion.

Beholden to Enlightenment dogmas, modern anthropology has presupposed that religion has and had no practical use. Its universality can only make sense if one considers religion to be parasitic, as Voltaire and Nietzsche so famously did. Modern anthropology has, by and large, excluded religious evidence in its attempts to answer its questions. Girard comments, "In the context of the rationalism espoused by anthropological studies, religion plays no real part and is of absolutely no use. It can only be superfluous, superficial, a secondary addition."[49] Bias, not science, explains the inability of the majority of anthropologists to follow Girard's lead. In this context the term *rationalism* implies the distortion of the faculty of reason. It perverts the knowing process through bias. On account of this bias, anthropologists have misread the most important data pertaining to the question of human and cultural origins.

Girard connects his brief for antireligious bias to a broader critique of postmodern relativism, especially in regard to religion. Relativism, according to Girard, precludes scholars from determining any difference between religions or cultures, and thus leads them to ignore the peculiarity of the biblical witness. Girard's rhetoric on this point is typically pointed: "This rationalist expulsion of religion continues to dominate contemporary anthropology, even though anthropologists and other social scientists now try to conceal somewhat the simplistic character of their views . . . The modern social sciences are essentially antireligious."[50] Unlike modern anthropology, which excludes religion *a priori*, Girard's offers a less dogmatic anthropology. Yet his theory has been attacked as crypto-apologetic. Contemporary anthropology, however, ignores the possibility that religion might provide the matrix that explains the origin of culture while at the same time avoiding the accusation of bias because the wider culture shares the same assumptions. Because it challenges these assumptions, mimetic theory has generated the excitement and backlash that it has.

There is an additional layer to Girard's analysis of how the social sciences study religion. As hinted at in chapter 1 (and developed further in chapter 4), Christianity demythologizes religion. Christianity also paves the way for the subsequent demythologization at the heart of so much of the social and human sciences. Girard states, "I conclude that the force of demythification in our world comes from the Bible. This answer is unacceptable to those who feel that anything that would place the Bible in a favorable light cannot be seriously envisioned by scholars because it must be a *religious*—and therefore an irrational—view, with no value whatsoever."[51] Such bias continues to prevent the kind of insight and openness needed for genuine discovery. Girard concludes, "This attitude is itself irrational, motivated by religious prejudice."[52]

In *I See Satan Fall Like Lightning*, Girard references the problem of religious evidence. If modern sociology and anthropology presuppose that religion represents an irrational incursion into human culture, then these fields will continue to ignore evidence that religion holds the key for understanding the emergence of cultural institutions. Like the geocentrists of the sixteenth century and earlier, these fields rely on an assumption that has become increasingly implausible: "This possibility is that religion is the heart of every social system, the true origin and original form of all institutions, the universal basis of human culture."[53] Girard reached this conclusion by shedding the antireligious animus that dominated these fields of study: "Modern research would have found their true origin long ago if it had not been handicapped by its irrational hostility to religion."[54] The social sciences, on Girard's reading, fall short of authentic rationality. This failure relates especially to academic anthropology's resistance to mimetic theory, as Girard outlines in *Evolution and Conversion*: "My feeling is that the real obstacle in the case of mimetic theory hasn't simply been the incompleteness of the record but the *unwillingness and inability of our world to question its own fundamental assumptions*. In particular, a real obstacle has been the inability of anthropology to deal with the questions I am addressing, even as hypothesis."[55]

Pope Benedict XVI's "Regensburg Lecture" gave Girard the opportunity to connect his critique of bias in the social sciences to a more general discussion of how faith and reason relate. Delivered to an audience at his hometown university, Benedict's lecture has been remembered mainly for a gaffe about Islam.[56] Girard's commentary on this speech offers his clearest distillation of how faith and reason relate.[57] At the beginning of his text, Benedict cited a negative comment by Manuel II Paleologus, the fourteenth-century Byzantine emperor, who assessed Islam thusly: "Show me just what Mohammed brought that was new, and there you will find things only evil and inhuman, such as his command to spread by the sword the faith he preached."[58] With no awareness of the wider context of the talk, or even the fact that the pope was only quoting and not approving Emperor Manuel's statement, protesters reacted angrily. Muslim groups attacked churches in Palestine, a Pakistani cleric issued a *fatwa* asking Muslims to kill the pope, and one fanatic shot a nun in Somalia.[59] Against this backdrop, Girard's ringing endorsement of the Regensburg lecture, in an interview titled "Ratzinger Is Right," struck a discordant note.

Those acquainted only with the backlash generated by the lecture would be dumbfounded by Girard's declaration that he "wholeheartedly approve[d] of this lecture."[60] The central thesis of the address, ignored by most commentators, concerned norms for how faith should relate to reason. More precisely, Pope Benedict attempted to demonstrate the essential openness of Christianity to the Greek philosophical tradition, before lamenting the modern tendency to separate faith from reason, either through a scientific spirit closed to religion or through the hostility toward science witnessed to by faith communities. The lecture attacked Western secularism far more stridently than Islam; the problem with modernity, for Pope Benedict, lay not so much in its preference for reason, but in its exclusive preference for a certain kind of reason. The modern concept of reason permits no space for religion outside the realm of private subjectivity—"The subject then decides, on the basis of his experiences, what he considers tenable in matters of religion." For Benedict, this means that religious experience and the knowledge gained by faith can no longer forge a reasonable community. "This," the pope continued, "is a dangerous state of affairs for humanity, as we see from the disturbing pathologies of religion and reason which necessarily erupt when reason is so reduced that questions of religion and ethics no longer concern it." By falling into a mutual distrust, lamented Benedict, both reason and faith will suffer.

Like Pope Benedict, Girard thinks that reason needs religion to be rational—*reason within the limits of mere religion*, as it were. Girard affirms that modern forms of reason have already manifested religious traits: "Christian truth is now facing two religions, which are all the more terrible because they are hostile to each other: rationalism and fideism."[61] Christianity—at least in the form of Christianity advocated by the pope—can broker the "dialogue of cultures" because it has successfully navigated a course between the Charybdis of rationalism and the Scylla of fideism. Reason stripped of its religious roots cannot solve the problem; it needs to reorient itself toward the divine. By brokering this impasse, which the Regensburg lecture did in outline, Christianity will "demystify rationalism and fideism," just as it demystified archaic religion by pointing to the charade of the scapegoat mechanism.[62] Like Benedict, Girard insists that reason and faith "not be disturbed by a complete separation. The orders should neither be mixed up, nor separated, but *understood*."[63] This imperative, which Girard sees as fundamental for Christianity, resonates with the pope's insistence that faith and reason come into harmony: "The fundamental decisions made about the relationship between faith and the use of human reason *are part of the faith itself*."[64]

As I stated in the introduction, Pascal posited that the purpose of reason was to show its limits. A thorough, rigorous application of reason to reality reveals an aporia between what reason can know, and the object of its search. Acknowledging this aporia results from an application of reason, and it cannot be dismissed as a religious judgment. Girard's reflection on the scientific status of mimetic theory helped prod him toward this Pascalian position.[65] In his 2004 conversation with Gianni Vattimo, the two discussed their adult return to the Catholicism of their youth. For Girard, Vattimo's return symbolized the dead end that philosophy can become if left to its own devices.[66] Here Girard's understanding of reason's limitations echoes Pascal: "Christianity values human reason but does not believe it can lead to some absolute truth."[67] Vattimo's autobiographical remarks, collected in a short work, *Belief*, situates his religious return more in affective than in rational categories. In their conversation it was Girard, not Vattimo, who insisted that Christian faith must be understood to include an openness to reason and truth. In response to Vattimo's focus on love, Girard adds, "I agree with Vattimo when he says that Christianity is a revelation of love, but I don't exclude that it is also a revelation of *truth*."[68] If it remains closed off from the divine, modern philosophy is at a dead end: "It is becoming clearer all the time that religion defeats philosophy and outstrips it. In fact, the various philosophies are dead on their feet."[69] Girard's critique of philosophy, like his critique of social science, does not depend on having privileged access to revelation, but on the failure of these fields to be open to what reality reveals.

Girard's gloss on the pope's Regensburg lecture marks an advance from his earlier thinking, which lumped together Greek philosophy and pagan culture. Chapter 4 of *Things Hidden* contrasts the Heraclitian and the Johannine *logos*.[70] In these pages Girard argues that the "Hellenization" of Christianity came belatedly: "The notion that Christianity could be translated into philosophical terms was only admitted very gradually."[71] The Girard of *Things Hidden* would have been an unlikely advocate of Pope Benedict's exaltation of the pre-Christian, Greek philosophical tradition, especially Plato. As Pope Benedict stated in the "Regensburg Lecture," the fusion of biblical faith with Greek philosophy preceded even the birth of Jesus. Biblical faith benefited theologically, if not practically, from its encounter with Hellenism, which resulted "in a mutual enrichment." Even the translation of the Hebrew Bible into Greek—the Septuagint—represented "an encounter between genuine Enlightenment and religion" that "proved decisive for the birth and spread of Christianity." For Pope Benedict, Christianity entails believing in the compatibility between faith and reason.

In *Things Hidden*, Girard contrasted Heraclitus's *logos* to the *logos* of John's gospel. Girard declared the former to belong to the same fallen order as all other culture: "Something common to all cultures—something inherent in the way the human mind functions—has always compelled us to misrecognize the true Logos. We have been led to believe that there is only one Logos, and that it is therefore of little importance whether that Logos is credited to the Greeks or the Jews."[72] The key, then, is to distinguish the Greek from the Judeo-Christian *logos*. Johannine *logos* entails the recognition that sinful human culture will always expel the truth of the victim's innocence—"He came to his own home, and his own people received him not" (John 1:10–11). Greek philosophy, for all of its insights, does not arrive at the truth of the scapegoat mechanism, and thus it can never really appropriate the Christian *logos*. In *Things Hidden* Girard applauded Heidegger's separation of Greek from biblical *logos*: "Heidegger makes the final gesture that disencumbers Western thought of all the pseudo-Christian residues that still clung to it; he separates the two types of Logos by showing that everything is Greek and nothing is Christian."[73] By distinguishing Greek from biblical reason, the Girard of *Things Hidden* expressed an opinion about the Greek that differed significantly from his position in *Battling to the End*.

Like the part of the Christian tradition associated with Tertullian and his dictum cited above ("I believe because it is absurd"), Girard has occasionally manifested a philosophobic streak. When I met with him in early 2008 and asked him about Eric Voegelin (whose bedside chaplain was Robert Hamerton-Kelly, a devout Girardian!), he volunteered that the problem with philosophers is that they never really experience anything. This anecdote corresponds to the casual antiphilosophical statements that Girard would often make. When pressed, however, he would qualify his claims.[74] I suspect that this suspicion came from his intuition that one cannot accurately account for the entirety of the knowing process without recourse to saving knowledge, which invites such words as conversion or grace. I also suspect that John Paul II's and Benedict XVI's emphasis on relating faith to reason had something to do with Girard's later revisions. To recall language from earlier in this chapter, this knowledge forms the upper blade. Without it, mimetic theory might be coherent, but it cannot be complete.

The Limits of Theory and the Need for Grace

The near total absence of any specifically Christian or theological language in Girard's first two books—*Deceit, Desire and the Novel* and *Violence and the Sacred*—lent the impression that those earliest works were pre-Christian. Since the publication of *Things Hidden*, however, Girard has consistently highlighted the Christian inspiration of his thought and has made explicit his attempt to unify mimetic anthropology with Christian orthodoxy. The final sentence of *The Girard Reader* lays it bare: "Mine is a search for the anthropology of the Cross, which turns out to rehabilitate orthodox theology."[75] Yet recent interviews have upended this claim, as Girard has insisted on the unity of his entire project. His religious conversion, which he dates to Holy Week 1959, preceded the publication of these works.[76] So it makes little sense to imagine mimetic theory, even in its "pre-Christian" phase, as something other than the reflections of an already converted thinker.

As a person of faith, Girard considers the biblical texts to be divinely revealed. The debt to biblical wisdom emerges in his titled work; three different books echo biblical verses: *Things Hidden* (Matt. 13:35), *I See Satan Fall Like Lightning* (Luke 10:18), and *Job: The Victim of His People*—the French original reads *La Route antique des hommes pervers* (Job 22:15). Additionally, both *I See Satan Fall Like Lightning* and *The Scapegoat* mainly consist in exegesis of scriptural passages. Even in works that take up other concerns—*Evolution and Conversion* and *Battling to the End*—Girard references biblical stories and insights.[77]

Concerns about Girard's unorthodox approach to anthropology likely derive from his use of scripture. Critics seem to understand the dilemma through the framework of cause and effect. Either Girard became a Christian, and his faith caused or generated his literary criticism/social science; or he began as a literary critic/social scientist and used the Bible solely for empirical validation. By recalling the metaphor of upper and lower blades—the upper being personal conversion, the lower being scientific plausibility—it becomes feasible to reconceive Girard's account outside of such a framework. His discussion of the relationship between ritual and myth reveals the problem of relating interpretation to data: "Normally ritual is more directly revealing than myth, and this is because it confirms the interpretation of the latter as the resolution of the mimetic crisis. This reciprocal interpretation helps to solve many hermeneutical problems. Ritual confirms that the victim is really killed. Myth suggests that the victim is killed in order to reproduce the effects of the first murder."[78] Girard does not question what came first. What is at stake, rather, is the relationship between evidence and interpretation. Believing in the violent roots of ritual alters the way one interprets myths; reading myths as concealers of violence compels one to look for violent rituals and origins. For Girard, "the problem itself is circular, and one has to choose a point of entry into this descriptive circle, which isn't self evident."[79] So too with the biblical texts. At times Girard states that the Bible is the source of mimetic truth. At other times, Girard applies mimetic theory to biblical stories, as if the theory were independent of its source.

Still, from *Things Hidden* onward, Girard has consistently underlined the exceptional quality and force of the biblical witness. Scripture is not only a source of truth for Girard; it is the locus for reconsidering the entire horizon within which he reads all other texts. On this point Girard is at his most theological. The biblical texts and the Jesus event so shook the foundations of archaic culture and religion as to render it impotent. In its wake has arisen a "Western" worldview, with its unique attitudes toward itself and other cultures, one manifestation of which is the field of anthropology.

Since Girard admits his debt to the insights of biblical revelation and allows the Bible to inspire so much of his writing, it is justifiable that scholars like Kevin Mongrain regard Girard as a theologian. Such judgments, however, do not make his anthropological theories extrascientific. The later Girard became more transparent about this debt. In *The Girard Reader*, for instance, he admits: "The main source of my intuition is the Gospels, which unmask the role of collective foundational murder."[80] He has also rebutted the impression that his early work was somehow pretheological: "The sequence leading up to *Things Hidden* . . . gives the erroneous view of a theoretical movement from mimesis to myth, then to the Gospels, whereas in fact, a more fundamental understanding goes in the opposite direction."[81] These claims seem counterfactual; *Violence and the Sacred* identified the foundational murder, after all, without any reference to the Gospels. Girard's insight about Christianity—that it reads archaic culture with greater depth than modern anthropology—makes it possible to make sense of this conundrum. He asserts, "It is Christianity that reads mythology better than any anthropologist, and allows us for the first time to unmask the mimetic mechanism. . . . The most decisive text for the understanding of the mimetic mechanism is the Gospels."[82] *Battling to the End* echoes these claims: "Judeo-Christianity and the prophetic tradition are the only things that can explain the world in which we live. There is a mimetic wisdom, which I do not claim to embody, and it is in Christianity that we have to look for it . . . The Crucifixion is what highlights the victimary mechanism and explains history."[83] These citations do not undermine earlier statements about the scientific status of mimetic theory. But Girard seems to be saying that Christianity made it possible to conceive mimetic theory. The social sciences cannot ever grasp the source of their truth if they remain beholden to a truncated view of reality.

The circularity of mimetic theory means that a mimetic account of desire can also inform biblical interpretation. Mimetic theory sheds light on how anthropological evidence indirectly attests to the founding murder and to the universality of the scapegoat mechanism. The Bible's witness to this truth offers apologetic fortification for Christians, should they want it. Girard's reflections on the Ten Commandments in *I See Satan Fall Like Lightning* exemplify his method for reading mimetic theory into the scriptural passages.[84] Here the mimetic reading reveals the text's deepest meaning. According to Girard, the final commandment (the tenth) in Exodus 20 unlocks the meaning of the previous commandments, but modern translators miss the point: "The verb *covet* suggest that an uncommon desire is prohibited, a perverse desire reserved for hardened sinners. But the Hebrew term translated as 'covet' means just simply 'desire.'"[85] With this insight Girard connects biblical law with mitigating the rivalry and the violent escalation that results from unchecked desire. The final commandment covers the previous commandments; well-ordered desires make the other commandments superfluous. The list, however, reveals the order of discovery rather than the order of importance: "In reading the tenth commandment one has the impression of being present at the intellectual process of its elaboration. To prevent people from fighting, the lawgiver seeks at first to forbid all the objects about which they ceaselessly fight, and he decides to make a list of these. However, he quickly perceives that the objects are too numerous: he cannot enumerate all of them. So he interrupts himself in the process, gives up focusing on the objects that keep changing anyway, and he turns to what never changes."[86] Such an interpretation shows the power of Girard's exegetical abilities. Yet the lukewarm reception of his work into biblical studies recalls the difficult encounter of mimetic theory with anthropologists.[87]

By using scripture to illuminate anthropological truths, Girard introduces readers into his theory of mimetic desire and shows its breadth. He interprets the order of the Decalogue in a way that highlights the truth of his own theory. This pattern continues several pages later: "Rather than beginning with the cause and pursuing then the consequences, like a philosophical account, the Decalogue follows the reverse order, tackling the most urgent matter first: in order to avoid violence it forbids violent acts."[88] This style of interpretation dominates Girard's *oeuvre*. His analyses of John the Baptist's beheading and Peter's denial bring out the mimetic underpinnings in these stories.[89] In these moments Girard really is doing theology, and he considers such activity of the same order as the literary interpretation that he had performed in his earliest work.

This chapter began by suggesting that faith and reason, or the natural and the supernatural, offer modes of knowing that, when not properly integrated, cannot give a complete account of reality, nor can they offer an epistemology that adequately explains how they arrive at this reality. Girard's remarks on science, bias, and the rationality of religion, when placed together, not only answer the questions raised about his method but also overlap with the theological efforts to relate faith to reason. By closing with an explication of Girard's account of faith, it will be possible to fill in remaining questions about how Girard relates faith to rationality.

On one level—natural faith—Girard believes in the truth of Christianity in a way analogous to belief in heliocentrism, or in the law of

natural selection. Girard went from being skeptical about Christianity
to being convinced of its veracity. Yet biblical faith also implies, as noted
above, that one has received this faith as a gift. Believing in the Resurrection, the divinity of Jesus, and the Incarnation operates on the same
level as a "natural faith" in things unseen, be it karma, the tooth fairy, or
the heroism of one's mother or father. Different in kind from this level
of faith is the surrender of one's whole life to God. Pascal implied this
difference when he famously wrote: "God of Abraham, God of Isaac,
God of Jacob, not of philosophers and the scholars."[90] The latter, supernatural faith is rooted in the experience of religious conversion. Girard's
insight into supernatural faith and his implicit distinction between it
and natural faith form a key element in understanding how faith and
reason relate.

Although mimetic theory possesses its own intrinsic intelligibility,
and although Girard thinks he has validly and coherently argued that
biblical texts deconstruct mythology, he does not cancel the supernatural
character of faith. Girard understands the biblical revelation of the scapegoat mechanism as "stem[ming] from a reason more powerful than our
own."[91] Rather than conceiving saving truth as a matter of simply following certain steps right up to the revealed truths of Christianity, Girard's
explanation brings out the graced quality of faith. Mimetic theory cannot be reduced to a truth that results from looking hard enough at the
anthropological data, or attending closely enough to the great novels and
to the Gospels. Mimetic theory is also a theory about conversion. One
must acknowledge one's own complicity or sinfulness if the theory will
ever be something more than just another social theory. Girard writes,
"Conversion means accepting the mimetic nature of desire. Otherwise,
one would fall back on the old authentic/inauthentic binary opposition . . . We have already seen how misleading and illusory this sort of
individualism is. The only way to overcome it is through a conversion,
which ultimately leads to a revision of one's own religious belief."[92] Such
statements confirm that mimetic theory, as a discourse for the converted,
operates within a theological framework.

Girard broached the topic of conversion long before his more explicitly confessional writings. Already in 1961, *Deceit, Desire, and the Novel*
addressed the conversion experience of certain novelists. Girard's central

insight into the great novelists was that at some point they underwent a conversion: "The novelist comes to realize that he has been the puppet of his own devil. He and his enemy are truly indistinguishable. . . . This experience is shattering to the vanity and pride of the writer."[93] In his treatment of Cervantes, Girard showed how the process of reading could inflame mimetic desire. As the novelistic type of conversion came into focus, certain novelists, especially Dostoevsky and Proust, initiated Girard's own conversion. Although he has been understandably hesitant to discuss his own conversion, in his interview with James Williams, he revealed, "I realized I was undergoing my own version of the experience I was describing."[94] Yet he categorized it as an "intellectual-literary" conversion, or simply an "intellectual" conversion.[95] The conversion was, in other words, not "religious."

The interview with Williams that concludes *The Girard Reader* and the interview with the French journalist Michel Treguer recount the insufficiency of Girard's initial conversion. Recalling Augustine's distinction between his intellectual and religious conversion, Girard confesses that he was incapable of conforming the way he lived to his new intellectual conviction.[96] He even admits that during this period of intellectual conversion he experienced an enhanced aesthetic appreciation, which included rapturously listening to Mozart operas. A cancer scare, however, shook Girard terribly, transforming his intellectual conversion "into something really serious in which the aesthetic gave way to the religious."[97] Girard's discovery that his scare was not lethal synchronized with the events of Holy Week 1959. Like Christ, Girard went through (the threat of) death only to be raised up through the undergoing of grace to a new life. Girard in no way compares himself to Christ, but his cancer scare gave him the opportunity to understand, on a nondiscursive level, how his own suffering during Holy Week gained meaning when understood as a palimpsest of Christ's suffering. Similar to Augustine's recollection, this religious conversion compelled Girard to take specific ecclesial actions: "Immediately after that experience, I went to confession and I had my children baptized. My wife and I were remarried by a priest."[98] Over the past fifty years, Girard has remained a practicing Catholic, even though, as a thoroughgoing anti-Romantic, he downplays his piety: "I am just an average Christian. I go to church."[99]

This description, coupled with his insistence on the necessity of conversion, lends credence to the claim that the metaphor of upper and lower blade is necessary to explain how faith and reason cohere in Girard's thought. One can, through reason, reach many right and true conclusions about individual and social morality, and even about the universe, the question of meaning, and the existence of God. Yet these truths more closely approximate something attained than something undergone. This distinction gets at the paradox of mimetic theory: one can easily observe the mimetic origins of rivalry between two opposing figures, or the use of scapegoats in a culture other than one's own. The real difficulty is to find these patterns within oneself: "We should never minimize our inability to recognize this reality. Our miserable autonomy is more important to us than anything else."[100] Girard notes elsewhere: "A deeper knowledge and self-examination are required. The knowledge of mimesis is really tied to conversion . . . A personal knowledge, fully rational and yet not always accessible to reason, is needed."[101] And again, "To truly repent the way Peter and Paul do is to understand one's personal participation in the expulsion of God."[102] From Girard's admission of the limits of reason, however, there does not follow a plunge into irrationality. An admission of reason's limits, for Girard, is part and parcel with understanding reality under a graced horizon.

Mimetic theory calls into question what it means to be rational. Girard insists that his reliance on biblical texts and his personal faith do not invalidate the scientific legitimacy of his research. One can understand mimetic theory on an abstract, objective level yet still not recognize when one becomes caught in its throes. By asking how much value should be attributed to understanding something on an abstract, "objective" level, mimetic theory deconstructs the image of the detached scientist or philosopher. Only religious conversion gives us the reality or the objectivity that reason desires so ardently. In extrapolating the difference between his intellectual and true conversion, Girard notes: "Conversion is a more objective reality than what we call objective the rest of the time."[103]

CHAPTER THREE

MIMETIC THEORY AND THE
THEOLOGY OF REVELATION

Despite trying on such diverse models of Jesus as teacher, wonderworker, healer, rebel, and guru, the Christian community has rarely dwelt very long with Jesus the exegete.[1] The Gospels, however, seem to invite such a model. Like any good rabbi, Jesus interpreted the Hebrew scriptures creatively and insightfully. Luke portrays Jesus the exegete early in his gospel:

> And he stood up to read; and there was given to him the book of the prophet Isaiah. He opened the book and found the place where it was written, "The Spirit of the Lord is upon me, because he has anointed me to preach good news to the poor. He has sent me to proclaim release to the captives, and re-covering the sight to the blind, to set at liberty those who are oppressed, to proclaim the acceptable year of the Lord." And he closed the book, and gave it back to the attendant, and sat down; and the eyes of all in the synagogue were fixed on him. And he began to say to them, "Today this scripture has been fulfilled in your hearing." (Luke 4:16–21; RSV)

Jesus takes this passage from Isaiah 61 and reads a revealed truth. He explains revelation here, in this case the witness of the Isaian community. His interpretation, which Christians hold as divine, constitutes a revelation of revelation. Both the original Isaian passage and Jesus' judgment that "today this scripture has been fulfilled" are revelatory. Interpretation in this instance *is* revelation, which makes revelation—at the very least when Jesus is the one doing the revealing—inherently hermeneutical.

Revelation is the process by which God communicates saving truth to humanity. Christ is the summit of revelation because, endowed with "the human consciousness of the incarnate Word," he was "the subject of both inexpressible and expressible knowing."[2] In other words, Jesus was the means by which humanity was able to understand God most fully. The theologian Charles Hefling insists that this kind of knowledge does not consist in sensations, information, or even judgment; like wonder or "the light of intellect," it is a thoroughly hermeneutical knowledge (but Hefling does not use this language)—"there is a sense in which this 'light' gives us knowledge of everything about everything."[3]

Underlying any attempt to claim canonical status for the New Testament lies the conviction that its revelatory power resides in its capacity to *read* the Hebrew scriptures. When Jesus says, "Today this scripture has been fulfilled" (Luke 4:21), he, like any reader, makes a claim about what the text means. Yet as the Word who shone in the darkness, Jesus offers the ultimate interpretation of these texts. In the Christian account (as in many other religious traditions), *revelation* submits itself to further interpretation. This function makes it imperative for any substantial theology of revelation to at least gesture toward the process of reading these texts and recognize their ability to reshape interpretive horizons. Yet mainstream theologies of revelation, as I shall show below, often fail to realize the full implications of the hermeneutical dimension of divine revelation, even when they emphasize the human element of revelation by talking about its "subjective" side.

Might insights from mimetic theory help deepen and expand recent theologies of revelation? This chapter explores that question, first by outlining the dominant theologies of revelation in Catholic theology over the past fifty years—those of Avery Dulles and René Latourelle—then by rendering a hermeneutical critique of the basic framework in which both Dulles and Latourelle imagine revelation. Doing so undermines the modern framework of subject and object within which Dulles and Latourelle imagine revelation. Additionally, I construct an account of revelation itself as hermeneutical and of Jesus as the revealing interpreter.

This twofold critique and reconstruction relies on familiar figures in hermeneutical theory: primarily Heidegger and Gadamer, in addition to the work of the great Jesuit communication theorist Walter Ong. The application of these ideas to a critique of the default framework for understanding revelation—a framework represented by the approach of both Dulles and Latourelle, permits a more concrete grasp of how a Girardian revelation works. Girardian revelation yields both a formal and material element. Formally, it initiates a process of re-reading; materially, it *reveals* or *discloses* a fundamental truth about humans and God that reverses the cultural momentum aimed at concealing these fundamental truths.

The Shortcomings in Recent Theology

Although they are not normally regarded as breathing the same rarefied air as twentieth-century Catholic theology's greatest luminaries—Rahner, Balthasar, Lonergan, Congar, de Lubac—it is difficult to overestimate the influence of Avery Cardinal Dulles (1918–2008) and René Latourelle (1918–) on the understanding of the doctrine of revelation. Latourelle's *Theology of Revelation* appeared in 1966 in English, three years after the French original.[4] For several decades (roughly 1955–85), Latourelle occupied the chair in fundamental theology at the Gregorian University in Rome, where he regularly taught his theology of revelation. Available in both French and English, his authoritative book offered the most accessible Catholic overview of revelation.

Among those influenced by Latourelle's work was Avery Dulles, who studied at the Gregorian after finishing his theological formation at the Jesuit seminary in Woodstock, Maryland. Dulles returned to Woodstock to teach theology in 1960. As the recent tribute by Patrick Carey recalls, Dulles relied on material he had learned from Latourelle when teaching a course on revelation: "These [class notes] helped Dulles introduce students to the historically sensitive dimensions of the theology of revelation. He also found Latourelle's work important as a starting point for his own research on the doctrine of revelation."[5] When Latourelle's work appeared, Dulles did not wait for the English translation; he reviewed the French original in 1964.[6] A few years later he published *Revelation*

Theology: A History, which sketched a historical overview of revelation.[7] Under the subject headings of his select bibliography, he lists Latourelle's *Theology of Revelation* eight different times.[8]

Along with Latourelle's *Theology of Revelation*, Dulles's *Models of Revelation* has dominated the direction of recent Catholic theologies of revelation. Although, as Carey's article points out, Dulles influenced the subject more as a synthesizer than as a constructive theologian, his synthesis has made a lasting impact. Not only are references to his work on revelation dominant in theological encyclopedias, but such diverse theologians as Gabriel Fackre, Neil Ormerod, John Montag (representing Reformed, Lonerganian, and radically Orthodox, respectively) also use Dulles's typology and approach as a central pivot in their own work.[9] Similarly, theologians attempting to recover premodern theologies of revelation have often used Dulles as a foil.[10] The theology of Dulles and Latourelle by no means constitutes a monopoly in Catholic discussions of revelation, but these two have no doubt exercised a broad influence and reach.

Although this chapter eventually points to the shortcomings of their work, it is important to linger a bit on their positive contribution to the field. Dulles and Latourelle sought to overcome what they saw as an impersonal account of revelation offered by neoscholastic theology. They addressed serious shortcomings in the Catholic theology of revelation with insight and scholarly rigor, incorporating research from biblical scholarship, philosophy of language, contemporary Protestantism—especially dialectical theology—and Catholic theological renewal found in *ressourcement* theology and transcendental Thomism. They also read Aquinas and Augustine anew and discovered in them a richness overlooked by the scholastic manuals. Yet they imagined this renewal within a modern horizon that provided a truncated framework of human knowing. Consequently, their critiques and proposals oscillate between objective and subjective, between being focused on the "really real" object out there and the subject "already in here."[11] A hermeneutical approach transcends this oscillation.

The neoscholastic account understood revelation strictly as "facts" or "data" necessary for salvation, thereby neglecting the personal encounter with God described in biblical theophanies. In addition, it ignored attempts to merge the theology of revelation with salvation history or with the subjective appropriation of these truths. Both Dulles and Latourelle considered this lacuna problematic. In a gust of frustration, Latourelle recounts his differences with Catholic theologies of revelation at the beginning of the twentieth century:

> Following Saint Thomas, they [especially Garrigou-Lagrange and Hermann Dieckmann] insist on prophetic revelation, but almost completely ignore revelation through Christ. In a general way, moreover, their biblical approaches to revelation remain hesitant, not to say non-existent. Revelation is defined on the basis of etymology or on the basis of the documents from the Church magisterium, which, moreover, are merely summed up rapidly; . . . They preserve an astonishing reserve on the interpersonal relationship which revelation establishes between God and men. These deficiencies, to all appearances, arise for the most part from an inadequate consideration of the data of Scripture.[12]

Latourelle goes on to align his own project with what he calls a "renewal" in the Catholic theology of revelation. This renewal sought to address the shortcomings of neoscholasticism while avoiding modernism and uncritical appropriations of Protestant categories, deemed hopelessly subjective by Latourelle.[13]

Although less polemical than Latourelle, Dulles shared his teacher's dissatisfaction with the propositional account of revelation. The first model in Dulles's *Models of Revelation* is the doctrinal model of revelation, which featured an apologetic approach in response to deism. These apologists imagined revelation "as a body of clear and distinct ideas from which conclusions could be deduced."[14] Dulles correlated the Catholic variation on this model with the neoscholasticism pilloried by Latourelle. His concluding criticism in his first chapter notes how the doctrinal or propositional model "has gone into a severe and possibly irreversible decline."[15] Dulles then remarks that biblical scholarship, especially form criticism, undermines assertions that all biblical statements should be read as propositional declarations: God's self-communication, which constitutes revelation, extends beyond merely propositional truth. Such a truncation of truth raises problems: "The propositional model rests on an objectifying theory of knowledge that is widely questioned in our time. . . . Propositions depend for their meaning upon a host of circumstances that can never be adequately stated in propositional form."[16] Appealing to insights from more recent theology, including Protestant efforts eschewed by Latourelle, Dulles responds to the insufficiency of neoscholastic manualist theology by offering a more biblical and narrative account of revelation.

After proposing the model of (1) revelation as doctrine, the next four models cover (2) revelation as history, (3) revelation as inner experience, (4) revelation as dialectical presence, and (5) revelation as new awareness. Exponents of the historical model (2) emphasized the event-based character of revelation: God bellows to Moses, hardens Pharaoh's heart, aids Israel and her enemies, takes on human form in Bethlehem, and raises up Jesus on the third day. This model emphasizes the deeds that made God present to various people in history. Perhaps the strongest advocate for this approach is Wolfhart Pannenberg, who argues that "historical revelation is open to anyone who has eyes to see."[17] Even more than the doctrinal model, the historical model stresses the objective reality of revelation. By emphasizing the event, this model corrects the biblical deficiencies of the doctrinal model, and it can also incorporate a theology of salvation history into its account.

Dulles contrasts the historical model with the model of "inner experience" (3). He ascribes this model to such nineteenth-century Protestants as Friedrich Schleiermacher and Albrecht Ritschl, and also to the Catholic modernists George Tyrrell and Friedrich von Hügel, who accented the mystical element of religious life. These theologians define revelation as "an immediate experience of God who inwardly communicates with each believer."[18] They locate revelation deep within human experience, as the personal encounter with God's transforming grace. God's action is marked more by a subjective turn in the individual than in the authority of an objective occurrence. God as *being*, not *a being*, can never be reduced to thing-ness or data. Dulles cites the French Protestant Auguste Sabatier: "God, not having phenomenal existence, can only reveal Himself to spirit, and in piety that He Himself inspires."[19] To some measure an heir to this tradition, Karl Rahner echoes this point: "Revelation is not possible in the original bearer of revelation without the occurrence of what may be called 'mysticism as the experience of grace.'"[20] Testimonies to this experience, and dogmatic formulae, figure as second-order reflections on the more primary experience of inner illu-mination. Doctrines can at most represent this inner reality symbolically. To take them for first-order revelations risks sliding into idolatry, since such an approach trades a simulacrum for the real thing.

Dulles locates the model of "dialectical presence" (4) in the dialecti-cal or *Krisis* theology of the post–World War I German Protestant theo-logians Emil Brunner, Karl Barth, and Rudolf Bultmann. Although these three towering figures would later part ways, in the 1920s they presented a united front against the three previously mentioned models. The di-alectical model shared many similarities with the first two models by emphasizing the "really real" aspect of revelation, yet it also wanted to account for the fact that any natural human witness to such an event is a fallen and thus an unreliable witness. There is an *absence* to the in-breaking presence of God in human experience. A divine encounter feels more like a loss than a breakthrough, like a meteor that leaves only con-cavity in its stead. Dialectical theology also promoted a robustly Christo-centric theology of revelation that downplayed any standpoint in which natural revelation temporally or logically precedes supernatural revela-tion. In the words of Flannery O'Connor's Misfit, "Jesus thrown every-thing off balance."[21] One experiences divine revelation or God's saving grace as more than a piece of information or as even good news about our salvation. To receive the revelation initiates being drawn up into sal-vific transformation.

More than any of the previous three models, the dialectical model does not opt for either an objective or a subjective stance. Yet its propo-nents found it difficult to explain just how it avoided doing so, notwith-standing Barth's rhetorical splendor. In the second edition of his Romans commentary, for instance, he writes, "The gospel is not a truth among other truths. Rather, it sets a question-mark against all truths. The gos-pel is not the door but the hinge."[22] Barth's cryptic explanation aside, dialectical theology's fundamental mistrust of any interior, cooperative action on the part of humans lent a metaphor for revelation as external in-breaking. To be really real, argued the dialectical theologians, revela-tion cannot be appropriated by any human category.

The fifth model imagines revelation as a new awareness (5). Like "inner experience," the model of new awareness "gives a new perspective or point of view on the self and on the world as they are experienced in the whole of life."[23] According to Teilhard de Chardin, "God never reveals himself from outside, by intrusion, but *from within*, by stimulation and enrichment of the human psychic current."[24] For these theologians—Dulles includes Rahner and Tillich in this category—God is already always present as the ground of being. By emphasizing divine in-breaking, dialectical theology fails to understand that God was never absent. The model of new awareness conceives God as having been present all along. It is similar to inner experience (3) in prioritizing the subjective pole in that the subject's interior awareness signals the revelatory event.

These models occupy a framework where revelation oscillates between internal and external. Theologians of revelation, for Dulles, emphasize either the objective reality of the really real or the subjective reality, in which the information becomes more real once inwardly appropriated. This visual metaphor of inner/outer underlies how Dulles frames the conceptual possibilities of revelation.[25]

Although he does not use anything like Dulles's "models," Latourelle summarizes twentieth-century efforts through a back-and-forth akin to Dulles: "The twentieth century . . . oscillates from one aspect to the other, always in danger of stressing one element to the detriment of the other. Revelation-reality or revelation-doctrine; revelation as event of salvation or revelation as knowledge; revelation as progressive history or revelation as immutable and definitive deposit of faith; revelation as act of God or revelation as human testimony; revelation as truth or revelation as personal encounter; . . . revelation as external message or revelation as inner word."[26] Latourelle's *Theology of Revelation* adjudicates these efforts fairly and critically. The same framework seen above in Dulles informs Latourelle. In his discussion of Johann Adam Möhler, for instance, Latourelle contrasts the Protestant, exclusively "interior revelation" with Möhler's insistence upon the necessity of "an exterior revelation."[27] Too much emphasis on the interior, subjective element leaves the objective, exterior insufficiently accounted for. Latourelle recalls efforts to integrate the subjective and the objective in his historical overview.

Integral to the event of revelation is not only a divine sign or word, but the inner movement of faith that receives this sign. Both Bonaventure and Aquinas stress the need for "inner illumination" in order for revelation to take hold. Latourelle notes about the former:

> This inner illumination which does not show a new object, but enables the mind to grasp this object as it should be, Saint Bonaventure calls, in the words of Scripture, "revelation," "testimony," "inner inspiration."
>
> What is communicated through revelation, that is, the object of faith, Saint Bonaventure calls: "the teaching of divine revelation," "the Gospel, apostolic, or prophetic teaching," the "truth of salvation," the "truth of the faith and of Holy Scripture."[28]

Like Bonaventure, Aquinas acknowledges revelation as an event in history, yet he deems this event dependent on an interior reception in order to have intelligibility: "God leads us to believe through external preaching and through miracles, but also through the interior activity of His grace, inviting us to adhere to the message heard. This activity of grace Saint Thomas does not, usually, call revelation, but . . . primarily, interior instinct."[29] In Latourelle's treatment of Suarez, who had rooted his understanding of revelation etymologically, the metaphor is ocular: "To *reveal* means to lift the veil which hides an object from view; but the veil can cover the object or the faculty of vision. . . . God lifts both veils."[30] The same metaphors dominate Latourelle's treatment of Matthias Scheeben. The reader learns of Scheeben's "care to integrate the exterior and interior elements of revelation. . . . This external speaking has a corresponding inner illumination which also bears the name of revelation."[31] Latourelle also uses these poles in his summary of Tridentine Catholicism: "One of the first currents of thought sees revelation, properly so called, in the phenomenon of interior illumination which opens the soul to the brilliancy of the supernatural world: thus Bañez and Cano. The Jesuits Suarez and De Lugo, on the contrary, reacting against the excesses of the Protestant Enlightenment, reserve the term revelation for the manifestation of the object, the light of faith deserving the name revelation only in a broad sense."[32] Visual metaphors abound among these authors, and Latourelle faithfully renders these metaphors in his review of their theology. The general framework in which Latourelle relates these theologies of revelation follows the polarity of objective and subjective, external and internal. His

constructive "Theological Reflection" (313–488) corrects the serious failings of the manualist tradition by integrating biblical and history of salvation approaches so utterly lacking in his neoscholastic predecessors.
Throughout his conclusion, however, Latourelle employs perceptualist
and ocularist tropes.

It is not possible to give a full account of Latourelle's "Theological
Reflection" here, though a recitation of three instances sufficiently demonstrates how Latourelle functions within this conceptual framework.
The first occurs when Latourelle notes that divine testimony "is not limited to this external manifestation which takes place through human
language and the signs of power. Its most profound dimension is a completely interior activity."[33] This metaphor of inner versus outer continues
in Latourelle's section on the historical nature of revelation: "The process
of revelation in its totality is thus made up of the following elements:
A. Historical event. B. Interior revelation which provides the prophet
with an understanding of the event, or at very least the reflection of the
prophet directed and illuminated by God. C. The prophet's word, pre-
senting the event and its meaning as objects of divine testimony."[34] Once
again, external and internal come together in order to render revelation
faithfully. The metaphor remains visual and perceptualist. Our final example comes from Latourelle's summary of the salvific act of revelation:
"But this external proclamation is accompanied by an interior activity of
grace which invites to the adherence of faith and which gives man the
power to deliver himself to the living God, in Himself and for Himself."[35]

Pointing to this polarity does not make Latourelle hostile to a
more hermeneutical approach, or to a less visual metaphor.[36] Nor does
it impugn Dulles, whose chapter "Symbolic Revelation" in *Models of
Revelation* articulates the heart of Dulles's own constructive theology
of revelation. Here Dulles upbraids Pannenberg for hoping to find a
"bare fact" of revelation in the historical event. Like Latourelle, he also
accepts the need to bridge subjective and objective accounts of revelation.[37] He later acknowledges that events, even salvific ones, do not interpret themselves: "For the correct interpretation of revelatory events a
prophetic grace or inspiration is a valuable, and in some cases indispensable, qualification. Yet the interpretation is not extrinsically imposed on
the events."[38]

As Dulles transitioned from a models-based theology of revelation into his more constructive work, the polarity of inner and outer continued to animate his descriptions. In his chapter on Christ as the summit of revelation, Dulles talks about symbols as either "real or mental," and later contrasts a "merely external fact" with a "quasi-sacramental reality."[39] The penultimate chapter describes how symbols reflect and affirm "what is antecedently real," thereby falling into a perceptualist language, almost in spite of his earlier statements.[40] Thus despite hints of transcending this framework, Dulles remained tethered to it.

It is not my aim here to malign Dulles and Latourelle for the kind of naïve thinking about revelation that they themselves sought to correct. Rather, it is to demonstrate that they do not take full advantage of the resources afforded them by certain strands of hermeneutical thinking and by basic reflection on the *process* of reading as itself revelatory, which the Christian scriptures exemplify, and which the opening of this chapter signaled. The next section offers a more targeted critique of a certain heuristic of knowledge.

The Hermeneutical Movement

Epistemologies, whether they prefer a more subjective or a more objective approach, share a desire to account for human experience. Analogously, religious epistemologies attempt to account for religious experiences. Hermeneutic theory problematizes the category of experience. In the concluding section of his *Foundational Theology*, Francis Fiorenza outlines and succinctly defines how hermeneutic theory accents the problem with a theology beholden to a naïve conception of experience: "Contrary to popular understanding, experience is primarily an act of interpretation. Experience takes place within the context of memory, the memory of previous examples and similar cases . . . Memory, tradition, and interpretation are as much a part of experience and as determinative of experience as are the acts of consciousness, sensation, or feeling."[41] This critique has particular import for any account of revelation. If this area of theology covers the possibility and actuality of the human encounter with God, it must acknowledge what hermeneutical theorists mean by *Vorverständnis*, pre-understanding. An appeal to "experience" absent any cultural or historical setting, says Fiorenza, "overlooks the extent to which human experience takes place within a cultural tradition that provides concepts and paradigms according to which that experience is interpreted. There are no experiences of the religious dimension of reality that can escape the influence of the historical tradition in shaping religious experience."[42] A hermeneutical approach both highlights and attempts to answer this problem. Below I make an especial appeal through a specifically Heideggerian approach.[43]

A term that served a pivotal role in Heidegger's hermeneutical revolution, *Vorhandenheit*, usually correlates to "presence at hand," and its cognates to some variation of this phrase.[44] Frederick Lawrence explains:

> The principal denotation of *Vorhandenheit* is present-ness and static constancy . . . As Heidegger clearly states in his 1940 Nietzsche lectures, precisely inasmuch as being or the really real is conceived as statically present, "seeing is preeminently suited to serve as explanation for the apprehension of the present and the statically constant." Correlative to the *Vorhandene* (as statically there on the objective pole of the horizon) is some form of seeing, whether as perception with bodily eyes or as some pure, non-sensible reception of the sheerly *Vorhandene* on the subjective pole.[45]

As a consequence, argues Heidegger, a certain naïve realism explains how knowledge happens: knowing is like taking a look. Within my discussion here, divine revelation is something to be seen or experienced as presence. Left as such, this critique would be no different from any idealist critique of realist, empiricist, or commonsense epistemologies. Heidegger and Gadamer show, however, that most "conceptualist" or idealist accounts are just the flip side of naïve realism. Paired with an object "out there" is a subject prior to these objects. Both naïve realism and conceptualism or perceptualism operate within the horizon of *Vorhandenheit*. Lawrence writes, "Both the thinker who is adamant about the reality 'out there' of, say, the universal triangle and the thinker who vigorously maintains the exclusively 'in here' or intramental quality of the universal triangle share this common pathology proper to the horizon of *Vorhandenheit*."[46]

Such accounts privilege seeing as the dominant form of cognition. Employing the category of *Vorhandenheit* to critique a default cognitional theory enables one to sidestep the pendulum between objective and subjective that informs Dulles's and Latourelle's positions on revelation. That spectrum, expounds Lawrence, leads to a mistaken understanding of knowing: "What is 'known' to be the case through sense perception is 'objective,' and what is added to this perceptual cognition by properly intellectual spontaneity and activity such as inquiry, imaginative schematization, understanding, extrapolation, conceptual articulation, the search for judicial warrants, and judgment itself, is merely 'subjective.'"[47] The visual model here dominates the entire knowing process. Echoing Heidegger, Gadamer criticizes Wilhelm Dilthey for wanting the mode of knowledge in the humanities to parrot the mode of knowledge in the natural sciences.[48]

Lawrence's reference to "judicial warrants" recalls Gadamer's discussion of judicial prudence in *Truth and Method*. According to Gadamer, a good judge does not simply know the letter of the law but is able to discern the spirit of the law, because law does not simply "apply." In the instance of a sentencing guideline for a particular crime, a good judge may apply a stiffer or milder sentence based on a judgment about what the law intends and what the particular instance demands. Societies enlist judges to make such judgments—otherwise we could have a sentencing structure by a computer program akin to TurboTax! Knowing the law does not simply equal knowing what the law states. Gadamer explains: "Inasmuch as the actual object of historical understanding is not events but their "significance," it is clearly an incorrect description of this understanding to speak of an object existing in itself and of the subject's approach to it. The truth is that historical understanding always implies that the tradition reaching us speaks into the present and must be understood in this mediation—indeed, *as* this mediation."[49] Gadamer's (and Heidegger's) postmodern critique of cognition rejects the notion of a view from nowhere. It also rejects an ocular model that posits knowing as a correct vision of the object by the subject—here Lawrence takes particular issue with Kant's notion that judgment is the "representation of a representation."[50] Through hermeneutic philosophy, Heidegger and Gadamer broaden the cognitional process. This approach recognizes that the judge does not simply read the law for its historical interest, as if she existed outside of the same historical stream in which the text exists. Nor does the judge reproduce the language of the law, or enter into the original spirit of the law, as in the Romantic hermeneutical approach associated with Schleiermacher.[51] The just judge "fuses" the horizon [*Horizontsverschmelzung*] of past and present by understanding the spirit of the law and translating it in a way that makes its meaning intelligible in the present particular case. Gadamer writes, "It is still the case that an interpreter's task is not simply to repeat what one of the partners says in the discussion he is translating, but to express what is said in the way that seems most appropriate to him, considering the real situation of the dialogue, which only he knows."[52] Such a mode of knowing falls outside the category of taking a look, and is not contained within the poles of a subjective "in here" and an objective "already out there."

For Gadamer the lessons of legal hermeneutics carry over into theological hermeneutics. To take human temporality seriously involves imagining oneself as a being in time, not as a being standing outside of time.[53] Knowing a text does not mean knowing it in a way I can know an object on my desk. Gadamer explains:

> Our *line of thought* prevents us from dividing the hermeneutic problem in terms of the subjectivity of the interpreter and the objectivity of the meaning to be understood. This would be starting from a false antithesis that cannot be resolved even by recognizing the dialectic of subjective and objective. To distinguish between a normative function and a cognitive one is to separate what clearly belongs together. The meaning of a law that emerges in its normative application is fundamentally no different from the meaning reached in understanding a text. It is quite mistaken to base the possibility of understanding a text on the postulate of a "con-geniality" that supposedly unites the creator and the interpreter of a work. If this were really the case, then the human sciences would be *in a bad way*. But the *miracle* of understanding consists in the fact that no like-mindedness is necessary to recognize what is really significant and fundamentally meaningful in tradition. We have the ability to open ourselves to the superior claim the text makes and to respond to what it has

to tell us. Hermeneutics in the sphere of philology and the historical sciences is not knowledge as "domination"—i.e., an appropriation as taking possession; rather it consists in subordinating ourselves to the text's claims to *dominate* our minds.[54]

The "line of thought" that Gadamer mentions includes Heidegger's understanding of *Vorhandenheit* and also the radical temporality of all human-being. According to the model of human understanding that Gadamer takes aim at, the subject always seeks to control or "dominate" the object. Here it appears that the opposite happens: the text reads the reader. The "miracle" has nothing to do with new information, but it is a radical transformation that the truncated horizon of *Vorhandenheit* does not permit. Yet it also does not imagine the subject as static or timeless, as if the text were lying in wait like a predator.

As a being in time, the person is wholly hermeneutical. Therefore she always comes to the text through another text. She reads the Qu'ran as a Christian, or as a late-modern American Christian with a Muslim husband, or as a devout Muslim woman in a study circle, but never *just so*. Human experience is thickly layered. A new e-mail is read through all past e-mails; a conversation is heard through a prior history of friendship or hostility. The "miracle of understanding" describes the process through which these layers become reorganized or reclassified. This is what Gadamer means by the "fusion of horizons" (*Horizontsverschmelzung*). The text reads the reader such that she reads everything else differently: not just other parts of the same "sacred" book, but other books, paintings, films, gestures, and symbols. The human being never stops reading. But she does not simply resign herself to past horizons when judging the present. The miracle of understanding means that a possible re-reading lies just around the bend. It would seem that Gadamer's miracle of understanding echoes the conversion experience of the disciples on the road to Emmaus (Luke 24:13–35).

For Heidegger and Gadamer, knowing could not be more different from "taking a look." Their account eradicates the need for drawing a bridge between a subject "in here" and an object "out there." Gadamer instead points to a connection between judicial prudence and reading because both examples involve making judgments that cannot be reduced to preprogramming. If this were so, to echo Gadamer, then indeed the human sciences would be in a bad way.

The critique of a subject/object heuristic laid out above also offers an understanding of conversion as a reconstellation of horizon. In light of this reconstellation, mimetic theory's particular contribution to theology of revelation gains greater relevance. Before laying out this explicitly hermeneutical theology of revelation, it will prove helpful to retrieve the work of Walter Ong. In two of his texts, *Orality and Literacy* and *The Presence of the Word*, Ong underscores the massive shift in consciousness initiated by the invention of written texts and the age of Gutenberg.[55] Ong notes how visual models of knowing coincided with the rise of printed text. Recapitulating Ong's position on the difference between oral and written culture will make it possible to recover Ong's insight into the cause of ocular models of cognition. Of particular interest is how Ong understands the "word" as event. My treatment of Ong concludes by highlighting the implications of his thought for a Christian theology of revelation. Despite operating in a different disciplinary corner, Ong ends up reinforcing much of what Heidegger and Gadamer say.

In pursuing this line of research, Ong followed in the footsteps of his mentor and collaborator, Marshall McLuhan, whose *Gutenberg Galaxy* explored the seismic, consciousness-altering impact the printing press had on Western civilization.[56] Following McLuhan, Ong emphasized how a given medium affects both what we say and how we hear. Oral cultures formed dramatically different relationships between humans and words than does our textual culture. Ong states, "Without writing, words as such have no visual presence, even when the objects they represent are visual. They are sounds . . . They are occurrences, events."[57] Unless pledged to memory, these words are forever lost upon being spoken.

Oral cultures, in comparison to written ones, experience the relationship between truth and time differently. Of all of the senses, hearing has the most difficulty "holding on" to reality. Ong notes, "Cultures which do not reduce words to space but know them only as oral-aural phenomena, in actuality or in the imagination, naturally regard words as more powerful than [do] literate cultures."[58] This difference has enormous religious implications. The God of Abraham and Jacob reveals Himself to them by calling their names (Gen. 22:1; 31:11). Ong notes,

"The word is not an inert record but a living something, like sound, something going on."[59] The Hebrew *dabar*, which means both "word" and "event," captures what Ong describes.

Building off the research of Eric Havelock, Ong regards Plato's visual metaphor of understanding as rooted in a fundamental assault on an older oral culture.[60] The association of the forms or the realm of the ideal as the "really real" signaled a shift in learning—no longer could one equate being educated with memorizing Homer's corpus. Plato shifted the pedagogic focus to the idea rather than the spoken word. Ong reports: "Plato's ideas were the polar opposite; not events at all, but motionless 'objective' existence, impersonal, and out of time. Forming the ultimate base of all knowledge, they implied that intellectual knowledge was like sight . . . Basically the Greek word *idea* means the look of a thing."[61] Similar to Heidegger, Ong finds the roots of modern cognitional assumptions in ancient Greece. The roots of both *Vorhandenheit* and the subject–object model of knowing lie in Plato and Aristotle. Ong contrasts the Greek visual model with the Hebrew auditory model: "The Hebrews tended to think of understanding as a kind of hearing, whereas the Greeks thought of it more as a kind of seeing, although far less exclusively as seeing than post-Cartesian Western man generally has tended to do."[62]

Ong considers John Locke's *Essay Concerning Human Understanding* (1690) the clearest marker of the transition to a visual metaphor for cognition.[63] Ong notes, "Locke assimilates the entire sensorium to sight and converts consciousness into a *camera obscura*, a hollow into which and through which light rays play. The visual simplicity of Locke's model is matched only by the naiveté of his assumption that the model is adequate to the real state of affairs."[64] After citing Locke's meditation on a dark room, Ong laments the reduction of any psychological experience to visual description. Words are sounds, and they cannot be broken down into letters as though one were disassembling Ikea furniture.

Ong connects the preference for visual metaphor with the shift in theological language following Locke's epistemological revolution. Instead of a God who communicates through sound, the eighteenth century opted for God the Great Architect: "The concept of God is itself affected. Eighteenth-century Deists, following the . . . spatialized accounts of language which make it a phenomenon rather than a communication, tend to think of God himself as no longer a communicator, one who speaks to man, but as a Great Architect, a manipulator of objects in visual-tactile space, or possibly as a 'force,' a kinesthetically based concept, also spatial in its implications. They are likely to consider this idea of God to be a notable improvement."[65] These thinkers preferred such a metaphor to older, audial–oral metaphors. The visual account of knowing seemed superior to the oral because of its claim to be "objective."

At issue here is not simply preferring one sense metaphor over another. Ong identifies a circularity in the predominantly visualist cognitional account. In equating knowing with seeing (empiricist), there arose a parallel tendency to prefer the inner to the outer (idealist). Instead of being polar opposites, empiricist and idealist models of knowing are simply the flip side of the same presupposition. Ong comes to a conclusion that mirrors Gadamer's: "'Real' means, in this way, not just something out there but something that I am involved in and that is involved in me. The objective reality of something is in this way measured by one's own subjective awareness, not merely by something out there but rather by something out there interacting with something in here."[66] Even more than sight, the sense of touch confirms our contact with the "out-there-ness" of the world or the object, but always through an immediate connection to us. This does not mean that an audial model is better; rather, it means that a theology that recalls the audial can move beyond naïve picture thinking: "Picturability," explains Ong, "is not the measure of actuality."[67]

To attempt to bring Ong's insight closer to home, consider what model of communication results from modern perceptualism: "My mind is a box. I take a unit of 'information' out of it, encode that unit, and put it into one end of the pipe. From the one end of the pipe the 'information' proceeds to the other end, where someone decodes it and puts it in his or her own box-like container called a mind." Ong's judgment follows in his next sentence: "This model obviously has something to do with human communication, but, on close inspection, very little, and it distorts the act of communication beyond recognition."[68] Divine communication, if imagined this way, is doomed to oscillate between the objective and subjective poles. A rich account of human communication, let alone of divine revelation, as Ong explains, cannot be contained by such a model. All knowing, and all speech, is conditioned by the interaction between a set of memories and present judgments that arise within the habits and expectations through which reality is filtered. Communication is not only profoundly interpersonal, but undeniably hermeneutical. There is a reason why Baptists do not report apparitions of the Virgin Mary!

Ong concludes *The Presence and the Word* with a section entitled "God's Word Today." Here Ong applies his findings to religious understanding. Revelation, as the Vatican councils teach, consists of "words and deeds," but history, even Western history, is not linear because time is not a visual line. Therefore, Ong points out, "Events are not outside one another at all. Rather, succeeding events, at least some of them, include and reconstitute earlier events without being identified with them."[69] Salvific and revelatory events—deeds and words—do not simply pile up on top of one another. Instead their intelligibility depends on continuity with previous revelation, while also possessing the capacity to reconstitute what has been revealed. Ong's findings, then, overlap significantly with Heidegger and Gadamer.

The Gospels, the Acts of the Apostles, and the Pauline epistles take great effort to re-tell Israel's history because its meaning has undergone a dramatic shift. The previously salvific events no longer *mean* the same thing. Ong continues, "In Christian teaching . . . the word of God comes to man in history which culminates in the coming of the Word in the person of Jesus Christ, and this necessarily means not simply after a given number of events have followed each other upon an imaginary line of time, but after the psyche has in certain ways reorganized itself in its relationship to the events and to the world around it. The word of God comes to man and is present among men within an evolving communication system."[70] Ong points to a profoundly hermeneutical view of the matter. The world of not only the written word but also of print and electronic media can never return to the primitive state in which God spoke to Abraham and to Jacob. The medium, the *Word*, is indeed the message.

How do such theories of cognition and interpretation apply to revelation? Hermeneutic revelation describes two processes: the first initiates the experience of conversion that makes possible a radical reorientation; the second is the insight and judgment of the person who looks anew at texts and constructs. Jesus initiates the first process in others and enacts the second process in various and sundry ways throughout the Gospels. Jesus is the Word who interprets scripture for us, and the New Testament is the record of that reinterpretation. Yet many leading theologians, in particular

Dulles and Latourelle, give too little attention to incorporating an analysis of this hermeneutical undertaking into their work. This current section has not only highlighted this failure, but it also anticipates how mimetic theory can contribute to a more hermeneutical theology of revelation.

Mimetic Theory in Practice

At the heart of mimetic social theory rests the claim that beneath any social order, any "civilization," lies a tomb. Human beings emerge from a mimetic escalation by means of the scapegoat mechanism, which restores order and peace. Religion begins with a ritual practice that remembers this initiatory event through its repetition, and all social institutions bear some lineage to this order. Religion also produces myths that conceal the original violence.

The end of chapter 1 presented Judeo-Christianity as the great demystifying, or demythologizing, tradition. More poignantly than any previous texts, the Gospels unveil or reveal the scapegoat mechanism and the lies upon which every human culture hitherto based itself. In the rest of this chapter, I dedicate myself to a closer examination, not only of *what* mimetic theory reveals, but *how* it reveals truths "hidden from the foundation of the world." Doing so animates the hermeneutical insights gained through Heidegger, Gadamer, and Ong.[71]

Mimetic theory contrasts mythic or cultural concealment with biblical revelation. Girard explains the Bible's hermeneutical impact: "The violence of the cultural order is revealed in the Gospels . . . , and the cultural order cannot survive such a revelation. Once the basic mechanism is revealed, the scapegoat mechanism, that expulsion of violence by violence, is rendered useless by the revelation."[72] Christian revelation compels a re-reading of all of human history. In a sense, this is what Augustine already accomplished in *The City of God.*[73] Biblical texts powerfully reveal the nature of primitive religion. This revelation, then, radically transforms humanity's future by re-reading its past and exposing the lies upon which so much of it rested.

Before turning to the scriptures, Girard sought insights from anthropology and ethnology, which applied their own hermeneutic to ancient cultures. Although Girard learned much from his interaction with these texts, he came to realize that the New Testament reads ancient myths and cultures better than modern anthropology: "It is Christianity that reads mythology better than any anthropologist, and allows us for the first time to unmask the mimetic mechanism, and, particularly, the nature of the scapegoat murder . . . The most decisive text for the understanding of the mimetic mechanism is the Gospels."[74] Modern culture recognizes scapegoating from the horizon opened by the biblical witness.

The Gospels recount the scapegoating of a sinless Jesus. As the narratives in all four gospels move toward the Crucifixion, each canonical gospel shows how the different groups—Romans, Jewish leaders, disciples, and "the crowd"—convinced themselves that Jesus deserved to die. The judgment made about Jesus' guilt drew from Roman and Jewish cultural (religious) understandings about the relationship between God and victims. This judgment also contained a mimetic element in human decision-making: after a few people say something, it becomes more difficult to disagree.

In *The Scapegoat*, Girard analyzes the mechanism of Peter's notorious denial of Jesus.[75] In Peter's declaration of fidelity and subsequent betrayal, Girard discerns continuity rather than contradiction. Peter is hypermimetic: "He cannot be counted on. He is changeable, impulsive, somewhat weak in character."[76] Although he did not chant with them for Jesus to be crucified, he eventually assented to the victim's culpability and sided with the crowd's pious disdain for the victim. Girard even deems Peter's subsequent shame as mimetic: after all, shame depends on the conviction that the other's opinion carries a certain weight. In his gloss on Peter's denial (Mark 14:71; Matt. 26:74), Girard writes, "Peter makes Jesus his victim in order to stop being the sort of lesser victim that first the servant girl and then the whole group make him . . . What is said to these others, on such occasion, varies very little: 'We are all of the same clan, we form one and the same group inasmuch as we have the same scapegoat.'"[77] The Gospels, however, tell the entire story from the perspective of the victim. In doing so they shed light on qualities that make scapegoating possible. Instead of another tale in which the sacrificial victim deserved or needed to die to appease an angry god, the Gospels point to an innocent victim who unveiled the mechanisms that lead to the victimization of the marginalized.

It is to this evangelical unveiling that Girard refers when he claims, "Every myth is a failed passion."[78] Every myth, by covering up this reality, conceals where the Gospels unveil. But by this act of unveiling, the Passion initiates the kind of hermeneutic revolution mentioned above. Girard describes this revolution through the metaphor of an X-ray, able to see inside what is hidden from the normally conditioned eye.[79] In another writing, he affirms this point: "[The Bible] teaches us to decode the whole of religion . . . The Gospels will be seen as that universal force of revelation."[80] They enable us to read anew mythic texts and ritual operations and thus to bring about their end.[81]

Girard repeatedly stresses how Christian revelation deconstructs and demythologizes the scapegoat mechanism and the mythic concealing of foundational violence.[82] In order to highlight the hermeneutical point, it will be helpful to recall Girard's exegesis of a few key scriptural passages. Early on in his engagement with biblical texts, Girard interpreted the "Curses against the Scribes and Pharisees."[83] The most relevant section reads:

> Woe to you, scribes and Pharisees, hypocrites! For you are like whitewashed tombs, which outwardly appear beautiful, but within they are full of dead men's bones and all uncleanness. So you also outwardly appear righteous to men, but within you are full of hypocrisy and iniquity. Woe to you, scribes and Pharisees, hypocrites! For you build the tombs of the prophets and adorn the monuments of the righteous, saying, "If we had lived in the days of our fathers, we would not have taken part with them in shedding the blood of the prophets." Thus you witness against yourselves, that you are sons of those who murdered the prophets. Fill up, then, the measure of your fathers. You serpents, you brood of vipers, how are you to escape being sentenced to hell? Therefore I send you prophets and wise men and scribes, some of whom you will kill and crucify, and some you will scourge in your synagogues and persecute from town to town, that upon you may come all the righteous blood shed on earth, from the blood of innocent Abel to the blood of Zechari'ah the son of Barachi'ah, whom you murdered between the sanctuary and the altar. (Matt. 23:27–35; for the Lukan account, see Luke 11:44–51)

Contemporary Christianity responds to such a text by pretending it is unrelated to the rest of the Gospels, or by isolating it as part of Matthew's larger issues with Pharisaic Judaism, and thus not truly revelatory.[84]

In light of mimetic theory, the passage takes on heightened meaning. It indicates how Israelite history encompasses all history. The reference to Abel (not an Israelite) and Zechariah (the last person killed in the last of the Hebrew historical books, 2 Chronicles) indicates that Jesus means all of human history. Girard adds, "It therefore looks as though the kind of murder for which Abel here forms the prototype is not limited to a single region of the world or to a single period of history."[85] These clues, easily gleaned from commentaries, indicate a broader meaning. Instead of a passage whose anti-Pharisaic drift should embarrass sophisticated readers, it becomes a passage that isolates the Pharisees because they represent the most advanced religious culture; if they are guilty, so is everyone else. Girard states, "If Pharisaism were not the highest mode of religious life yet attained by man, it could not stand for every other form; the words uttered by the gospel would not reach all cultural forms at the same time."[86] Rather than singling out the Pharisees unfairly, Jesus employs the trope paraenetically to indict all human cultures.

The fecundity of the passage justifies lingering with it a bit longer. The textual clues manifest how Jesus interprets sacred religious structures as sites of injustice. The sacred location of the killings, *between the sanctuary and the altar*, recalls prophetic truth. Perhaps the most insightful phrase comes from the response that Jesus puts in the mouths of the Pharisees: *If we had lived in the days of our fathers, we would not have taken part with them in shedding the blood of the prophets.* The mentality attributed to the Pharisees also applies to current circumstances, and experiments performed by Stanley Milgram and Philip Zimbardo (Stanford prison experiment) reinforce the capacity for normal, good people to act like Nazi prison guards. Mimetic theory helps realize the full revelatory power contained in the passage.

Mimetic theory provides the anthropological insight necessary to discern how these and similar passages bring the reader to the heart of Jesus' message. Girard connects this passage with its nearest Johannine correlate:

"I know that you are descendants of Abraham; yet you seek to kill me, because my word finds no place in you. I speak of what I have seen with my Father, and you do what you have heard from your father." They answered him, "Abraham is our father." Jesus said to them, "If you were Abraham's children, you would do what Abraham did, but now you seek to kill me, a man who has told you the truth which I heard from God; this is not what Abraham did. You do what your father did." They said to him, "We were not born of fornication; we have one Father, even God." Jesus said to them, "If God were your Father, you would love me, for I proceeded and came forth from God; I came not of my own accord, but he sent me. Why do you not understand what I say? It is because you cannot bear to hear my word. You are of your father the devil, and your will is to do your father's desires. He was a murderer from the beginning, and has nothing to do with the truth, because there is no truth in him. When he lies, he speaks according to his own nature, for he is a liar and the father of lies. But, because I tell the truth, you do not believe me." (John 8:37–45)

Even more than the previous passage, this section of John's gospel causes immeasurable embarrassment to modern Christian readers. Its anti-Judaism appears even more strident than in the Matthean passage. Yet the purported anti-Judaism, as much as it embarrasses the modern reader, should not blind us to its deeper meaning. The first clue about an expanded meaning comes from an earlier verse, which identifies the audience with "those Jews who believed in him" (John 8:31). Although such scholars as Nils Dahl have pointed out the connection between this passage and Abel's killing in Genesis 4, Girard contends that the full import of the passage has not been brought to light.[87]

Just as in Matthew 23 and Luke 11, the eighth chapter in John moves from the particularity of Jesus' interaction with adversaries to a cosmic point about human history. The identification of a primal murder rests at the heart of all three passages, in addition to a conflation between a resistance to Jesus and a denial of culpability. Girard notes "a triple correspondence . . . between Satan, the original homicide, and the lie."[88] Girard's reading conjoins the scapegoating to the mythic concealment. The Gospels do not simply expose human culture's violent origins, they also reveal the violent attempt to keep these origins hidden.[89] The inability of Christian churches to recognize the reference to the violent origins of previous culture has led to the paradox of Christian anti-Judaism based on these texts.[90] After centuries of using these texts to scapegoat Jews, Christians have finally ceased to read the texts this way, but they have sustained a sacrificial logic by blaming the violence on the texts! Girard proclaims, "We find that the text has become a stumbling block even to the Christians themselves who see it as the cause of their own past violence (to Jews)."[91] These passages highlight the potential *mis-recognition* between text, or Jesus, and the reader. If a failure to acknowledge one's role in scapegoating happened in Jesus' day, and it happened throughout the history of Christian persecution of Jews, then it certainly can happen today.

The gap between the message and its reception gets to the heart of a mimetic theory of revelation. Jesus signaled the unconscious quality of scapegoating when he cried from the cross, "Father forgive them, they know not what they do" (Luke 23:34).[92] Jesus not only unveiled the mechanism, but he even told his disciples and the crowds that it would be used against him. Yet the revelatory power of this information did not take effect. The ineffectiveness of Jesus' message points to a particular quality of the truth being revealed: it more closely resembles an interpersonal truth requiring a conversion than an objective piece of information whose acceptance requires no particular effort. Girard points to this problem in the section entitled "Love and Knowledge" of *Things Hidden*. Riffing on 1 John 2—*he who loves his brother abides in the light*—Girard adds, "There is no purely 'intellectual' process that can arrive at true knowledge . . . Love is the only true revelatory power because it escapes from, and strictly limits, the spirit of revenge and recrimination . . . Only Christ's perfect love can achieve without violence the perfect revelation toward which we have been progressing."[93] One cannot make a merely intellectual assent to mimetic theory any more than one can make a merely intellectual assent to the gospel.

It says something about the hearers of divine revelation that the divine "content" was not transmitted solely in a text. The real meaning of humanity was revealed through the person of Jesus and the dramatic events of his life, death, and resurrection—what *Dei verbum* calls "words and deeds."[94] Holy Week dramatically enacts all of the events of a mimetic crisis: tension, scapegoating, and a restoration of peace through the victim. Girard notes, "Without the Cross, there is no revelation of the fundamental injustice of the scapegoat mechanism . . . with all its repercussions in our relationships with each other."[95] In other words, because of our belief in Jesus' innocence, it becomes possible to believe in the innocence of others. This knowledge has minimal impact, however, unless one comes to see one's own role in scapegoating.

Dulles's and Latourelle's theologies tried to account for this interpersonal quality of revelation through a conception of revelation as a new awareness and through attention to the interpersonal element of revelation. Girard also recognizes this dynamic in a late interview: "Most people are perfectly capable of seeing the mimetic theory as a mere social satire that does not implicate them personally . . . It takes a kind of personal conversion, an acceptance of humiliation, to say to oneself: 'I was terribly mimetic on such an occasion.'"[96] Here, and on many other occasions, Girard accents this personal element of the kind of knowing at stake in cases where traditional theology would employ a term like *gratia sanans* ("healing grace").[97] Revelation occurs not so much in the suddenness of an event, but in the slow and painful coming-to-understand that unifies being forgiven with becoming conscious of one's sinfulness. The revelation transforms what it means to understand: not so much to conceive, but to undergo change: "Understanding no longer depends on merely justifying the mechanism; it is meant to increase our resistance to the temptation of the victimization, to the representations of persecution that surround it, and to the mimetic consequences that favor it."[98] The nature of the knowledge or meaning revealed determines the manner of its appropriation. And the extent to which Christians have understood the meaning of Christ's words and deeds manifests itself in the way they live their lives. Girard concludes *The Scapegoat* on a prophetic note: "Those who come after Christ will therefore bear witness as he did, less by their words or beliefs than by becoming martyrs and dying as Jesus died."[99]

The biblical texts reveal a disparity in awareness between Jesus and his disciples. The disciples fail to grasp the full or even main import of the message, which Jesus understood the whole time (see John 8:37–45, above). James Alison's reflection on this disparity formed the central point about the "intelligence of the victim" in his first book, *Knowing Jesus*. Although the texts that reflect this disparity were written by the disciples (or their disciples), they illuminate how Jesus had this understanding before the Resurrection, and the disciples received it only after the Resurrection. Alison concludes by describing the formal quality of that revelation: "The intelligence of the victim is the discovery of the sort of human beings we are, and how we tend to build our personal and social identities on a series of exclusions. This discovery was and is made possible because Jesus had the intelligence of the victim from the beginning."[100]

Alison's description of this discovery parallels the hermeneutic conversion described above by Gadamer, among others.[101] This conversion initiates a re-reading of one's life and one's sacred texts. Alison clarifies, "Revelation is the process of the discovery of who God really is that is subversive of the culturally developed understanding of who humans are . . . [This discovery is] an apprenticeship which involves learning to see the same reality from a different perspective."[102] The process that the disciples undergo after the resurrection sets the standard for later and contemporary readers of the Gospels.

For both traditional Christian theology and for Girard, Jesus functions as the divine manifestation of revealed truths. He is both message and messenger: "The revealer and what is revealed are one . . . the mimetic war of all against one, concealed in Satan and the powers, is revealed in the crucifixion of Christ."[103] In *Things Hidden*, Girard analyzed the famous chapters in the Johannine texts on love and the word—1 John 4 and John 1. Here Girard sets John's *logos* against the Greek *logos* of Heraclitus, which he connects to a violent *agon*. John's *logos* is not only from "the beginning," thus identified with God, but it is also love (1 John 4:8). Even more, *as* love it expels the fear that accompanies the urge to scapegoat— "perfect love drives out fear" (1 John 4:16). It is contrasted with the sacrificial *logic* of Caiaphas—"it is expedient for you that one man should die for the people, and that the whole nation should not perish" (John 11:50; see also 18:14). The truth of the Johannine *logos* ultimately manifests itself when Jesus reveals himself on the cross as life-giving truth, thus answering Pilate's infamous question: *What is truth?* (John 18:38).

Girard identifies three instances in John's prologue where the lack of comprehension and reception indicate expulsion. He notes, "The Johannine Logos discloses the truth of violence by having itself expelled."[104] Elsewhere he connects this revelation with the transformation it paradoxically induces: "The expulsion of the Logos is the beginning of the end of the 'reign of Satan.' Defeat in the world is really victory over the world."[105] The entire arc of John's gospel follows what the prologue already declares, "that the darkness did not comprehend it" (John 1:5). Earlier in this section I examined one manifestation (John 8:37–45) where John's gospel unpacks this record of noncomprehension. The gospel plays out the story in which the lie of violence expels the truth of love. John's true, evangelical *logos* reveals the nature of the false *logos* of violence, strife, and domination.

The gospel revelation not only uncovers the scapegoat mechanism, but it also radically distinguishes the true God of Jesus Christ from earlier divinities. This discovery, of course, reverses the order of traditional Christian theology, which begins with truths about God and then draws human consequences.[106] Girard notes, "There is an absolute separation between the only true deity and all the deities of violence, who have been radically demystified by the Gospels alone."[107] The gospel revelation marks a definitive turn in the history of religion.

Although Girard's explanation interweaves social science with scriptural interpretation, he casts doubt, already in *Things Hidden*, on the possibility of a natural discovery of such an insight. At the end of "Book I: Fundamental Theology," he writes, "The revelation of the surrogate victim as the founding agent in all religion and culture is something that neither our world as a whole nor any one particular 'gifted' individual can claim to have discovered."[108] The revelation is not the fruit of a genius. Such a Romantic notion of revelation would undermine Girard's novelistic critique of Romanticism. At this point, mimetic theory requires assent to a worldview where the supernatural interrupts the natural order, the divine becomes human, and the most important truths come to, rather than generate from, humanity. Girard's writings sometimes presuppose this. *The Scapegoat* proclaims: "At the [gospel] text's origin there must have been someone outside the group, a higher intelligence that controlled the disciples and inspired their writings."[109]

The nature of the gifted shape of this discovery presupposes a Christian ontology in which people can experience graces from a divine origin. Girard does not begin his analysis with grace, but he aims to show, apologetically, how the most realistic account of humanity makes grace necessary for sustained human flourishing. In the words of Wolfgang Palaver, grace functions as an "outer boundary" for Girard's ontology.[110] By examining Girard's theology under the auspices of revelation, it becomes easier to mark that outer boundary. Alison seems to agree that an influx of divine grace most plausibly accounts for the groundbreaking nature of the discovery in question. He writes, "Clearly, my own approach, and Girard's, does not seek to do without celestial intervention. Indeed, it is one of the primary tenets of the approach that I have been outlining that it becomes possible to develop the sort of anthropology I have set forth only *because* there has been a divine revelation."[111] Mimetic theory, then, posits that this anthropological insight comes from a supernatural source. Yet the revelation itself takes on a human form. Here it follows the old scholastic dictum: *quidquid recipitur ad modum recipientis recipitur*, "that which is received is done so according to the mode of the one receiving it." Coming from a divine source, it is not only supernatural but also anthropological: "The commentators take it for granted that this revelation is exclusively related to supernatural matters. The supernatural dimension in the gospels is essential but it cannot be assessed properly . . . if the human aspect of the revelation is not perceived."[112] Yet this revelation into anthropology also tells us about the God who both makes humans and redeems them: freely, lovingly, nonviolently, noncoercively.

The gospel's *anthropological* claims, whose revelatory power Girard seeks to highlight, coincide with revelatory *theological* claims. The Gospels reveal God to be the victim whose death reconciles humanity to God. The Eucharistic prayer for the Roman rite mass used to read: "See the victim whose death reconciles us to yourself."[113] Girard remarks on the connection between the anthropological and the theological: "There is an anthropological dimension to the text of the Gospels. I have never claimed that it constitutes the entirety of the Christian revelation, but without it Christianity could scarcely be truly itself, and would be incoherent in areas where it need not be."[114] Expulsion originates in demonic powers, not in the one, true God who is known through both Testaments. Jesus, who is God, is also identical to the God of the Hebrew scriptures, which point to him while also being the object of so much of Jesus' pointing. The biblical construal of how God relates to victims marks its difference, in kind, from most other religions.

It is now possible to return to several biblical passages in order to highlight how the scriptures describe the hermeneutical revelation realized through Jesus. Modern hermeneutical theory points out, in the

words of Sandra Schneiders, "that there is no such thing as presuppositionless understanding."[115] Reference to the Gospel of Matthew's use
of Hosea helps to demonstrate Schneiders's point. Twice in Matthew's
gospel, Jesus implores his audience to find the true meaning of the verse
from Hosea 6:6: "I desire mercy, not sacrifice" (Matt. 9:13; 12:7). The
first reference to Hosea 6:6 rebuts accusations about Jesus' friendship
with Matthew. The second instance refers to the disciples picking grain
on the Sabbath. In these and many other locations, Jesus gives a much
different interpretation than his opponents do.[116] The New Testament
revises, often in fundamental ways, how people had interpreted the
scriptures, bringing to light the presuppositions that had claimed to be
"presuppositionless" in their search for the true meaning of different passages. The revelation that Jesus gives of passages like Psalm 118:22—"the
stone that the builders rejected has become the cornerstone"—is a profoundly hermeneutical revelation. Jesus also inspires Peter's and Paul's re-
readings concerning the Gentile role hinted at in the prophet Isaiah. This
type of hermeneutical revelation dominates the New Testament, which
contains more than three hundred instances of direct citation, and many
more indirect citations of and allusions to the Hebrew scriptures.[117]

Mimetic theory not only points out this re-reading of Hebrew scriptures but even claims that Jesus enables the re-reading of all religion and
culture. In his final chapter of Girard's *Job*, he compares the persecution of Jesus to Job, who constitutes an interesting case study for Girard,
and an easy comparison to Oedipus.[118] The dialogue between Job and
his friends highlights the contrast between the mythical and the biblical worldview. From the perspective of his friends, Job's suffering demonstrates his guilt, whereas Job himself protests his innocence. Yet the
book of Job still retains traces of a mythical perspective, especially in its
prologue. Here Girard describes how the New Testament helps re-read
the Old: "If the Christian text is allowed to intervene in the interpretation of the Dialogues, we immediately achieve decisive results. The fu-
tility of the boils and the lost cattle is apparent. The incredible originality
of the Dialogues becomes more visible. The enigma of this text comes to
light. And the Gospels provide what is needed to resolve that enigma, the
knowledge of the Passion that is responsible for the essential articulation
of the text, and reveals the true nature of the drama of Job's life."[119] After

having received the reconciling witness of Jesus' resurrection, readers of the latter "revealed" Testament can finally read the revelation in the book of Job in its fullness. The horizon of meaning expands after the revelation of Jesus Christ in a way hitherto impossible, and according to the arc prescribed by Gadamer.

Girard's demythologizing differs from other ethnological and anthropological approaches because the Christian revelation, not the social scientific method, receives privileged interpretive authority.[120] These two approaches need not be exclusive, but from *Things Hidden* onward Girard privileges the hermeneutical capacity of the gospel: "We can no longer believe that it is we who are reading the Gospels in the light of an ethnological, modern revelation, which would really be the first thing of its kind. We have to reverse this order. It is still the great Judeo-Christian spirit that is doing the reading. All that appears in ethnology, appears in the light of a continuing revelation . . . that enables us little by little to catch up with texts that are, in effect, already quite explicit."[121] This comment has a triumphalist undercurrent that can distract from the point Girard makes about the hermeneutic nature of Christian revelation. It enables anthropological and sociological insights into other cultures, and even makes these disciplines possible.

The *locus classicus* of revelatory re-reading is the Emmaus story (Luke 24:13–35).[122] Here the disciples learn how to connect the Passion with the events of Israelite history. Christ opens the scripture and thus puts alight the disciples' hearts. The upshot, according to Alison, is that "Jesus became their living hermeneutical principle."[123] The revelation is a revelation *into* interpretation. Girard notes how fecundity of revealed truth after the Resurrection is based on "the power of interpretation that is bestowed on humankind by the Passion of Christ."[124] Passages that hitherto had only an otiose or obscure meaning now reflect or refract key insights into the nature of God and humanity.

The hermeneutic power of evangelical revelation also stretches into the future. Mimetic escalation, scapegoating, and mythic concealment continue after the biblical revelation, and they often manifest themselves within Christian structures. The re-reading encouraged by the resurrected victim does not limit itself to the Hebrew scriptures and archaic myths of origin. Girard insists that hermeneutic revelation persists into current times: "The Christian revelation clarifies not only everything that comes before it, the religion and culture of myth and ritual, but also everything that comes after, the history we are in the process of making."[125] As Girard makes clear in the opening chapter of *The Scapegoat*, modern readers bring a hermeneutic of the victim to these texts. This hermeneutic changes the way people read later texts of persecution, which the Gospels have demystified: "No one is deceived any longer by the accusations of incest or infanticide made against the Jews during the Black Death."[126] The revelatory power of Christianity, in other words, continues.

Mimetic theory not only points out the way that Jesus opens the scriptures to his audience, but it also embodies this opening by attending to it. Alison confesses the convergence of Girard's and Jesus' approach: "What Girard does with texts is in itself an education in the art of 'doing things with texts' which is what we see Jesus do in the New Testament."[127] Especially after *Jesus the Forgiving Victim*, which enacts the same principle of hermeneutical revelation, what Alison says about Girard applies in equal measure to Alison himself.[128] The staying power of the exegetical work of such mimetic theologians as Robert Hamerton-Kelly, James Williams, and Raymund Schwager lends testimony to the ability of mimetic theory to capture the hermeneutic quality of biblical revelation.[129]

Conclusion

This chapter began by highlighting the intertextual nature of biblical revelation. The passage from Luke 4 pointed out how the intensity of the moment of revelation cannot be identical with proximity to an event; propinquity does not determine how powerfully or certainly one can experience a revelation. Revelation does not merely transmit data; it communicates meaning that reshapes horizons and reorders worldviews. Bernard Lonergan contrasted meaning with data in his book on theological method, noting, "Meaning is an act that does not merely repeat but goes beyond experiencing. For what is meant, is what is intended in questioning and is determined not only by experience but also by understanding and commonly, by judgment as well."[130] Yet the ability to apply this realization to a theology of revelation has proven problematic.

The importance of the need for something like a "subjective appropriation" of objectively or divinely revealed words and deeds did not escape leading Catholic fundamental theologians of the post–Vatican II era. Despite efforts to account for subjective appropriation, the approaches offered by Avery Dulles and René Latourelle, and many other leading theologians, failed to solve the problem adequately. The perceptualist epistemology that undergirded their work severely truncated their theologies of revelation. Phenomenological and hermeneutical approaches point to the problem of, and offer some way beyond the impasse of, modern, Lockean polarities between subject and object.[131] I have reviewed the hermeneutical approach, especially that articulated by Hans-Georg Gadamer and Walter Ong, to point toward a new way of understanding a Christian theology of revelation.

The upshot of such an extensive ground-clearing becomes manifest in the final and most substantial section of this chapter, which treats a mimetic theology of revelation. Jesus, I posit, reveals the nature of God through the manner of his reading sacred texts. The New Testament canon, in turn, reads Jesus' words and deeds in the spirit of Jesus' own reading of past events. Mimetic theory points to this process of reading and its relationship to an uncovering or unveiling of both personal and political forestructures that cripple paths to understanding. Girard's own interpretation of scripture, and its effect upon his readers, demonstrates how revelation works.

A mimetic theology of revelation can never be a method. The great irony of Gadamer's *Truth and Method* is that the book itself systematically undermines the modern privileging of method.[132] A mimetic theology of revelation does not guarantee the right results for those who follow the necessary steps. Instead it invites and initiates a destabilizing discovery. Thus mimetic theory offers a fecund resource for future attempts at a Christian systematic theology of revelation, and those theologies that ignore mimetic theory may be the poorer for it.

REALIZING A MIMETIC
THEOLOGY OF RELIGION

Problematic Assumptions

As a positive religion, Christianity makes claims about God's action in human history. These actions, according to Christian theology, reveal the order and nature of the universe. Christian fundamental theology aims to articulate how revealed truths and creedal claims predispose Christians toward other religious traditions. Since the Second Vatican Council, and in particular the groundbreaking document on the relationship between Christianity and other religions, *Nostra aetate*, Catholic Christians have intensified their engagement with other religious traditions. *Nostra aetate* boldly declared that the Church "rejects nothing of what is true and holy" in these traditions, which "reflect a ray of truth that enlightens all men" (sec. 2). This document initiated a transformation in Catholic attitudes about other religions. Catholic theology since the Second Vatican Council has increasingly undertaken comparative studies in order to relate Christianity to other religions.

Mimetic theory seems peculiarly ill-suited to this task: after all, Girard himself has asserted the superiority of Christianity and downplayed the value of nonbiblical insights. His reading of myth and of violence appears to minimize whatever rays of truth might derive from these traditions. In *Things Hidden*, he declared, "Violence is the controlling agent in every form of mythic or cultural structure, and Christ is the only agent who is capable of escaping from these structures and freeing us from their dominance."[1] Such claims imply that only biblical revelation can resolve the injustice of scapegoating and the deception of religious myth-making.

Although one might assume that such triumphant-sounding remarks made early in his career have given way to a kinder, gentler René Girard, such an assumption does not hold up to scrutiny. In a 2005 response to a question about the "dictatorship of relativism," a phrase that Joseph Ratzinger had used in a homily, Girard stated, "All of my work has been an effort to show that Christianity is superior and not just another mythology." Later in the same interview he added, "The whole point of the Incarnation is to say that the human and divine are interrelated in a way that is unique to Christian theology, unthinkable in any other religion and, in my view, absolutely superior."[2] Such statements make it seem that, in comparison to topics like sacrifice or atonement theory, the later Girard made no revision to his earlier judgment.

Many Girardians have already noted the contrast between Girard's orientation and that of Catholic theology, broadly construed. In his summary of Girard's attitude toward other religions, Lucien Scubla stated, "Having shown sacrifice to be the cornerstone of all religious systems, René Girard has undertaken to construct, on this basis, a new apologia for Christian religion. For, of all religions Christianity is in his eyes the only one to reveal the violent foundations of every human society and, most importantly, the only one to point to a remedy."[3] Similarly, Michael Kirwan added a note of alarm: "There is a concern to be addressed about Christian exclusivism, since a rigorous assertion of this hermeneutical key would seem to devalue and depreciate what other religions may have to say about the overcoming of sacred violence."[4] Scubla and Kirwan, representative of a larger, sympathetic contingent, worry how Girard's statements on nonbiblical religion could undermine how mimetic theory might otherwise contribute to Christian theology.

Critics have also noted Girard's religious exclusivism. Some have responded to Girard's claims with empirical arguments to the contrary. Already in a review of *Violence and the Sacred*, Ninian Smart noted that Girard's failure to deal with Eastern religions would explain "why historians of religion are unlikely to take Girard's theory very seriously."[5] Likewise, Markwart Herzog said, "It is peculiar that Girard demonstrates the benefits of Christianity in light of its difference to the religions of 'ethnological' societies, and thus obviates a comparison to other great religions."[6] Others have objected more specifically to the following claims by Girard: (1) only the Judeo-Christian scriptures denounce sacrifice as a founding element, and (2) only the gospel offers a truly nonviolent response to cultural violence. Claude Dussault, for instance, demonstrates that Buddhism already offered this denunciation and a nonviolent response five hundred years before Christianity.[7] Indeed, Buddhism even has an incipient understanding of desire as mimetic.[8] Buddhism, notes Dussault, combines a forceful and profound critique of the Hindu system of sacrifice with a call to renounce violence through the love commandment. One of America's leading comparative theologians, Leo Lefebure, like Dussault, points to examples in the Buddhist tradition that seem to foretell mimetic theory's analysis of desire and scapegoating.[9] Yet the brunt of his critique centers on Girard's purported exclusivism: "Girard is also vulnerable to the charge of continuing the tradition of Christian triumphalism. He typically finds true religion only in Jewish and Christian texts and neglects the resources of other traditions, such as Jainism, Hinduism, and Buddhism, for renouncing violence and fostering forms of life free from mimetic rivalry and violence."[10] If mimetic theory persists in its exclusivism, then whatever it births, despite the insights that it might bring to a theology of religion, will be stillborn. Lefebure summarizes the problem: "For Girard, all non-biblical religions turn to epiphanies of sacred violence to resolve social crises. Girard asserts that there is no common ground between the violence-ridden mythologies that dominate all other religions and the revelation of God in Judaism and Christianity."[11] Echoing Lefebure, Mark Wallace warns that "however alluring" Girard's approach may be, it "should be resisted as insensitive to the capacity for truth-unveiling outside the biblical environment."[12] Questions follow from such critiques: Are followers of mimetic theory bound to Girard's apparent exclusivism? Is not such an exclusivism the left hand of any Christian apologetic?

Besides noting this problem in mimetic theory, scholars have also questioned whether mimetic theory should relocate the privileged place that Girard has given to the biblical tradition. The Colloquium on Violence & Religion (COV&R) at Boston College in 2000 was devoted to the subject "Violence and Institution in Christianity, Judaism, Hinduism, Buddhism, and Islam." It was the first communal attempt by mimetic theorists to think about the implications of mimetic theory for interreligious dialogue.[13] A 2011 conference in Berkeley, California, sought to advance the discussion from the previous decade.[14] In *Girard and Theology*, Kirwan treated the relationship between Girard and other religions by revisiting the 2000 COV&R meeting and summarizing its contents.[15] Even Girard himself, despite his remarks in the 2005 interview on Ratzinger, has modified his stance toward other religions. A brief overview of the most important of these statements is in order.

The strongest normative claims by mimetic theorists to reexamine the relation between mimetic theory and other religions have come from the last two COV&R presidents: Wolfgang Palaver and Sandor Goodhart. In his remarks on the 2011 Berkeley conference, Palaver cited a statement by Goodhart about the relationship between Girard and other religions:

> I will quote part of Sandor's letter from May 2007 (*Bulletin* 30): "The second danger is the idea that Girardianism privileges Christian or Judeo-Christian matrices. It does not. It remains open to other religious orientations . . . Judaism and Christianity may be our way into these understandings, our access to them, but that does not mean other ways— via Hinduism, Buddhism, Islam, or other religious orientations—are not available and as valuable."
>
> I agree with Sandy. The question of how mimetic theory relates to other world religions is important and deserves a careful exploration.[16]

Palaver's and Goodhart's comments reflect the spirit of the 2000 COV&R meeting. The proceedings point to an agreement that mimetic theory in no way prohibits the insights gained from other cultures concerning how best to temper the patterns of desire that lead to conflict. Goodhart, for instance, underscored how mimetic theory, since it makes a universal claim about the hardwiring of humans, can be understood in any culture. He remarked, "One might claim these [ethical questions resulting from mimetic dynamics] as being specifically Christian, or Jewish, or

Islamic, or Buddhist. *But*, the way in which mimesis opens itself into a scapegoating process seems to be ineluctably human. We are hardwired for that. So, regardless of religion, we have to respond."[17]

Goodhart's remarks at Boston College foretold his 2007 *Bulletin* comments, which affirmed that mimetic theory need not belong to any particular religious tradition. Robert Hamerton-Kelly responded to a Muslim scholar aligned with Goodhart's position: "Islam's monotheism is a powerful antidote to this pagan sacred, indeed, in terms of mimetic theory, all the great religions are more or less in reaction against the pagan sacred, against generative violence; and one of the marks of their greatness resides in the candor with which they address the problem of the residual sacred violence in themselves."[18] Hamerton-Kelly seemed to identify the "great religions" with the Axial religions, which, according to Karl Jaspers, developed an ethical system that transcended simple group-think. Hamerton-Kelly associated this emergence with the monotheism of postexilic prophecy, but he identified the same process at work in the East. In both cases, Hamerton-Kelly concludes, the great religions have found resources to avoid the violent patterns of exclusion and scapegoating.

It should be noted that references by Palaver, Hamerton-Kelly, and Goodhart are not arbitrary—these scholars represent leading voices, perhaps the leading voices, of the Roman Catholic, Protestant, and Jewish integrations of mimetic theory. More authoritatively, Girard himself seemed to concur with their judgments both at the conference in 2000 and in subsequent reflections. In *Evolution and Conversion*, composed shortly after the 2000 conference, Girard acknowledged that nothing in mimetic theory prevented discovery from other religious traditions: "Mimetic theory does not exclude the possibility that a given society or religious group could reach a form of radical awareness of the violent nature of human beings." In the same response, Girard admitted that Jainism reached an asceticism "compatible with a Christian understanding."[19] When his interviewer followed up with a question about Hinduism and Buddhism, Girard confessed, "I fully acknowledge that the Eastern traditions have contributed in making those societies less violent. They know that the human being should withdraw from anger, resentment, envy, and violence, but they are not fully aware of the scapegoat mechanism."[20]

Girard's last decade of writing, from 2000 to 2010, also included a textual encounter with another tradition. In 2003, Girard published a short essay, *Le sacrifice*, which compared Christianity to Vedic Hinduism.[21] These Vedic scriptures have received little attention in the West, save the Rig Veda. Girard's own analysis stems from the second stratum of Vedas, the Brahmanas, which focus more on sacrifice.[22] Girard's analysis of these texts, though hardly that of an expert, showed an openness to their revelatory capacity. The Brahmanas reflect a profound commitment to sacrifice. They would seem to confirm Girard's prior statements about the omnipresent connection in archaic thought between religion and scapegoating, yet Girard's generous reading of these texts leads him to posit that their insights into desire parallel mimetic theory's: "The Brahmanas are more perceptive than our human sciences, and [they] see the mimetic nature of desire."[23] Girard's evaluation mirrors his earlier statements about the Gospels, wherein he proclaimed the anthropological superiority of scripture to social science. In contrast to the numerous myths that conceal the process of sacrifice, Girard lauds the brazen quality of the pro-sacrificial Vedas, noting, "The Brahmanas are especially perceptive about the genesis of religion in that they exalt the sacrificial process itself above its victims."[24]

Girard's positive assessment extends to a Brahamanic Veda, which illuminates the relationship between the rival and the substitute victim. This relationship must remain unconscious for scapegoating to remain efficacious. The text reads, "When he deals the deathblow to Soma, he thinks of his enemy; in the absence of an enemy he aims his thoughts at a blade of grass."[25] Girard comments that this passage contains "a full and complete revelation of the real function of sacrifice." Since the text inverts the relations between substitute and victim, "it reveals the real function of sacrifice."[26] He later summarizes, "Of all the sacrificial reflections on sacrifice, this one, I think, is the most revealing of all."[27] The conclusion of Girard's *Sacrifice* returns to a Brahamanic text that deconstructs the sacrificial culture of ancient India. He notes its similarity to the critique in prophetic Judaism, in particular of Micah.[28]

Although Girard's encounter with Indian religious texts came very late in his life—he was eighty when the book was published in French—the recapitulation provided here should dispel the quite legitimate claims

that Girard vacillates between ignoring and disparaging the great religions of the East. Yet legitimate questions persist: Why does Girard make
the 2005 statement about the superiority of Christianity? And why does
he continue to sound triumphalist notes in late texts, especially *Battling
to the End*? Perhaps most fundamentally: Does this "correction" really
align with Girard's monistic theory of the origins of culture?

I answer this question by offering the following hypothesis: The purported difficulty of relating mimetic theory to non-Christian religions
rests on a category mistake. Girard offers an understanding of religion so
at odds with our own, that it is more helpful to hear "culture" when he
says "religion." Further, Christianity functions in Girard's system less as a
religion and more as a demythologization of religion. Most basically, for
mimetic theory, Christianity is a critique of religion. The remainder of
this chapter builds on an earlier article that called for a wider notion of
religion.[29] As I shall show below, mimetic theory's notion of religion overlaps with Pope Benedict XVI's call for "dialogue of cultures" in the spirit
of Vatican II's *Nostra aetate*.[30] The first task, then, will be to revisit how
Girard recalibrates the relationship between religion and culture before
examining how several leading scholars understand the nature of religion.

Deconstructing Religion

Religion normally connotes sacred scripture and places, ethical imperatives, and such activities as worship and prayer. All of these phenomena
fall into the sphere of personal and social activity called "religious." An
examination of Girard's corpus, however, shows that Girard himself destabilizes such an understanding. Girard's own occupation in religion
grew out of his earlier, more primary interest in culture and its origins.
Indeed, his understanding of the relation between religion and culture
deconstructs in a serious and profound way the very category of religion that serves as a default understanding in the modern West. According to Charles Mabee, Girard declared this interest to him in their first
encounter: "Girard's first . . . utterance in my presence immediately became canonical for me: 'I am interested in the origins of culture.' I have
always maintained that these simple words contain a key insight into

René's thought."[31] Girard's shift from literature to anthropology signaled his desire to understand the origins of culture. He reached the conclusion—in contrast to those who presupposed that religion is subsequent to culture—that religion birthed culture. Girard declares, "One of the central points of the mimetic theory which could contribute a good deal to the debate [between Darwinists and creationists], if we take it seriously, is that religion is the mother of culture."[32] Rather than being a product of culture, archaic religion generates culture. Girard repeats this claim in *Sacrifice*: "Human culture is fundamentally and originally religious rather than secondarily and supplementally."[33] This radical assertion does not accept the modern, Western presupposition that religion is merely one unfortunate part of culture, rather than the generative force behind culture.

Girard's blanket statements about religion function as summaries of his cultural anthropology. Archaic religion results from humanity's attempts to calibrate hypermimeticism. On this point, Girard's account of religion resonates with Robert Bellah's natural explanation of religion—it requires neither affirmation of the transcendent nor any faith claim.[34] Girard declares, "Mimetic theory renders an account of sacrifice and archaic religion in terms of a purely natural force, human hypermimeticism."[35] Because of the capacity of the human brain for mimetic reciprocity, humanity always held in its very genetic constitution the possibility of self-destruction. The same hypermimetic quality made it possible to avert the looming crisis by first sacrificing a victim and then repeating this sacrifice in order to achieve the same peaceful effect as the first sacrifice.

Although Girard calls these processes natural, they are not deterministic. Indeed, he posits that several prehistoric societies may have collapsed not from climate change or food shortages, but from the inability to deal with mimetic crisis: "We can hypothetically assume that several prehistoric groups did not survive precisely because they didn't find a way to cope with the mimetic crisis; their mimetic rivalries didn't find a victim who polarized their rage, saving them from self-destruction. We could even conceive of groups that solved one or two crises through the founding murder but failed to re-enact it ritually, developing a durable religious system, and therefore succumbing to the next crisis."[36] In contrast to such a thinker as Jared Diamond, who argues that societal collapse results from a failure to adjust to environmental changes, Girard attributes collapse to intrahuman failures.[37] In *Battling to the End*, he notes: "Only religion has been able to contain the conflicts that would have otherwise destroyed the first groups of humans."[38] Like Bellah, Girard develops his theory of religion by first looking at biological factors. Whereas Bellah ignores evidence of a religion "red in tooth and claw,"[39] Girard posits violence as the indissoluble fact in need of a theory. Bellah feels no need to explain why religion was so violent, even when treating incidents of obvious religious violence, which seem to belie the argument that religion evolves from the play instinct. Girard, by contrast, explains the data in a way that takes the violence seriously. The earliest humans worked their way gradually from extreme fragility to a more stable social footing through the invention of religion. Hence Girard's assertion that "humanity is the child of religion."[40] Religious practices gave humanity the capacity to learn how to live together, east of Eden. Religion allowed humanity to survive its earliest, most fragile era, while humanity adapted to its evolving, hypermimetic brain that contained a newfound capacity for mutual destruction.

If Girard is correct about how all surviving human culture owes its existence to religion, then certain questions follow. From what standpoint could one be so free of religion as to look at it objectively? Can one demarcate the religious from the secular if religion birthed culture? To address these questions, I will examine the work of Wilfred Cantwell Smith and William Cavanaugh, who provide a wider basis for understanding the ramifications of Girard's restructuring of the relation between religion and culture.

In his classic text *The Meaning and End of Religion* (1962), Smith asks whether the concept "religion" is still adequate. His first two chapters trace how the understanding of religion—a uniquely Western concept—has undergone enormous change. Smith asserts: "Man is everywhere and has always been what we today call 'religious.' Yet there are today and have been in the past relatively few languages into which one can translate the word 'religion'—and particularly its plural, 'religions'—outside Western civilization. One is tempted, indeed, to ask whether there is a closely equivalent concept in any culture that has not been influenced by the modern West. I think that the answer to this is 'no' with the partial and highly interesting exception of Islam."[41] For Smith, *religion* has reified the fluid, religious reality that led Westerners to assume mistakenly that religion both exists as a stable entity and has been understood in the same manner throughout history. Smith hoped his research would lead at the very least to a change in taxonomy: "This much, at least, would seem evident: that humanity is now reaching a stage of awareness in the religious realm where it may, and its leaders of thought perhaps must, decide whether or not in the future to use the concepts 'religion' and 'the religions' as fundamental elements for understanding. This awareness is now historical, in immense sweep. It is also conceptual, as self-awareness."[42] Alas, Smith's hope did not come to fruition. Twenty-first-century Western nomenclature still clings to the early modern notion of religion. Smith's call for a change in taxonomy, now over half a century old, seems not to have trickled down to most default understandings of religion. Despite Smith's anticipation of a new "stage" fifty years ago, the old categories still animate popular discussion of religion.[43]

Before modernity, very few cultures, even Western ones, seemed to find the category of religion useful. Indeed, even such places as India, equipped with a sophisticated theological vocabulary (e.g., Sanskrit), had no word that corresponded to the Western word *religion*. Nor did they even have a name for their own religion, even though they named foreign religions as such. The Chinese coined the word "Shinto" to describe the native traditions in Japan; eleventh-century Muslim invaders invented the term "Hindu" to describe Indian religion.[44] As Smith shows, those outside of a given tradition felt a greater need to name that tradition than those inside it. Analogously, Smith posits, those occupying a space "outside" of the religious realm felt compelled to name an entity called "religion." Only modernity made it possible for people to conceive their lives "so that the religious seems to be one facet of a person's life alongside many others."[45] There was no way to be an eleventh-century French peasant without being Catholic, or an Aztec tribesperson without assenting to its sun god. In modernity, especially its current iteration, one *chooses* to be religious, either from an early age in one's life, or, somewhat later, when one is free of parental influence. People from Lower Saxony may be more likely to become Lutheran, but

being Lutheran differs from being a Saxon in the imagination of even
the most pious Saxon Lutheran.

Despite the implications, Smith did not explore either the apologetic or the theopolitical ramifications of his research. The more recent
work of William Cavanaugh fills this lacuna. Cavanaugh's *The Myth of
Religious Violence* builds on Smith's research by demonstrating how early
modernity "invented" religion in order to replace it with a nation-state.
This new nation-state vouchsafed for itself an authority, hitherto unknown, to raise an army, levy taxes, and wage war with increased vigor.[46]
Cavanaugh notes, "Religion, in modernity . . . is said to be half of the
religious–secular binary into which all human pursuits are divided."[47] In
other words, the demarcation of a "religious" sphere originated with the
nation-state's power grab in early modern Europe. For better or worse,
modernity made it possible to imagine loci where religion played no
role. Modern thinkers were the first to name "religion," which enabled
a social imaginary that reified the secular.[48] Only since this period, and
only in the West, has there been any systematic attempt to study religion and to name "religions." For Cavanaugh and Smith, this result is
not coincidental.

These arguments bring into focus Girard's thoughts on religion's
relationship to culture. Additionally, and more importantly, they show
that the current starting point for discussions about religion is arbitrary
at best (Smith) and, perhaps more plausibly, a politically motivated effort to grant legitimacy to the nation-state (Cavanaugh). These points
raise questions: Does secularity constitute a new kind of religion?[49] And
if it has domesticated religion by naming it, should it not be opposed
vigorously?

Attempts to point blame or to heap praise in response to these developments depend both on how one evaluates the "secular age" and
on what one's relationship is to Christianity. Most evaluations since the
seventeenth century have been forged out of a dialectical tension: the
goodness of the secular age depends on the evil of premodern theoc-
racy, in its Western manifestation. Or if Christian Europe is the good,
then the secular age clearly initiated a period of decline. This zero-sum
tug of war still animates many secular intellectuals and a good number of Christians. It was Nietzsche who notably posited a more genetic

relationship between Christianity and modernity, but he saw both as forces for evil, the "Last Man" resulting inevitably from the Sermon on the Mount's slave morality. Since Nietzsche's critique, many Christian thinkers have exchanged a defensive assessment for a more neutral stance toward modernity and secularism.[50] After they recognized secularism's complicated relationship to Christianity—marked by a seemingly decisive rupture, yet simultaneously inconceivable without many centuries of Christendom's spadework— the stakes become far less dramatic.[51]

What *is* inconceivable to moderns is the notion that an individual could have opted for or out of religion in a premodern society. Modernity opened up the horizon in which one could see religious identity as something chosen rather than given. This quality, according to Charles Taylor, defines what it means to be in a secular age. Being religious or pious, or having faith, means something different than it used to because, gradually but inescapably, this quality does not overlap entirely with other identities, especially cultural and national ones. Instead of dismissing this development as simply one of loss or decline, Taylor views it positively, or at least neutrally. On par with the Axial Age, the secular age, suggests Taylor, ushered in another "great awakening," on par with the Axial shift that Karl Jaspers had identified. The "secular age" names a paradigmatic shift that comprises one of the greatest pivots in human religious history.[52]

Mimetic theory also posits a causal link between secularism and Christianity. For mimetic theory, biblical revelation creates the space or the time—the *saeculum*—that makes the identification of religion possible. Only within the context of an overcoming of religion can one comprehend the liberating news of the gospel. By recognizing these "epochs" in religious history and the way they radically transform presumptions about the nature of religion, mimetic theory is able to articulate in a new way how Christianity relates to religion.

Christianity and Archaic Religion

For heuristic purposes, it helps to distinguish two kinds of religion before the secular age. Girard calls the first kind of religion "sacrificial" or "archaic," which others label "pre-Axial" or "tribal." Girard derives the meaning of religion from its function: religion, which includes rituals, taboos, and myths, serves as the glue for culture. Axial, or biblical, religion contains the resources that societies develop and employ, consciously or unconsciously, in order to minimize scapegoating and sacrifice, with some understanding that sacrifice, and its treatment of victims, is wrong. These resources comprise the stories, prayers, meditation techniques, and ascetic practices. Girard's positive assessment of the second type of religion becomes manifest to his later thought. Unless we distinguish between the two meanings of religion, however, Girard's readers may conclude that his theory of religion (1) promotes Christian exclusivism, or that it (2) no longer does so openly and does not specifically outline why his fundamental argument about religion does not lead to such an exclusivism.

In order to understand Girard's mature position, it is necessary to examine some of his later works. In *Evolution and Conversion*, Girard contrasts his own view with the Enlightenment's view on the origin of the clergy. For the Enlightenment, the religious aristocracy represents an irrational intrusion into the natural, primitive order of farming or hunting. Priests are parasitic on the rest of the community, which ekes out a *rational* living by reaping what it sows.[53] The religious aristocracy, or priestly class, demands the fruit of these labors based on the *irrational* notion that religious activity benefits the community's labor. What can explain the survival, let alone the flourishing, of this aristocracy? Following Voltaire, Nietzsche posits a priestly ruse, but for Girard, the answer lies in restructuring the premise: "There are two possible views of ritual. On the one hand, the Enlightenment view for which religion is superstition, and if ritual is everywhere, it's because cunning and avid priests impose their abracadabras on the good people. On the other hand, if we simply consider that the clergy cannot really precede the invention of culture, then religion must come first, and far from being a derisory farce, it appears as the origin of the whole culture."[54] Recent archeological discoveries, like Göbekli Tepe in modern-day Turkey, support Girard's claim. The structure, according the archaeologist who dug it, Klaus Schmidt, dates from around 10,000 BCE and precedes even the invention of the wheel and of agriculture. He gave a provocative paper in 2000, titled "First Came the Temple, Then the City."[55] Although it would be a mistake to oversell the importance of such discoveries, Schmidt's groundbreaking work only serves to make Girard's theory of culture more, not less, plausible.

Girard locates the elements distinguishing human from animal culture in the scapegoat mechanism. "Religion," says Girard, "is the mother of culture."[56] As he explains in both *Violence and the Sacred* and *Things Hidden*, the scapegoat mechanism forms the foundation for a variety of institutions, including marriage, kingship, farming, and the domestication of animals. Humanity and culture are birthed through this mechanism. Girard continues: "If you simply reject religion, then how does one account for the fact that the only things that are common to all cultures are language, ritual and God? Therefore, religion is the mother of everything."[57] In other words, biological causes cannot fully account for the *evolution* from advanced primates into human beings. Through the scapegoat mechanism, the earliest hominids not only learned to coexist peacefully, but they also adopted language-symbols, habits, and rituals that transcend the merely biological. From these activities come the hopes and dreams, or desires, that result from being together and sharing a language, history, ritual symbolic system, and a collective memory. As a "midwife," religion does not negate the biological, but rather it works from within it to create human culture, and is just as indispensable to it. Girard avers, "Of course men, like animals, have to feed themselves, but it is religion that makes them human."[58] Contra Huizenga and Bellah, Girard argues that man is man *homo religious*, not *homo ludens*.

A Christian Hermeneutic of Religion

It would be hermeneutically naïve to accept Girard's claim that his Christian convictions can be divorced from his scientific theory. As chapter 3 demonstrated, experience is never just experience; it is always understood through some filter or set of filters. Although one need not assent to any creed or doctrine to accept Girard's argument about the origin of archaic religion, it would be mistaken to presume one could arrive at these conclusions without the moral grammar that Christianity made available. Analogously, one would not need to be a

Freudian to call somebody repressed, or to notice that somebody is in a state of latency. Yet such an observation would only be possible from a post-Freudian perspective. Although Girard continued to maintain that the theory held *qua* theory, as he became more deeply entrenched in defending Christianity, he became more adamant that only Judeo-Christianity made possible the insight into the scapegoat mechanism. Christianity differentiates itself from archaic religion by showing the latter's structural features. Girard notes, "All archaic religions grounded their rituals precisely around the re-enactment of the founding murder. In other words, they considered the scapegoat to be *guilty* of the eruption of the mimetic crisis. By contrast, Christianity, in the figure of Jesus, denounced the scapegoat mechanism for what it actually is; the murder of an innocent victim . . . That's the moment in which the mimetic mechanism is fully revealed."[59] Archaic religion mystifies and mythologizes; it makes the sacred *sacred* by recalling for the community the way in which it found its original order.

In *Battling to the End*, Girard recalls Christianity's effect on the sacred. By revealing the scapegoat mechanism, "Christianity demystifies religion."[60] Rather than acknowledging this fact, scholars of religion make a category mistake by reading the Gospels as another mythical account: "Absurdly, [Christian revelation] is conflated with myth, which it clearly is not, and doubly misunderstood by both its enemies and partisans, who tend to confuse it with one of the archaic religions that it demystifies. Yet all demystification comes from Christianity. Even better: the only true religion is the one that demystifies archaic religions."[61] Pregnant with meaning and implications, this quotation captures how Girard relates Christianity to archaic religion. Christianity exposes archaic religion for the lie that it is. Girard continues, "Christianity reveals the central role of religion in the genesis of culture. Christianity truly demystifies religion because it points out the error on which archaic religion is based: the effectiveness of the divinized scapegoat. Revelation *deprives* people of religion."[62]

It will be helpful to read "religion" as "archaic religion." By uncovering the purpose of these rituals, Christianity anticipates work of such the nineteenth- and early twentieth-century luminaries as Sir James Frazer (*The Golden Bough*), and Henri Hubert and Marcel Mauss (*Sacrifice: Its*

Nature and Function).[63] Indeed, it surpasses their work: "It is Christianity that reads mythology better than any anthropologist, and allows us for the first time to unmask . . . the nature of the scapegoat murder."[64] Because of this unmasking, Girard considers Christianity to be a religion "demythified."[65]

By offering an interpretive framework to read religion nonmythically, Christianity is less a religion than a hermeneutic of religion. Christianity's powerful perspective changes the course of world history. Once it pulls back the mythic curtain, it becomes less feasible to close the curtain and pretend that nobody saw what lay behind it. The shift that Karl Jaspers, Charles Taylor, and Robert Bellah attribute to the Axial religions, Girard attributes to biblical religion.[66]

From Girard's argument a question arises. If Christianity is merely a theory of religion, then is it really a religion? Girard's interpretation of Christianity returns the focus to the fraught conversation about "religion" discussed earlier in the chapter. In addition, as several commentators have noted, Girard's critique of religion, and his argument that Christianity is functionally antireligious, echoes the claims of dialectical theology of nearly a century ago. Already in 1980, Hans Urs von Balthasar correlated Girard's position with Barthian dialectical theology, both in his treatment of Girard in *Theo-Drama* and in a book review. Balthasar summarized his views on Girard: "There is therefore no such thing as a 'natural' concept of God. This brings us back to the 'theology' of the young Karl Barth."[67] In the review, Balthasar concluded that Girard, despite his Catholicism, reaches a conclusion that leads to "an extreme Protestant position."[68] Similarly, Rowan Williams observed: "It must be by some concrete transaction that puts religion itself to the test that God as God, God free from religion, appears. And if that makes Girard sound unduly like Karl Barth, that too may suggest some further work of comparison."[69] Markwart Herzog made a similar point, even positing an influence of Barth on Girard.[70] Finally, in his response to Gil Bailie's article in *Communio*, Roch Keretzky noted that Girard's negative attitude toward religion "fits a more Barthian approach to world religions than the Catholic approach."[71] Such a collection of associations likely merits a brief explanation of the Barthian position on religion that formed a central tenet of dialectical theology.

For dialectical theology, "religion" signifies the idolatrous attempt of humanity to understand God from within its fallen, natural resources. Barth opens his famous section on religion in *Church Dogmatics* by declaring, "We begin by stating that religion is unbelief. It is a concern, indeed, we must say that it is the one great concern, of godless man."[72] Echoing Barth's screed against religion, his most important disciple, Dietrich Bonhoeffer, famously called for a "religionless Christianity."[73] These theologians understood religion as part of the sinful remainder of *post lapsum* humanity.

Although dialectical and mimetic theology provide resources and arguments for contrasting Christianity and religion, they arrive at this conclusion through quite different methodologies. Barth would have likely frowned upon mimetic theory's reliance on the social sciences to gain religious insight. And it is doubtful whether Barth would condone Girard's importing of mimetic theory into biblical hermeneutics. Still, it is noteworthy that Barth and Girard, both intellectual giants, came to the same conclusion about the disharmony between Christianity and religion. More relevant to the task at hand, the similarity gives mimetic theory an avenue for advancing the theological discussion of "religion" in theology.

Christianity and Religion Revisited

It is not enough to say that Girard is negatively disposed toward archaic religion and more positive, or at least neutral, to Axial religion. Such a position would not do justice to the relationship between Christianity and the archaic. In *Things Hidden*, Girard contrasted Christianity with religion by arguing that Christianity was a "non-sacrificial" religion, at least in its essence.[74] This meant, paradoxically, "sacrificing" the Letter to the Hebrews as an intrusion of sacrificial logic into the biblical text.[75] In *Things Hidden*, Girard seemed to advocate removing the Letter to the Hebrews from the Christian canon. In order to highlight the gulf between Christianity and archaic religion, Girard sought a new Christian taxonomy that would eliminate "sacrifice" (and thus the Letter to the Hebrews) from the Christian theological vocabulary. He took this position, despite the fact that Christian theology had a long tradition of utilizing "sacrifice," especially in Eucharistic theology.[76] Girard later came to revise his thinking about sacrifice, especially regarding the Letter to the Hebrews, to make the contrast between sacrificing the Other versus self-sacrifice.[77] Despite this shift, Girard always maintained an essential chasm between the archaic and the biblical.

Although Girard has maintained that Christianity demystifies archaic religion, he still upheld a structural similarity between the two. The similarity lay in the role of the victim: "This is where the unity of religion lies . . . The God of Christianity isn't the violent God of archaic religion, but the non-violent God who willingly becomes a victim in order to free us from our violence."[78] Sacrifice is the point at which the archaic and the Christian come into a consonance that seems to highlight their difference. Girard continues, "A similarity is also at stake here. . . . We have then to use the word 'sacrifice' as self-sacrifice, in the sense of Christ. Then it becomes viable to say that the primitive, the archaic, is prophetic of Christ in its own imperfect way."[79] It is not the case that Christianity merely unveils the true nature of archaic religion. The archaic, in leading humanity to solid footing, prepares the way for its own undoing. Girard explains, "One can regard archaic religion as a prior moment in a progressive revelation that culminates in Christ."[80] This same logic is at work in the Catholic Church's liturgical calendar, when the second Sunday of Lent juxtaposes the binding of Isaac (Gen. 22) with Romans 8:31–34. In the first story, it is God who demands a sacrifice, only to withdraw this demand, whereas in the reading from Romans, Paul reminds his audience that God "did not spare his own son but handed him over for us all." The aborted sacrifice of Isaac prepares hearers to receive the self-sacrificial love of Jesus.

Christianity, for Girard, does not consist in a pure idea unhooked from its historical existence. Although clear-eyed about the failures of historical Christianity, he still connects this history with what Christianity sought to overturn: "Christianity fought against the archaic religions, and it still struggles against more or less explicit forms of the sacred. Historical Christianity has maintained elements of archaic religion."[81] The growth and expansion of Christianity has occurred amidst archaic forces. Indeed, the scapegoat mechanism has been able to operate with particular efficiency during many periods of Christianity. The ambiguity about how the sacrifice "works" in much of atonement theology demonstrates this confusion. Girard at one point even uses the phrase "archaic Christianity" to express this violent surd in Christian history.[82]

Only in concert with this similarity between archaic and Christian sacrifice does Girard think that one can properly articulate the difference between Christianity and religion in general. Even calling Christianity a religion comes with severe qualifications. Undergoing the demystification process makes people less religious. After millennia of archaic religion, Christianity initiated a break that forever altered the religious landscape. Girard explains, "I link secularization and Christianity essentially because Christianity caused a break in the cultural history of mankind, in particular the history of mankind's religions, which for tens of thousands of years had allowed primitive communities to avoid self-destructing."[83] Despite an obvious similarity, Christianity initiates a dissimilarity that fundamentally alters humanity's relationship to religion. In large part, postarchaic religion deprives its adherents of the scapegoating mechanism they had hitherto clung to so fiercely. To be religious had meant believing in the healing power of violence. This changed with the gospel. Girard explains, "Christ took away humanity's sacrificial crutches and left us before a terrible choice: either believe in violence or not; Christianity is non-belief."[84] The revolutionary nature of this truth depended on, yet overturned, humanity's need to believe in the redemptive power of violence. Christianity's magnificent revolution ultimately destroys the old order: "Christianity is destructive of the type of religion that brings people together, joining them into a coalition against some arbitrary victim, as all the natural religions have always done, except for the biblical ones."[85] This makes for a dissimilarity that manifests itself only in the context of sacrificial similarity.

Christian Particularity and the Matter of Truth

In this final section, I return to a key set of questions hinted at earlier in this chapter, which are of particular import for the larger argument of this book. If mimetic theory admits that the great religions have found ways to curb violence by identifying its root in mimetic desire, and by discouraging scapegoating, what makes Christianity special? Why should one be a Christian? This chapter concludes by arguing that the revelatory quality of Christian truth matters, both in terms of the way it is received and how this revelatory quality distinguishes it from other postarchaic religions. This feature explains why, as late as 2005, Girard had maintained the exclusive uniqueness of Christianity.

One would have good reason for regarding mimetic theory as a kind of gnosticism. After all, it claims to possess a "hidden" knowledge that unlocks the key to understanding every religious ritual and taboo, every text of persecution and every myth. At the end of *Girard and Theology*, Michael Kirwan summarizes this critique. After citing Charles Davis, Gillian Rose, and Jean-Marie Domenach, Kirwan concludes that although these thinkers distort Girard's thought, "the gauntlet [of gnosticism] has been thrown down by too many critics not to be taken seriously."[86] Here one can add Paul Valadier's judgment that for Girard, "Our salvation comes from a knowledge, not from a faith."[87] These claims are understandable, for Girard's three-step project—mimetic rivalry, scapegoating, Christian uncovering—seems to require a secret insight about the way things are.

One gains some daylight in these matters when taking up Girard's last major work, *Battling to the End*. When comparing Carl von Clausewitz, the Prussian military theorist, with Hegel, Girard notes: "[Clausewitz's] view of history is more accurate, more concrete [than Hegel's]. You cannot view it from above, or get an eagle-eye view of the events. I myself thought that was possible, when I was writing *Things Hidden Since the Foundation of the World*."[88] This passage points to the problem of a theoretical position that posits a pure objectivity. In the next paragraph he declares, "I repeat, absolute knowledge is not possible."[89] Indeed, the naïve goal of pristine objectivity seems quintessentially modern and thus atypical of Girard. Although he does not use the term "gnostic" here, Girard points to a problematic model for knowing the relationship between truth and reality. The model that Girard had applied in *Things Hidden* seems to be one where truth floats above reality, and when one grasps it, one becomes a veritable gnostic saint.

Later in *Battling to the End*, Girard recalls the distinction made in *Things Hidden* between "essential" Christianity and actual, lived Christian history. He notes, "The criticism [in *Things Hidden*] of an 'historical

Christianity' and argument in favor of a kind of 'essential Christianity,' which I thought I had grasped in a Hegelian manner, was absurd. On the contrary, we have to think of Christianity as essentially historical."[90] Girard considers absurd the notion that one can achieve an intellectual grasp or essence of some truth and thus remove oneself from the historical manifestation or distortion of it that one might call "being-in-the-world." Choosing otherwise leads to a certain essentialism. But there is no essential Christianity separate from historical Christianity because the truth of Christianity is historical.

Girard reaches the same conclusion when he treats Hegel's almost fatalistic notion of reconciliation. Girard writes, "This faith in the necessary reconciliation of men is what shocks me most today. I was a victim of it, in a way, and my book *Things Hidden Since the Foundation of the World* expressed confidence that universal knowledge of violence would suffice. I no longer believe that for the reasons I have just explained and which I did not see at the time."[91] The saving knowledge ushered in by biblical revelation does not suffice. Girard's mistake, in his own account, was to believe that if he explained the essence of Christianity in such a manner that people grasped its antisacrificial quality, then everything else would follow. Girard came to grasp the necessity of a more dramatic enactment of the *gnosis* of mimetic theory.

Since Girard only points to this problem in a late writing, it will be helpful to understand how other mimetic theorists address the nature of Christian truth and what it means for a theology of religion. The English Benedictine monk Sebastian Moore gives an important witness by renouncing his earlier work that had not taken into account the real history of the Gospels.[92] In his most popular book, *The Crucified Jesus Is No Stranger*, Moore interpreted the Cross as a psychic event.[93] The transformation of the disciples made possible through the *events* of the Passion, as Moore later realized, could have been worked just as well through a fictional *dream*. Moore's *The Fire and the Rose Are One*, published three years later, retracted parts of *The Crucified Jesus*. Moore asks whether it was necessary that the history happened, or whether, perhaps, it is more important that we have a story that we can believe in, irrespective of the event. He insists on the former: "To settle for the [latter] is to say 'It's the story that matters,' in a way which implicitly denies the necessity of the *event* of salvation. There is a danger that the contemporary fascination, in theological circles, with 'stories' will obscure the event-requirement in the great story."[94] Moore insists that, prior to any universal truth or religious archetype, an actual event took place. Just as prior to any theory about society, or culture, is a real victim, a real event of scapegoating. Moore admits *The Crucified Jesus* had opted for what can be called the "gnostic temptation," which identified salvation with the knowledge derived from it, not the acts that happened during it. Though Moore does not advance a theory in which the "pure data" of an event somehow exists as a substratum of the "meaning extracted," he insists on the priority of the event over any truth abstracted from it:

> [*The Crucified Jesus*] did involve a real, sinless Jesus. It obviously involved real crucifiers, but they were merely representative of the human evil. They were not, to use a medical analogy, the patient who at the end of the story would be cured. Thus they were not in the drama of sin and its redemption the way Jesus was. . . . So the story was not a story of salvation, meaning a story of definite people being saved or at least experiencing salvation . . . The [sinner] must enter the story as sinner and exit from it as saved. That is to say, his sin must be somehow made over by the event and, thus made over, be cured in the event.[95]

Moore's emphasis on the historical event parallels Girard's. Mimetic theory does not reduce Christianity to merely a theory of desire and a framework for avoiding it. Nor does it offer a parable, like Aesop, to show us how we imitate one another's desires in a way that leads to rivalry and scapegoating. Instead it remembers an event in which a real, sinless God-man is denied, betrayed, and crucified by real human beings.[96] From this event truths can be realized, conceived, and ascertained, but the event stands prior and fundamental to what follows. If mimetic theory privileges an essential, unhistorical Christianity, then Christianity has at most a set of moral precepts to offer. If, however, it coheres more to the position outlined above in Girard and Moore, then it differs in important ways not just from the archaic but from the Axial traditions, too. Girard points to this difference when he writes, "[Non-biblical religions] know what sacrifice is, and they progressively tried to forbid it. The difference that I see between them and Christianity is that the latter was able to formulate the Gospels and unmask in a full light the anthropological mechanism of mimetic scapegoating and sacrifice."[97] The unmasking consists in the dramatic enactment of real events in history, not in hermetic or secret teaching. The salvific truth of the Gospels more closely resembles a graced undergoing than a cognitional grasping. The event also distinguishes Christianity from religions like Buddhism, which elevate a universally available insight over a historical occurrence.

Conclusion

The "great religious traditions" have been able to reduce scapegoating, to offer resources for combating the dangers of mimetic desire, and to proscribe violent resolutions. These accomplishments constitute genuine goods from the perspective of mimetic theory. There is nothing in mimetic theory that prevents it from openly acknowledging the good of other religious traditions. At the panel on Girard's *Sacrifice* at the November 2012 meeting of the American Academy of Religion, noted Sanskritist and comparative theologian Francis X. Clooney offered comments about Girard's treatment of the Brahamanic Vedas. He pointed out the limited nature of Girard's engagement and the problem of commenting on Sylvian Lévi's abridged edition rather than on the primary documents. He concluded by saying that nothing should prevent the next generation of mimetic theorists from continuing Girard's initial but limited attempt to engage these traditions.[98]

By problematizing the very category of religion and the notion that Christianity is a religion, I hope to have shed light on how mimetic theory regards Christianity as a theory of culture. Insofar as mimetic theory argues that religion lies at the basis of culture, it cannot help but be a theory of religion too. The other great religions, with the exception of Judaism, do not perform the same unveiling and thus make a comparison problematic. Yet if mimetic theory downplays the consonance between Christianity and the great religions, it perhaps opens the door to a renewed dialogue between Christianity and culture.[99]

Girard himself reached this conclusion in *Battling to the End*, when he discussed Benedict XVI's "Regensburg Lecture." Here Girard expands the meaning of *religion* beyond its normal use: "Christian truth is now facing two religions, which are all the more terrible because they are hostile to each other: rationalism and fideism."[100] Girard discerns a compatibility between Pope Benedict's argument for aligning Christianity to reason and mimetic theory's understanding of Christianity as rationally demythologizing archaic religion.[101] Christianity allows for an integration of biblical revelation and *logos* that prevents reason from devolving into rationalism, and religion from becoming fideism.

Such an understanding of Christianity provides the optimal framework for a "dialogue of cultures and religions." In his gloss on the conclusion to Benedict's speech, Girard adds, "It is less *reason* that needs to face *religion* than one form of religion that has to face the other."[102] These forms of religion are Christianity and archaic religion. Girard has spilt much ink explaining this religious contrast, and only when one has taken it into account can a fruitful dialogue emerge between the modern, secular West and Christianity. A faithful interreligious dialogue—so desperately needed—not only rises to the challenge issued by Clooney above, but it also extends to a dialogue between Christianity and secularism, a topic that forms the central topic of chapter 6.

CHAPTER FIVE

IMAGINING A MIMETIC ECCLESIOLOGY

One of the great ironies in apologetics concerns the role given the Church. For much of the history of apologetics, the existence of the Church has been an argument in favor of Christianity. More recently, especially since the outbreak of the Catholic Church's cover-up of priestly sexual abuse, the Church itself has been more of a stumbling block to accepting Christian doctrine.[1] As a result, the Church has become something for which to apologize rather than a demonstration of Christian truths. Still, fundamental theology needs to ask: Can the Church still be an argument for Christian truth? If so, what kind of argument?

Mimetic theology makes inroads into this topic by examining the Church in light of mimetic theory. For mimetic theory explains the cause and the structure of human social dynamics. It also articulates how Christians derive their identity from the forgiving gesture of the victim to the crowd. By demonstrating the integral relationship between the most basic understanding of the gospel and any understanding of the Church, a mimetic ecclesiology reimagines the space created by the Church as an essential consequence of the religious revolution called Christianity.

Fundamental Theology, Apologetics, and Ecclesiology

In the introduction to this book, I suggested that the category of grace, especially as part of the sin–grace dynamic, offers a heuristic structure for positioning Girard's work on the Christian theological canvas. The category of grace also invites a distinction between what is natural and what is graced or supernatural. Of course, discussions about the relationship between nature and grace have a long and dense history in Christian theology. A few words are necessary, however, to understand how mimetic theory's anthropological narrative presents an avenue for rethinking the ecclesiological questions pertinent to fundamental theology.

According to one account, arguments for Christianity precede any specific theological commitments and thus, in theory, work for the non-believer just as well as they do for the believer. An alternative approach affirms the truthful and reasonable quality of these arguments, yet it also insists that the capacity to receive them is not simply natural. Instead, their reception follows from a *graced* place and thus are not value-neutral claims. The arguments either fit or do not fit into one or another person's particular story; this does not make arguments arbitrary or purely relative: some arguments work better than others.

Whatever its shortcomings, this second account gives a place of privilege to the operative grace of God, who not only "first loved us" (1 John 4:19) but also poured into our hearts the grace of the Spirit, through which believers profess salvific truth in love (Rom. 5:5). There is a similarity between this second account and Girard's juxtaposition of novelistic and romantic conversion. The wordplay in Girard's original French title for *Deceit, Desire, and the Novel*—*romanesque* vs. *romantique*, "romantic deceit vs. novelistic truth"—captures how an apparently slight difference can in fact be profound. Both types of conversion understand the unhealthy ways that human beings become locked into one another. Yet the romantic subject imagines she can escape this dilemma by sheer strength of will or conviction. The novelistic convert makes the same diagnosis but realizes she is part of the problem; any salvation happens by the grace of something or someone else; if she gains a certain freedom, she recognizes how passive she was in the gaining of it: *there but for the grace of God go I.*

The matter of grace helps bring into focus the need for a discussion of the Church in a work of fundamental theology. Attention was first given to this connection in the sixteenth century, when apologists sought to disprove the legitimacy of competing ecclesial confessions. If all creedal Christians professed their belief in the "one, holy, catholic, apostolic church," then it was the duty of apologists to show how their particular church best embodied these four *marks* or *notes*. This presupposition underlay many of the volleys exchanged between Catholic and Protestant theologians.[2] The so-called *via notarum*—emphasizing "one, holy, catholic and apostolic" as loci of demonstration—involved a basic syllogism, which for Catholics went like this:

* Major premise: Christ outfitted his Church with four signs.
* Minor premise: these signs are found exclusively in the Catholic Church.
* Conclusion: only the Catholic Church is the true church of Christ.[3]

When the interlocutors were Protestants, Catholic apologists assumed agreement on creedal matters and a reverence for select Christian sources. By the eighteenth century, Catholic apologists no longer had only Protestants to contend with. As deism gained legitimacy, apologists began making stronger claims about the miraculous nature of the Church itself, evidenced by miracles in the Church, in an effort to combat arguments that wanted to delimit Christianity within the realm of natural theology. These *notes* continued to feature prominently in ecclesial apologetics. Francis Sullivan attests, "In the course of the eighteenth and nineteenth centuries, the *via notarum* became a standard feature of Catholic apologetics."[4] Ecclesial apologetics used two different approaches to explain this syllogism. Besides the *via notarum*, writes Salvador Pié-Ninot, they implemented two additional approaches: the *via historica* and the *via empirica*. The *via historica* sought to connect the authority of the bishop of Rome with the authority that Jesus grants to Peter—made most explicit in Matthew 16 and John 21. The *via empirica*, on the other hand, emphasized "the value of the Church in itself as a moral miracle functioning as a divine sign confirming its transcendence."[5]

Although Catholic apologetic theology developed these three arguments, the *via empirica* began to gain momentum in the nineteenth century. This shift was the result of the theology developed by Victor Dechamps (1810–83), the Belgian theologian and later archbishop of Mechlin. Dechamps, as one commenter has noted, "preferred to begin with the Church as a present and obvious fact. The Church, by its marvelous qualities, deserves to be called a 'subsistent miracle.'"[6] This "subsistent miracle" morphed into later claims, especially in the late nineteenth and early twentieth century, which identified the Church as a "moral miracle."[7]

At no point was the Church's preference for the *via empirica* more pronounced than at the First Vatican Council (1870).[8] Here, through the constitution *Dei filius*, the Church declared the reasonability of the Christian faith by insisting on the compatibility between the naturally attainable truths about God and the revealed mysteries received supernaturally. In its third section, titled "De fide" ("On faith"), *Dei filius* shifted the focus to "miracles and prophecies that clearly signify divine omnipotence," and it confirmed that the Church guards and reflects these truths.[9] It declared:

> To the Catholic Church alone pertain all those things, so many and so marvelous, which have been divinely ordained to make for the manifest credibility of the Christian faith. What is more, the Church herself, by reason of her astonishing propagation, her outstanding holiness and her inexhaustible fecundity in every kind of goodness, by her Catholic unity and her unconquerable stability, is a kind of great and perpetual motive of credibility and an incontrovertible evidence of her own divine mission. So it comes about that, like a standard lifted up for the nations [Is 11:12], she both invites to herself those who have not yet believed, and likewise assures her sons and daughters that the faith they profess rests on the firmest of foundations.[10]

The First Vatican Council attributed to the Church an unequivocal "motive of credibility" for the truths of Christianity. After chronicling different miracles that convince people to believe, *Dei filius* defined the Church not simply as a repository of miracles or chronicler of holy lives but as itself a miracle. The official commentary called the Church a "*quasi* concrete divine revelation."[11] *Dei filius* grounded this claim in the perpetuity of the institution ("unconquerable stability"—*invictam stabilitatem*) and in the holiness manifested in believers. *Dei filius*'s third section declared, "Nobody who has accepted the Catholic faith as given by the magisterium of the Church can ever have a just cause [*iustam causam*] to abandon this faith or to retreat into doubt [*in dubium fidem eandem revocandi*]."[12] The First Vatican Council concluded that the Church itself offers empirical evidence for Christian truth, and that believers are morally bound to remain Catholic since they know too much to do otherwise.

Fundamental theologians since the Second Vatican Council have commented with more than a little chagrin on this section of *Dei filius*. One particularly unflinching critique comes from Avery Dulles. His 1982 article on the Church outlines the glaring shortcomings of the *via empirica*: "[Academic historians] are not persuaded that either the longevity of the Church or any of the other attributes pointed out by Dechamps is such as to defy all natural explanations."[13] The arguments no longer convince in the way that they seemed to, in part because of a greater skepticism about miracles. Dulles then adds a moral critique of those who would believe in the gospel primarily on the authority of its messenger, the Church: "Christians who implicitly accept whatever . . . the Church teaches on the basis of allegedly miraculous accreditation are frequently uncritical, rigid, defensive, and complacent. They take an attitude of arrogant superiority over members of other religious communities. They close their eyes to evils in the Church and resist the very idea of reform."[14] This strong rebuke, let it be noted, comes from the only American theologian ever elevated to the honorary position of cardinal, by John Paul II no less. Not only can the Church be a stumbling block to believers or potential believers by promoting a too easy triumphalism, but this triumphalism can facilitate a culture within the Church that paradoxically undermines the very *via empirica* it extols.

René Latourelle offers a more measured assessment of the older apologetic. The Church's role as sign, says Latourelle, "is in fact more ambiguous and infinitely more difficult to present than the sign of Christ."[15] Unlike the Church, Christ is both sign and the reality signified. The Christological avenue also provides a more effective medium because of the way Christ lived his life. One does not need to be Christian to recognize Jesus as an exemplary person. The Church, on the other hand, is a paradox, holy yet full of sinners. In discussing *Dei filius*, section 3, Latourelle posits that "the Church seems an abstract, ideal church with absolute attributes, rather than a fragile and sinful pilgrim community of the faithful. The adjectives applied to the church's characteristics evoke intensity rather than paradox."[16] Although less strident than Dulles, Latourelle remained nonplussed by *Dei filius*'s adoption of the *via empirica*.

Before turning to the ecclesial apologetics of the Second Vatican Council, it behooves us to examine the logic of *Dei filius* more closely. The text opts for a maximal claim rather than a quiet admission of the Church's failure. Such an approach can obfuscate the Church's fundamental role: to point to Christ. It makes the witness of the Church more important than it need be. The whole purpose of the Church, as mediator of holiness, is to facilitate the union with God for which humans were made. If one oversells the Church as the *res* instead of the *signum*, one had best be sure that the Church is as good as advertised.

Ecclesial apologetics presents two additional problems. The first, and more banal, has to do with the danger of hypocrisy. One could in fact read *Dei filius*, section 3, and make an amendment like the following: "Because of its exposed lack of sanctity, of its ambivalence toward all that is good, because of its very shaken stability, does the sex abuse crisis not then provide great credibility and irrefutable proof of the Church's *flawed* human mission?"[17] This paraphrase of *Dei filius* exposes how the claim to manifest divine truths necessarily cuts both ways. If the lives of the saints, the stories of the martyrs, and even the ordinary decency of a professing Christian engaging in pacific imitation can re-present Christ's self-emptying revelation, then the hypocrisy of Vatican officials, the greed and careerism of clerical leadership, and the ordinary meanness of a middle-class, American Christian can *mis*represent or conceal the presence of the resurrected Lord in the lives of believers.

The second problem recalls the difference between novelistic and romantic conversion. *Dei filius* nearly follows the Romantic or Pelagian way of thinking about faith. The reasoning goes something like this: Although faith is a gift, God in his infinite goodness has provided humankind with supernatural data. This data has been recorded in scripture and in the history of the Church. The Church, as both guardian of this truth and dispenser of sacramental goods—a sort of "value-added" element of religious belief—successfully mediates the relationship between God and individual human beings. Moreover, its magisterium provides true teaching and credible reasons for the beliefs to which Christians must assent. The individual believer, then, especially if raised Catholic, has *no excuse* to reject this belief. The logical underpinning of this reasoning points to faith no longer being a gift, even though the official teaching declares it so. The implication of *Dei filius*'s ecclesial apologetics seems to be that all reasonable, open-minded people, upon being given proper instruction, should come to believe all that the Church teaches. Indeed, lack of belief becomes an occasion for *j'accuse*. The believer in *Dei filius* reaches the conclusion, justifiable if not explicit, that he can scorn the unbeliever for not *achieving* what he has achieved; the unbeliever, especially one raised in the same faith as the believer, lacks what *Dei filius* calls a "just cause." Very quickly the Church takes shape as a community of the righteous.

The Church as Sign of Paradox

Fundamental theologians have outlined the problems with the older attempts to connect the church "founded" by Jesus with one's own ecclesial communion, which usually fell short of the standards of sound historical research. According to Francis Sullivan, "[This approach] meant returning to the sources in order to prove a pre-established thesis, rather than an inquiry that would allow the sources themselves [to] determine what kind of properties a church must have in order to be true to its New Testament origins."[18] By the twentieth century, the purported objectivity of these historical arguments became more difficult to maintain. Historical research that was more sophisticated with sources produced higher rates of qualification and lower rates of perfect confirmation. The arguments made by older apologists rarely met the standards that would come to mark professional historical work.

Leading fundamental theologians since the Second Vatican Council have tried to address the shortcomings of earlier ecclesial apologetics, while rethinking how best to understand the *four marks* in the context of fundamental theology. Heinrich Fries's 1985 *Fundamentaltheologie* critiqued the ecumenical upshot of prior approaches from the perspective of ecumenical efforts. The older ecclesial apologetics eliminated any chance for real ecumenical dialogue by arguing via a *demonstratio catholica* or *protestanta*.[19] Such demonstrations sought to show how the four signs existed exclusively in one (true) Church alone. Indeed, Hermann Josef

Pottmeyer complemented Fries's work by noting that this exclusivist method was the "point of departure" for the older ecclesial apologetics.[20] Such arguments proved unpersuasive to more historically learned readers, let alone nonbelievers, who often dismiss Christianity wholesale upon witnessing acrimonious and vicious interchange between Christians. Fries surmised, "As a result of the great difficulty of actually proving [the exclusive location of the signs in the Roman Catholic Church], the argument of the *demonstratio catholica* was oversimplified . . . Briefly put, this [approach] results in the following argument: only the Catholic Church possesses the marks which are at the same time the characteristics of the Church of Christ: unity, holiness, catholicity, apostolicity. It, therefore, is the one and only Church of Jesus Christ."[21]

Although Vatican II–era fundamental theologians voiced a broad and substantial critique of the older ecclesial apologetics, they shared with those apologists a common presupposition that the Church should bear some kind of witness to the truth of the Gospels. Following the lead of the fundamental theologians cited above—Pottmeyer, Dulles, Latourelle, Fries, Pié-Ninot, Sullivan—and of an essay by Walter Kasper, in the following pages I point to the Vatican II's understanding of the Church, along with two recent refractions of this understanding, in order to frame mimetic theory's contribution to fundamental ecclesiology.

Like Vatican I, Vatican II calls the Church a "sign and instrument" of revealed truth. Famously, in the first paragraph of *Lumen gentium*— the "Dogmatic Constitution on the Church"—the Council Fathers declared the Church to be "in the nature of a sacrament, that is, a sign and instrument."[22] The theme of sacramentality reverberates throughout the discussion of the Church in this and many other conciliar texts.[23] *Lumen gentium*, section 1, even explains what it means by calling the Church a sacrament: that it signifies and serves as an instrument of saving truth. The declaration of the Church's sacramental reality does not undermine the claims from the Council of Trent: that there are seven sacraments, no more or no less. Kasper clarifies this point: "The church is not an eighth sacrament, in addition to the other seven . . . By using the term sacrament in this merely analogous sense, the council is going back to the older sacramental concept of patristic theology. At that time . . . *sacramentum* was the Latin word used to translate the biblical term *mysterion*."[24] The term *mystery* implies depth and complexity while denoting the manifestation of a divine reality. Pié-Ninot adds that the First Vatican Council understood sign in the context of miracle, whereas for the Second Vatican Council, sign "is concentrated . . . in the category of witness."[25] *Lumen gentium*, section 8, supports Kasper's reading. The Church—both a visible society and a spiritual community— is "a complex reality (*realitas complexa*) that comes together from a human and divine element." As a complex reality, the Church manifests divine truths less straightforwardly than *Dei filius* suggests.

Lumen gentium signifies the upshot of this complexity by distinguishing between the ideal of "one, holy, catholic, and apostolic church" and the real Catholic Church that we encounter. The ideal church, "although constituted and organized as a society in the present world," is not *identical* with the Catholic Church. Instead it "subsists in (*subsistit in*) the Catholic Church" (*Lumen gentium*, sec. 8). This qualification might elide the casual reader. Francis Sullivan, however, remarks, "The term *subsists in* does not have the exclusive sense of the word *is*, which it replaced in the conciliar text. To say that the church of Christ subsists in the Catholic Church does not mean that it is not found elsewhere."[26] Sullivan highlights the consequence of this distinction: "Post-Vatican II Catholic apologists have no reason to indulge in the triumphalism that marked some preconciliar apologetics."[27] Dulles, again, gives a blunter reading: "The Catholic Church's claim that in it subsists the Church of Christ provides no ground for smugness or complacency."[28] At the very least, *subsists in* means that future treatises on the *notes* of the Church need not preclude these *notes* from other churches. *Lumen gentium* says as much when it continues, "Many elements of sanctification and of truth are found outside the Church's visible confines" (*Lumen gentium*, sec. 8). Although unity and holiness subsist in the Catholic Church, and thus its members and its visibility signify divine truth, elements outside the Church can also signify this reality.

Lumen gentium thus encourages Catholics to engage in ecumenical dialogue and to find the good in the theology and traditions of non-Catholic churches. A fervent Catholic must not hedge about the manifest holiness of her non-Catholic neighbor. A dedicated Catholic educator need no longer qualify how a nonreligious school has been able to instill in its students a love for the poor, which is wanting in her own parochial school. A Catholic intellectual can now officially embrace with joy the Protestant author whose most recent book received high and deserving praise for its courageous portrayal of Christian faith. Vatican II enshrines such an approach in its "Degree on Ecumenism" when it declares, "For the Spirit of Christ has not refrained from using the separated Churches and communities as a means of salvation"; further, their "liturgical actions most certainly can truly engender a life of grace, and, one must say, can aptly give access to the communion of salvation" (*Unitatis redintegratio*, sec. 3).

From the perspective of mimetic theory, it is easy to see how this shift in ecclesial language disposed Catholics to receive what it means to belong, absent any sense of superiority over against another. In reflecting on the mark of holiness, *Lumen gentium* qualified the Church's holiness: "The Church, however, clasping sinners to her bosom, at once holy and always in need of purification [*sancta simul et semper purificanda*], follows constantly the path of penance and renewal" (sec. 8). Although a sign of God's presence, the human community called "Church" also contains sinful people in need of redemption. *Lumen gentium* nods toward this paradoxical "holiness" in subsequent sections (see, esp., secs. 9, 15, 65). Vatican II also qualifies the note of holiness in *Gaudium et spes*, which says that although the Church "will never stop being a sign of salvation [*signum salutis*] in the world," the Church does not always live up to this sign: "The Church is not blind to the discrepancy between the message it proclaims and the human weakness of those to whom the Gospel has been entrusted . . . We cannot ignore these shortcomings and we must combat them earnestly" (sec. 43). The Church is a *human* community, despite its exalted status and possession of "the fullness of the means of salvation" [*omnis salutarium mediorum plentitudo*] (*Unitatis redintegratio*, sec. 3).

Latourelle, among others, has used this recalibration of the *notes* to revisit how the Church itself might be an argument. He takes the empirical evidence as problematic, "unless we think of the church as an idealized hypostasis separated from the believers themselves."[29] Yet such a view can lead to the dead end of "ecclesiological monophysitism." In the early Church, the monophysite heresy argued that Christ only had one nature; the Council of Chalcedon in 451 clarified that Christ had both a human and a divine nature. What Chalcedon rejected was the notion of Christ's divinity overshadowing his humanity, such that the latter was not really what made Jesus *Jesus*. Ecclesial monophysitism, analogously, expunges the human element of the Church. Vatican II recalibrated the ecclesial *notes* in order to reckon with this danger.

The heart of this recalibration centered on acknowledging sinfulness in the Church, which qualified the Church's capacity to signify. The sinful actions of Church members prompted such leading fundamental theologians as Latourelle and Dulles to ask whether the Church is not instead "an antisign, a countertestimony."[30] It can only maintain its status as sign, and not as a countersign, by acknowledging its paradoxical nature and permitting a healthy self-scrutiny. In spite of its weaknesses, the Church continues to preach the gospel and to demand evangelical perfection of the sinners whom it welcomes. Additionally, it continues to produce saints despite its failures. Although it can appear to be a countersign, the Church also "makes itself the judge and reformer of its own weaknesses."[31] As paradoxical, "the church, in spite of its infirmities, constantly and regularly produces saints great and loyal enough to be put forward for universal imitation."[32] Post–Vatican II fundamental theologians like Latourelle still make an argument for the Church, but it differs significantly from nineteenth-century precursors.

Like Latourelle, Dulles notices Vatican II's evolving theology of sign. From these texts Dulles surmises that Catholic fundamental theology can no longer make the same triumphant arguments embodied in *Dei filius*. The paradoxical quality of the Church's holiness permits fundamental theology, on good theological grounds, to jettison the older *via notarum* or *via empirica*. Even making such arguments can function as a countersign.[33] Dulles suggests the only way to be "an efficacious sign of God's redemptive work" is to become a "fellowship of reconciliation."[34] He states: "[The Church] must undergo constant conversion to the gospel, purifying itself of its faults, and incessantly pursuing the path of penance and renewal."[35]

Before turning to what mimetic theologians say about the Church, it behooves us to recall more recent instances of ecclesial rethinking at the prompting of Vatican II's teachings. One of the more compelling ecclesiological constructions has come from John Dadosky. In a series of articles, Dadosky argues that communion ecclesiology must be supplemented with an ecclesiology of friendship in order for the Church to be in a real dialogue with the world.[36] In the mid-1980s, then Cardinal Ratzinger, Pope John Paul II, and the 1985 Extraordinary Synod of bishops convened by John Paul II all deemed *communion* "the central ecclesiological concept of the Council."[37] For Dadosky, the metaphor of communion cannot adequately address those outside the Church who might, as the Vatican II documents cited above indicate, enrich the self-understanding of Christians. For Vatican II declared that the Church "not only mediates grace, salvation, Good News, and healing *to* the Other, but that she is also enriched *by* the Other."[38] Dadosky wants to employ the category of friendship in order to capture "that aspect of the Church's self-understanding as enriched by the Other."[39] He considers it an imperative to think theologically about what kind of metaphors help Christians understand this enrichment.

Dadosky appeals to the language of friendship because it allows for the loving capacity for self-correction. Only a good friend can deliver the news that one needs to drink less, lose weight, speak with greater magnanimity, and so on. The Vatican II's documents state explicitly that the Church can teach something to the world, and that the world can also, on occasion, teach something to the Church. Picking up on Vatican II's frequent use of *mutuality*, Dadosky writes, "The Church [at Vatican II] officially recognized that it could be enriched and influenced by the other."[40] As a complement to communion ecclesiology, an ecclesiology of friendship can facilitate Christian self-understanding that signifies holiness precisely through its orientation toward the other.

Because my words are being finalized in the fourth year of the Francis papacy, it is perhaps apt to say a word about Francis's own interpretation of Vatican II's ecclesiology. Like Dadosky, Richard Gaillardetz, in his 2014 "Presidential Address" on Francis's ecclesiology at the Catholic Theological Society of America, advocated a shift away from communion ecclesiology. Gaillardetz notes that Pope Francis, though not operating with the same theological firepower as his predecessor, has nonetheless managed to tilt de facto papal ecclesiology in a direction that more adequately captures the dynamism of Vatican II: "It is not difficult to recognize [Francis's] shift away from an exclusive reliance on an ecclesiology of communion to capture the deepest reality of the church."[41] Francis's vision of a missionary Church overlaps with Dadosky's emphasis on the other. Francis's sermons and addresses have stressed the missionary nature of the Church through such words as "encounter" and through such imperatives as requiring bishops and priests to have the "the odor of the sheep."[42]

Although it is important to recognize that Francis's statements do not reverse the ecclesiologies of the two previous popes, one can still discern a shift in emphasis. The old *via empirica* encouraged the Church to look inward. Pope Francis has implored just the opposite: "A self-involved Church is a sick Church."[43] The missionary nature of the Church impels encounters with the other, and with the poor. Its sacramental logic, therefore, must not center solely on affirming unity, as the Eucharist certainly does, but also in mediating grace. Francis writes, "The Eucharist . . . is not a prize for the perfect but a powerful medicine and nourishment for the weak" (*Evangelii gaudium*, sec. 47). Such statements as these have compelled two of the leading theological commentators on the Francis papacy, Richard Gaillardetz and Walter Kasper, to note a shift in the "root metaphor" for the Church to the "itinerant people of God."[44]

Mimetic Fundamental Ecclesiology

The previous section focused on the paradox of the Church's sacramentality: What kind of sacrament is the Church in light of its sinful members? *Gaudium et spes*, section 43, says the Church is a sign of *salvation*. Mimetic theory helps to highlight how the Church signifies what it means to be and to belong. The Church tells and lives the discovery of our identity and meaning. Just as the Eucharist—the source and summit of the Christian life (*Lumen gentium*, sec. 11: *totius vitae christianae fontem et culmen*)—is the sacrifice that undoes sacrifice, so the Church is the community that radically reorients community. It provides a space and time in which to grow into this new being, to unlearn patterns of false being, and to settle into and to undo false ways of belonging.

Despite an open confession of his Catholicism and of his admiration for many Catholic leaders, including John Paul II and Benedict XVI,

Girard himself says very little about the Catholic Church, admitting: "Catholics have very often criticized me for not having an ecclesiological theory, and in a way they have a point."[45] This lacuna in his corpus has been filled by James Alison. Spread over many works, Alison intuits what I in this chapter call a "mimetic fundamental ecclesiology" by describing this new way to be and to belong, and how the Church facilitates this process. Although a different author is under examination here, the same ontology of grace—made explicit in chapter 1, and referenced throughout the book—seeps through our analysis. For the Church not only mediates grace, but it names the grace that it mediates. Different aspects of Alison's ecclesiology have been gathered under seven related subheadings.

The Gratuity of Forgiveness

Alison's first book, *Knowing Jesus*, recounts how the crucified and risen Jesus appears to the disciples as gratuity. It also shows the quality of knowing by grace. Perhaps the clearest summary of how this works does not come from Alison but from his longtime admirer and "shadow" mentor, Sebastian Moore.

In a densely packed paragraph of *The Crucified Jesus Is No Stranger*, Moore lays out the central insight of *Knowing Jesus*. Both books deal with the entanglement of sin and forgiveness. Moore writes:

> In the ultimate order the ultimate sin, of crucifying the Just One, reverses itself, the victim giving life to the crucifiers . . . This solution is uniquely God's. . . . For we have to experience God coming into us, taking our shape of sin, making explicit our sin, making sin work our salvation. The ultimate truth, which is God's unique embrace, is that the essential *effect* of sin—the crucified—is, identically, the healing. What sin ultimately *is*, is seen in the crucified. What sin ultimately *is*, is forgiven . . . The crucified, therefore, *as* signifying sin's *ultimate* meaning, signifies its *forgiveness*. To *see* sin is to see its forgiveness.[46]

Moore's description indicates the twofold nature of this salvific truth: one discovers this truth in recognizing the entirely wrong way that one has been going about things. Alison locates the same tension in *Faith beyond Resentment*: "To each step of the clearer and more complete revelation of God, that is to say, to each purification of faith, there is a corresponding and simultaneous collapse of a whole series of elements which seemed to have been indispensable bulwarks of faith. For these elements turn out to be parts of an idolatrous order of things which had previously been confused with the worship of the true God."[47] Or as Moore puts it, to see sin is to see its forgiveness. Thus the insufficiency of grasping or excogitating this reality.

Only in the act of being forgiven for their participation in Christ's crucifixion do the disciples really come to know God. Alison declares, "The resurrection has turned our victim into our forgiveness."[48] Once awoken from a dream one can realize that (1) I am awake and no longer dreaming, and (2) I am no longer part of the dream in which I was late for class. This is quite different from waking up and still being late for class. Alison affirms this twofold recognition when discussing the gratuity of the Resurrection. Concerning the Resurrection's gratuitous interruption, Alison comments, "And it happened as forgiveness. This is the second great category of the experience of the resurrection. Part of the utterly gratuitous other is that it is entirely outside any system of retribution and desert, and is therefore experienced by us as loosing us from being tied in to the 'customary' other . . . It is both as forgiveness of our sins and complete restructuring of our virtues that the gratuitous other reaches us."[49] This kind of double act describes the process of reconciliation. A normal person cannot untangle two different emotional actions in the case of sin: a sense of dislike for oneself and a sense of God-as-Judge disliking me. When reconciliation happens, one not only feels forgiven from that particular sin but also feels that the God who only loves you when you are good slowly fades away as one comes to know a God who simply likes you.[50] The act of reconciliation allows for a reimagination of a relationship not rooted in reciprocity.

From Resurrection to Community

There is an ecclesiological upside to this being-forgiven. *Knowing Jesus* stitches together how the gratuity of the Resurrection relates to the community called Church. To *know* Jesus, for Alison, means to experience forgiveness from a sin of which one had not been fully conscious. Not just *a* sin, but a *sinfulness*, which entails unhealthy rivalry and a reciprocity that governs individual relationships. On a social level, sinfulness manifests itself in a manner of belonging that requires exclusion or expulsion of some other person or group of people. One comes to understand the way one belongs, and this way of belonging is rooted in an anonymity. Being known by Jesus means coming into an identity. The place this happens is the Church. Alison explains: "The only unity to which he or she can escape belonging is the unity of humanity that the Holy Spirit creates out of the risen victim, the unity which subverts all other unities . . . The Church is the universal sacrament of that kingdom (of heaven). That is to say that it is the efficacious sign of a reality that has been realized only in embryo. As such, it is radically subversive of all other forms of belonging, all other ways of constructing unity. But it is so *as* a gift from God."[51] If one does not experience this new kind of unity as graced or gifted, then one does not experience it at all.[52] Alison's description sheds light on what it means to call the Church a sacrament of salvation.

Being such a sign in embryo means that the Church does not equal the Kingdom. At best the Church points to the Kingdom of God, or heaven. Alison insists, however, that the Church cannot be just another group: "It is particularly sad when Catholics turn belonging to the Church into a sectarian belonging, into a definable cultural group with a clearly marked inside and outside, and firm ideas as to who belongs outside . . . By their very sectarian insistence on the unique truth of Catholicism, these people cut themselves off from access to the truth which they think is theirs, but which is only true when it is received as given."[53] *Received as given*: this phrase requires a bit of meditation. By this phrase Alison means something that we cannot return or pay back, that was neither earned nor deserved. We cannot receive grace any other way. On this point so many stumble because they are more likely to think they can earn whatever good things come their way. The citation at the beginning of this section from *Knowing Jesus* makes this point in its final sentence. God reaches us in the forgiving of our sins. Being forgiven *as* sinner lets the believer experience this grace in such a way that makes grace the coefficient in front of any account of human goodness.

The experience of being forgiven (soteriology) and the discovery of a new way of belonging (ecclesiology) constitute two sides of the same coin. Alison makes this point most explicitly in his short summa, *Jesus the Forgiving Victim*. The book's sixth and seventh essays link atonement with ecclesiology. Here Alison writes, "Do you see how it is that the Atonement and the birth of a new people are different dimensions of the same thing?" One paragraph later he adds, "Automatically the hearing of the voice of the Forgiving Victim is the inauguration of a new sort of relationship. The coming into being of the Church is not an add-on, but what the whole project was about."[54] Thus a discussion of the Church becomes essential to any Christian theology or apologetic.

A Paradoxical Apologetic

According to mimetic fundamental ecclesiology, the Church is a sacrament for a particular kind of being and belonging. Both the fundamental theologians mentioned above and Alison himself have noted the Church's failure to articulate a compelling fundamental ecclesiology. The historical context of ecclesial discourse qualifies its particular bent:

> It is worth noting that what is called "ecclesiology," or the discourse about the Church, is a fairly modern discourse, invented in the wake of the Reformation . . . It was born in the midst of a controversy, and on account of this still bears the scars of its defensive and apologetic birth. That is to say it was born to defend the truth of the Church against the devastating critique of the Reformation and for that reason had to have recourse to a series of proofs about Jesus founding the Church in its institutional form . . . In order to be maintained [these truths] were decked out in a whole way of conceiving of the Church which we're only now learning to get beyond.[55]

This passage echoes the argument made in post–Vatican II fundamental theology, and in what follows it will be shown how Alison even outdistances the aforementioned efforts.

To unpack Alison's nondefensive ecclesial apologetic, it will be helpful to review what Alison says about being and belonging. The revelation of Jesus permitted a transmission of knowledge from Jesus to the disciples. Alison explains, "The revelation that brings about the intelligence of the victim is creative of and constitutive of a new historical, linguistic, representational community, which is simultaneously seen to have been originary: what humans were always meant to be."[56] The Church allows one to belong in a way that throws into question earlier ways of belonging. Hence the Church's insistence that if one is to profess belief in it, one must profess belief in its catholicity, or universality. Only belief in such a catholicity can sublate a false belonging that insists on an exclusion; to be a member of a country club is by definition exclusive. To be a fan of the St. Louis Cardinals *is* to detest the Cubs. For Alison, the Resurrection overturns such presuppositions of belonging: "What is given in Christ's victim death is a subversion of the old human way of belonging, and the possibility of our induction into a new human way of belonging, of being-with, without any over-against."[57]

Of course, numerous people experience the Catholic faith as anything but universal. For many, being Catholic has meant *not* being something else. Such an attitude, according to Alison, exhibits a failure to undergo the Church's catholicity: "The unity that is created in this way—even the laughing emotional bonding that seems to have no practical consequences—is created at the expense of a victim or victims, at the expense of an exclusion . . . [Such a unity] betrays the very deepest truth of the Catholic faith, the universal faith, which by its very nature, has no over-against."[58] Alison retrieves the note of catholicity in arguing how the new community called "Church" demands that believers settle into a belonging without exclusion.

A further danger persists in assenting to this universality without making any attempt to undergo it. Alison points toward this undergoing when he relates the imaginative exercise of experiencing the Church as one big party. Most people have been at a party and wondered: "How did *that* person receive an invitation?" Too often Catholics have been able to attend a self-segregating weekly party. I do not mean only older ethnic parishes but also parishes that become bastions for progressives or traditionalists. For Alison, the universality of the Church "means that I am always going to have to be in communion with fundamentalists as a condition for staying at the party. Any tendencies I might have to belong to a group of people like me, who think like me, agree with me, and with whom I could form a nice friendly like-minded clique, are constantly being smashed."[59] Alison casts what many imagine as a foretaste of the kingdom negatively; such a community of the like-minded—that great country club in the sky—is only a more refined form of the kind of belonging of which Christ came to free us. The Church impels one to practice a new way of belonging to, not over against, the other.

Biblical Witness

Alison bases much of his ecclesiology on his exegesis of key New Testament passages. Read as a whole, the New Testament sends mixed messages about this new sense of universality and belonging. The Acts of the Apostles, the Johannine letters, and the Pauline letters describe communities fairly eager to keep certain people out. Mimetic theory suggests reading scripture as self-corrective and highlighting particular passages to demonstrate how God reveals through scripture. Alison unpacks the importance of the baptism of Cornelius in Acts 10. This chapter tells how Peter received a vision to eat nonkosher animals (Acts 10:15), which compelled Peter to extend this vision to Gentiles.[60] In the same chapter, Peter declares, upon sitting down to eat with Cornelius, "God has shown me not to call any person profane or impure" (Acts 10:28). Gentiles can enter the communion of Israel now called the Church.

For Alison the passage implies much more than a permission, following a very strange vision, to allow the baptism of a non-Jewish man. He calls Acts 10:28 "one of the most important lines in our history" and "an extraordinary anthropological earthquake."[61] The connection to the revelation of the scapegoat mechanism is direct: once one realizes the innocence of the victim, then the need for excluding individuals or whole groups of people dissolves. Rather than simply switching sides, like a liberal who becomes a conservative, now even more convinced that the entire fault lies with the other, biblical revelation calls into question such patterns of identity-seeking. This transformation means the creation of a universality hitherto unimagined. Acts 10 reveals the particular quality of Christian universality: "This is the great secret of catholicity: while every local culture tends to build its frontiers by means of victims, it is only if we begin from the forgiving victim that we can build a culture which has no frontiers because we no longer have to build any order, security or identity *over against some excluded person.*"[62]

To my knowledge, Alison does not offer any commentary on Ephesians 2:11–21, yet it is a passage that perfectly summarizes the effect of the Christ event on the community Paul addresses: the Gentiles. The letter sets out to explain how the Christ event changes everything for non-Jewish believers. Prior to Christ's resurrection, the Jewish community had understood Gentiles only in a negative capacity ("uncircumcision," 2:11). Christ, who "is our peace," proceeded to "break down the dividing wall of enmity" (v. 14). The metaphors that Paul uses to describe this reconciliation—"brought near by the blood of Christ" (v. 13), "reconcile both groups to God in one body through the cross" (v. 16)—interweave the soteriological with the ecclesiological. As a sacrament of salvation, the Church's catholicity, which fulfills the Christ's intention to "create in himself one humanity in place of the two, thus making peace" (v. 15), points to the new belonging liberated from a process of exclusion. The Church, paradoxically, is a community that undermines the logic of community as commonly practiced, much as the Eucharist is a sacrifice that undermines the logic of sacrifice. The Cross, according to Ephesians 2, makes this community possible.

Ecclesial Virtues

Alison's Church feels no sense of accomplishment by confessing Jesus' real achievement. To do so would misrepresent the gratuity of Christ's action for us. By modeling Jesus, the Church, for Alison, cultivates in its members the virtue of indifference needed to prevent such distortion.[63] In chapter 8 of *On Being Liked*, Alison shows what it means for Jesus to have founded the Church and for the Church to signify this founding. He does so by recalling Jesus's indifference to the temple; a hatred of the temple would give it more meaning than Jesus thinks it should have. This indifference, says Alison, "is of vital importance for fundamental ecclesiology."[64] Adopting an attitude of indifference permits believers to *be in* and *belong to* the Church in a new way. Understanding Jesus' attitude toward the temple as one of indifference lets us relate indifferently to supposedly sacred structures. The Church, he explains, "is not a 'Temple' at all. It is the constant undoing of the human tendency to get sucked in to centres of mimetic fascination . . . and the constant opening up of our intellects and imaginations toward the engaging in a new form of shepherding, leading people away from being trapped in sacred structures and forms of behaviour run by stumbling blocks. And *this is what the Church is*."[65] There can be a tendency after reading such a passage to say, "That is not the Church that I know; or, the Church is nothing like Alison's description of the Church." Mimetic theory helps us to avoid this judgment. Alison here writes for those ministering to gays and lesbians. In other words, for people who might be more justified in identifying the Church with violent sacred order. But for Alison's application of mimetic theory, such an act would itself constitute a failure to regard "The Temple" indifferently: "In fact we will not have left the Temple at all . . . but will still be utterly locked in to the centre of mimetic fascination, with its draw and its repulsion, and our sense of being good and bad will be utterly dependent on it."[66]

In this current section, I have thus far tried to show how Alison's writings serve a kind of "ecclesial apologetics" by making the Church itself a kind of argument. There's a way in which, despite talk of "undergoing" (a conversion to the gospel), one can "receive" the point here as something to be grasped. One can distinguish between Alison making a point and the reader getting the point. But Alison himself hints at a different process, because in the autobiographical section of his chapter, key insights happen on an Ignatian retreat, and in front of the Blessed Sacrament. Alison credits his capacity—he would surely call a grace—to this retreat, which liberated him from a prior reactive relationship with the Church.[67]

Eucharistic Abiding

Although much of my discussion in the earlier subsections concerned signification, in the final pages of this chapter I exchange "signification" for "abiding." The Church is not the Department of Motor Vehicles—it does not demand sufficient knowledge of the rules or doctrines, after the demonstration of which one would never dream of going back. The ecclesial faithful feel compelled to stay and repeat the celebrations and the rituals. As sinful humans, we regularly fail to see ourselves as victimizers because we would rather see ourselves as victimized, and thus let off the hook. Of this point, Alison writes, "Constantly to be brought up face to face with the forgiving victim is constantly to be encouraged into not being frightened of telling the truth, of having the myths stripped away. Because it is a reminder of how we are victimisers, when we thought were being good and holy and just . . . There is no true worship except in the presence of the true victim, because it is only from the victim that the voice which can undo the lies will come."[68] *Constantly*. This means understanding the celebration of the Eucharist not so much as something to entertain or to excite us, but to pull us out of a force field of romantic self-regard and into a remembering of our being forgiven by the innocent victim. It is only by *abiding* that we can experience the slow process of coming to understand how we are caught up in unhealthy being and belonging.

Sometimes this reckoning entails coming to see our original impulse toward the Church as wrongheaded. There's no better community to join for the wrong reasons than the Church. The liturgy of Word and of the Eucharist permit the grace that transforms the way we read the biblical stories, whose "whole purpose," writes Alison, "is to enable us to inhabit a 'we.' This we do not by detecting others' errors and hypocrisy, but by becoming aware of what I might call a mechanism of bad religion in which we all tend to be involved."[69] Abiding in the Church permits us to come to see how we have been mixed up in "bad" religion *as* Christians. We are the Pharisees. Texts that had formerly convinced us of the Other's evil now "become a gift which both shows us what an idolatrous building of our home looks like, and how to move beyond it in charity."[70]

Alison's discussion of the Eucharist describes the grace that God makes present as real presence. It is important that Alison presumes an abiding in the liturgical space. When this happens, "The Eucharist gets detached from either form of group belonging, and we begin to discover . . . the real presence of the re-creating heart of love which makes available to us a dynamic of detecting and moving beyond the mechanisms of violence that we set up for ourselves and inhabit so doggedly."[71]

Sacramental abiding in the Church catechizes believers into a new being and belonging. Without this abiding, for Alison, it seems nearly impossible to imagine how real conversion could work. During the mass, Christ's body and blood made really present graces our process of undergoing. Alison continues, "I'm not talking about anything magic here. Just the slow drip, drip, drip of regular participation at Sunday Mass mysteriously yielding the real, non-resentful presence of the risen Lord who . . . keeps alive the dynamic of enabling us to find ourselves within a catholic story."[72] This formation process enables participants to habituate themselves into a nonrivalrous belonging with the Other.

In the space provided for abiding, individuals not only grow in holiness but also come to understand the Church as the paradoxical sign discussed by the abovementioned fundamental theologians. As a "somewhat conservative Catholic," and also a gay man, Alison has outlined his own way of navigating the painful experience of what he calls an "area" or "field" of mendacity.[73] The Church, says Alison, has inherited a "field of mendacity" concerning its understanding of homosexuality akin to fields of mendacity in race and or gender. In other words, the Church itself has been part—even been at times a large part—of the cultural and institutional machinery describing gay people as defectively heterosexual. The Church, says Alison, has been a witness to this machinery, but it also "has an evangelizing role to play," which is as a "witness to and part of its overcoming."[74] Implied here is that Catholics should not equate the Church with the magisterium. Such an equation enables judgments about its holiness and catholicity to stand or fall at a distance. Alison suggests imagining the Church as the group of people—however haltingly or invisibly—not totally opposed to receiving the graces needed to abide peacefully with one another. One sign of this peaceful abiding is the capacity to react nonviolently to the magisterium when not in immediate agreement. Alison advocates that Christians avoid the dialectic between "pathological loyalty" and "pathological rejection."[75] The former cannot disentangle belonging to the Church from "an act of sacrifice of the 'other.'"[76] But the latter position, perhaps easier to justify, has its own pathology. It must not remain stuck in this reaction, however, lest it stop at "a symmetry of enemy twins." In reflecting on what many groups in the Church must have experienced as the unexpected shake-up initiated by Pope Francis, it would be a great failure if one's deepest joy in his papacy consisted in wondering how miserable he is making certain *bad* Catholics. Surely, to undergo no deeper joy would constitute a missed opportunity and would signal a shallow pattern of Christian belonging.

The Victimless Sacred

Alison imagines a "victimless sacred" space, in which one learns to receive an identity "without resentment." Alison does this, in his own words, by reading the gospel "eucharistically."[77] The kind of ecclesial belonging that brings about this new space understands the Church fraternally instead of paternally.[78] This belonging also requires a letting go of the need for human approval, because such approval can never mediate the graced sense of approval that can come only from God. Being wrapped in the dialectic of approval/disapproval indicates "a failure to accept the fullness of responsible involvement for bringing into being the project."[79]

The project takes time. The apostolicity of the Church gives witness to the Holy Spirit's creative work in history. In many and diverse ways, the Church has paradoxically signified the overcoming of an inherited mendacity. Worship and prayer, for instance, help participants experience time in a new way: "The True Worship of the True God is in the first instance the pattern of lives lived over time, lives which are inhabited stories of leaving the world of principalities and powers, and gradually, over time, giving witness to the True God."[80]

Christians have been fortunate in recent years to have True Worship portrayed accurately on the screen. The 2010 French film *Of Gods and Men* depicts how a group of Algerian monks pray communally and, as a result of their life together in quietude and prayer, learn how not to be wrapped up in the violent sacred. The film itself, I am convinced, can be viewed as a sacrament of true worship on account of its sluggish pace, especially for those inducted into recent American patterns of viewing. By drawing the audience into the deliberate rhythm of Trappist liturgical life, the film permits the viewer to experience, perhaps only dimly, how the monks learn not to be caught up in the violent tug of things. In one poignant scene, a younger monk blurts an obscenity at an older monk, whose nonresponse suggests how the angry reactive mode of relating can be overcome by prayer and asceticism. This portrayal overlaps with Alison's comments about worship. True worship, he notes, "enables us to dwell more freely and creatively within (the world of principalities and powers), a lifelong therapy for distorted desire."[81] Perhaps Catholics should consider religious life as an acute form of the "lifelong therapy" required for all of fallen humanity.

Understanding the Church as a dwelling place for lifelong therapy may be a good way to conceive lived Christianity, but is it any kind of argument for the truth it claims to teach? Alison's application of mimetic theory to fundamental ecclesiology proves especially helpful because it substitutes the perfunctory categories used to steer this topic. Judging which church or group most embodies the *four marks* means that one has not yet undergone the kind of transformation of desire that the Church teaches. To judge a community as beneath one's own is already to abandon the kind of belonging into which the risen Lord invites us.

The Catholic Church requires that one confess one's sins in order to be a *good* Catholic. This in itself is a paradox that Alison helps make sense of. Rather than leading to an overwrought scrupulosity, a sustained attention to sinful habits can lead the believer into a space where she is less easily dominated by them.[82] The Church brings one into a set of practices and names God's graces in ways that encourage us to exchange our anonymity for an identity. Although Alison's discussion of the sacramental life generally focuses on baptism and the Eucharist, I would suggest that penance might be a place where one could slowly "cook" in therapy, and in this way exchange sincerity for honesty. In his discourse on honesty, Alison argues that the main quality of honesty is that one is possessed by it. Real reconciliation means being loved into a more relaxed way of being and belonging.

I might also suggest the sacrament of marriage as a locus for this living out of ecclesial reality. Nothing quite embodies the gradual undergoing as does marriage, and the Church's theology of marriage especially underscores how God's grace unites the freely assenting couple in their bond. At a point when we are most likely to believe in the Romantic notion of our autonomous choosing, the Church suggests that, even here, the love really felt and expressed is subsequent to the God who loved us first and made us loveable to the other. Further, the ability to be faithful to this promise depends, primarily, not on the strength of our wills but on the auxiliary grace that overcomes rivalry and reciprocity to make possible a life together. Moreover, the command to be open to the fecundity of the sexual act, can, at its best, help couples see that God mediates his life-giving goodness through a couple's love.

On their own, the two discussions in this chapter—of the shift in how the Church signifies salvation and of how James Alison applies mimetic theory to fundamental ecclesiology—form coherent arguments. But if one considers these two approaches as a diptych (and indeed the chapter has been so conceived), then the mimetic fundamental ecclesiology presented in the second half advances the fundamental ecclesiology championed in the first half of the chapter. Mimetic theory advances the conversation to these topics by explaining the inner dynamics of what the Church is and how it comes to be, which condition the kind of argument that the Church can make for Christianity.

CHAPTER SIX

TRAJECTORIES OF MODERNITY

Girard and Taylor in Conversation

Christianity and Modernity in Tension?

The previous four chapters have covered "proper" theological topics and have discussed how mimetic theory, from the perspective of fundamental theology, enriches Christian theological understanding of these topics. By covering modernity and atheism, the final two chapters do not treat topics within theology; instead, they venture into arenas that alter, or perhaps even threaten, the Christian theological project *en masse*. Here too, mimetic theory has much to contribute and is at its most apologetic.

Theological and genealogical accounts of modernity are nothing new. A canon of genealogies has emerged to explain the Christian roots of modernity and secularism.[1] In this chapter, I do not bring mimetic theory into conversation with the entire body of literature devoted to theology and modernity. Instead I align René Girard with Charles Taylor as genealogists of modernity, and I argue that Girard's account helpfully supplements Taylor's. Only mimetic theory explains how evangelical revelation unveils the process of concealment that orders nonbiblical cultures and thus distills the essential qualities of Christianity in revealing the identity of God with Jesus the victim.

Modern secularism and loss of belief present a vexing challenge to contemporary Christians. This challenge comes into focus against the backdrop of the long Christian attempt to construct a theology of history.[2] The expansion and flourishing of the earliest Christian communities facilitated a teleological account of history where the Church Militant eventually triumphs against pagan or other non-Christian forces. Already in the fourth century, Eusebius of Caesarea argued that Constantine's conversion and the corresponding elevation of Christianity within the Roman Empire evidenced Christian truth claims—its triumph was its best argument. One century after Eusebius, Augustine, especially in the *City of God*, dissuaded his listeners from making such facile connections. Although by 390 CE the now-Christian empire had seemingly rid itself of paganism under Theodosius I, thus fulfilling Eusebius's manifest destiny, Rome would be sacked by barbarian hordes two decades later. Christian theology now had to answer the same question that eighth-century BCE Israelite theology had attempted after the collapse of the Davidic throne and the Assyrian invasion: How does one square divine election with terrestrial defeat? Augustine cautioned that neither triumph nor defeat definitively manifest God's will. In the fallen world, attempts to bring heaven down to earth, more often than not, manifested the same sinful *superbia* that motivated Adam and Eve.[3]

Many centuries later, Christian apologists and their interlocutors have tried to understand how a Christian civilization could devolve (or evolve) into a society in which belief in God and church attendance experienced such precipitous declines. A society with a secular worldview took its place and replaced God, at least in the public sphere, with purportedly theologically neutral entities, such as markets, nation-states, and secular reason. The massive shift, encompassed by modernity, has made it nearly impossible to impose a Eusebian interpretation on the formerly Christian West. Yet finding a satisfactory replacement model has proven difficult, despite the exalted status that Augustine shares.

The interpretation most likely to have staying power is Charles Taylor's. His writings have captured the problematic nature of much of the discourse about the secular age. Before describing his interpretation of the secular, it behooves me to spend some time developing a key polarity in Taylor's work. He notes, "As I have indicated, this debate tends to become polarized between 'boosters' and 'knockers,' who either condemn or affirm modernity en bloc, thus missing what is really at stake here, which is how to rescue admirable ideals from sliding into demeaning modes of realization."[4] According to the boosters, the Enlightenment ushered in the long, slow march of secularization. A triumphant scientific worldview, coupled with social changes like urbanization, linked secularization to technological progress. Although this progressive, upward-rising reading of history has come under criticism since at least 1949, when Karl Löwith published *Meaning and History*, it has maintained a certain resilience. Of course, the rise of Islamic fundamentalism in this century—bookended by the 9/11 attack and the emergence of the Islamic State—and the political emergence of evangelicalism in the United States provide counter data to the thesis of inevitability, but they do not overturn the primary contrast in worldviews—on the one side: premodern religious irrationality; and on the other: modern, secular reason.

The work of the highly regarded historian of the Enlightenment, Jonathan Israel, has come to the forefront in this debate. Israel's massive, three-volume project represents a towering achievement in Enlightenment studies. Here he relentlessly attempts to portray the Enlightenment and Christianity in the greatest possible contrast.[5] In *Enlightenment Contested*, he juxtaposes two irreconcilable worldviews, modern and premodern: "From its first inception, the Enlightenment in the western Atlantic world was always a mutually antagonistic duality, and the ceaseless internecine strife within it is . . . the most fundamental and important thing about it."[6] Although Israel incorporates various strands and stratifications within his general narrative, there can be no question about what lay at the opposite end of the Enlightenment, which promised both to emancipate individuals and to transform entire societies. The Enlightenment project, Israel notes, was met with stiff resistance: "Most men had no more desire to discard traditional reverence for established authority and idealized notions of community than their belief in magic, demonology and Satan."[7] According to Israel, the eighteenth-century failure to reconcile traditional theological convictions with the new science and with philosophy was less tragic than inevitable. Twenty-first-century efforts share the same fate. The true Enlightenment of Spinoza, posits Israel, has paved the way for the arrival of the secular and the planting of Enlightenment values across the West and parts of the developing world.

Now is not the time for retreat, as the concluding salvo to *Enlightenment Contested* declares:

> It is precisely this continuing, universal relevance of [the Enlightenment's] values on all continents, and among all branches of humanity, together with the unprecedented intellectual cohesion it gave to these moral and social ideals, which accounts for what Bernard Williams called the "intellectual irreversibility of the Enlightenment," its uniquely central importance in the history of humanity. Parenthetically, it might be worth adding that nothing could be more fundamentally mistaken, as well as politically injudicious, than for the European Union to endorse the deeply mistaken notion that "European values" if not nationally particular are at least religiously specific and should be recognized as essentially "Christian" values. That the religion of the papacy, Inquisition, and Puritanism should be labeled the quintessence of "Europeanness" would rightly be considered a wholly unacceptable affront by a great number of thoroughly "European" Europeans.[8]

Israel's viewpoint, which he summarizes here, encapsulates the dissonance between modernity and Christianity.

Certain Christian intellectuals have responded to secular modernity with an inverse triumphalism. Alasdair MacIntyre, for instance, has reshaped the field of theological ethics by arguing persuasively that modernity's understanding of moral goodness has made it impossible to present a coherent account of human flourishing, or to defend its claims for objective rationality.[9] Similarly, Leo Strauss, a secular Jew, contrasted the modern to the premodern in such a way that led many to prefer the classical over the modern articulations of moral goodness and political theory.[10] These countermodern thinkers greatly influenced the "knockers" of the past several decades, who neither accept the inevitable triumph of modernity nor judge Christianity as the intellectually inferior partner.

One popular strategy in this camp involves pinpointing a deviation in doctrine or practice that predated modernity proper. John Milbank's provocative and in many ways illuminating account of modernity is the most influential. For Milbank, late medieval nominalism instigated the decline: "Now this [late medieval nominalist] philosophy was itself the legatee of the greatest of all disruptions carried out in the history of European thought, namely that of Duns Scotus, who *for the first time* established a radical separation of philosophy from theology . . . The very notion of a reason–revelation duality, far from being an authentic Christian legacy, itself results only from the rise of a questionably secular mode of knowledge."[11] Here Milbank judges modernity to be an abrupt departure from what preceded it. Milbank's stridency reaches almost Manichean tones in his concluding paragraph to this foundational essay: "It is indeed for radical orthodoxy an either/or: Philosophy (Western or Eastern) as a purely autonomous discipline, or theology: Herod or the magi, Pilate or the God-man."[12] Modernity relates to Christianity as darkness to light.

More recently, David Bentley Hart, another of contemporary theology's most imposing voices, made a juxtaposition similar to Milbank's:

> The only cult that can truly thrive in the aftermath of Christianity is a sordid service of the self, of the impulses of the will, of the nothingness that is all that the withdrawal of Christianity leaves behind. The only futures open to post-Christian culture are conscious nihilism, with its inevitable devotion to death, or the narcotic banality of the Last Men, which may be little better than death. . . . And we should certainly dread whatever rough beast it is that is being bred in our ever coarser, crueler, more inarticulate, more vacuous popular culture; because, cloaked in its anodyne insipience, lies a world increasingly devoid of merit, wit, kindness, imagination, or charity.[13]

Like Milbank, Hart contrasts Christianity and modernity as forcefully as possible. These citations, from two of the most important contemporary theologians, would seem to ensure a trickle-down effect of their interpretations and narratives. The battle between Christianity and modernity in both instances emerges as a zero-sum game, in which the latter's gain can only mean a loss for the former, and vice versa.

An appeal to the categories of Bernard Lonergan will facilitate the transition of the previous battles over secularism to Taylor's approach. Lonergan's heuristic for analyzing differences of horizon distinguishes between the complementary, the genetic, and the dialectical. Using these categories, both Israel's and Milbank's position fall under the dialectical model—"what for one is good, for another is evil."[14] Although not treated here, a complementary approach attempts to minimize the differences by showing how compatible certain preeminent modern expressions—those of Kant or Rawls, say—are with Christianity. Taylor and Girard, meanwhile, offer genetic accounts of the difference between modernity and Christianity. As Lonergan describes it, "Each later stage presupposes earlier stages, partly to include them, and partly to transform them."[15] Modernity and the secular age—as problematic as they may be from a Christian perspective—are best understood when analyzed in conjunction with the Christian culture that birthed them.

At this point it is worth asking, from the perspective of mimetic theory, what kind of suspicions should arise in looking at different approaches to the relation between Christianity and modernity? Girard overturns the logic of most conflict resolution by insisting that similarity, not difference, drives conflict. Are the competing voices that insist on absolute contrast unable to discern a deeper similarity driving the conflict? Likewise, mimetic theory inclines one to question the attempts that link all modern evils to a single figure—Scotus, Ockham, Luther, or Suarez—or to an idea—univocity, nominalism, or instrumental reason. These kinds of arguments, especially when absent of scholarly rigor, share a structural similarity to scapegoating. So the question arises as to whether a mimetic reading of modernity offers a more fruitful approach. Precisely at this point, the projects of Taylor and Girard, which account for the emergence of modernity, can offer a more apologetically advantageous interpretation of modernity.

In what follows I do not aim merely to compare Girard and Taylor; I also argue that Girard's position, which can be best appreciated when studied in concert with Taylor, also goes beyond Taylor on certain key points. In this regard, the chapter builds on the recent work of Scott Cowdell, who notes that, for Girard at least, modernity does not result from a deviation within Christianity, but rather from an iteration that the earliest realization of Christianity made possible: "The seeds of secular modernity are to be found in the Bible and in the ministry of Jesus rather than where they are usually sought: in the late medieval period, the Renaissance, and the Reformation."[16] Christianity itself enables possible the modern, secular story.

Revisiting the Pre-archaic and the Christian Revelation

In order to address how both thinkers locate the relationship between Christianity and modernity, it will prove helpful to begin earlier—first with an analysis of how they relate Christianity to archaic religion— what Taylor calls "pre-Axial"—and then with their accounts of the essence of Christianity. In both *A Secular Age* and its forerunner, *Modern Social Imaginaries*, Taylor develops a theory of religion in order to illustrate the breakthrough of a religious vision central to Christianity.[17] Taylor borrows Karl Jaspers's famous distinction between pre-Axial and Axial religions.[18] The former, notes Taylor, are characterized by "a relation to spirits, or forces, or powers, which are recognized as being in some sense higher, not the ordinary forces and animals of everyday."[19] These belief systems engender a set of experiences quite foreign to us. In addition, these early religious forces are intensely social. God works on the group as a whole, and the group's or tribe's consciousness of well-being depends on the divine. Archaic religious practice imbues members with a heightened sense of communal belonging, which Taylor calls "social embedding." He elaborates, "Because their most important actions were the doings of whole groups, articulated in a certain way, they couldn't conceive themselves as potentially disconnected from this social matrix."[20]

Consequently, having a proximate and visceral religious experience meant seeing God as intimately bound to this world. It was not always the case that this God was "with us," but God's beneficent intentions, whatever their extent, became manifest in ordinary human flourishing. This pre-Axial God wanted a worshipper to be a king, or to have several sons, or to have a particularly glorious experience in battle.[21] In transposing Jaspers's contrast between archaic religions and the subsequent "Axial" religions that emerged between the eighth and fifth century BCE, Taylor posits some continuity between pre-Axial and Axial religion—not the least of which was the role of worship and belief in a ready exchange among the supernatural and the natural.[22] Still, the shift toward Axial religion cannot be understated: it was dramatic and transformative.

These Axial religions, which include Buddhism, prophetic Judaism, and the later Indian Vedas, distinguished themselves through "a notion of our good which goes beyond human flourishing."[23] Axial religions differentiated between goodness in an ultimate sense and the goods that benefited their own particular communities. At the same time there emerged a monotheistic understanding of the divine, at least in the Near East; the pre-Axial God would never let it rain on both the wicked and the righteous. The dignified, transcendent Axial God, however, seemed hesitant to call for even one plague against the wicked.

Since the notion of human flourishing was so imbedded in theological presuppositions, Axial religion permitted a corresponding shift in human flourishing. Post-Axial human flourishing became, over the course of many centuries, disengaged from a more immediate social context. St. Paul flourished, but through a mystical participation in Christ's crucifixion; Polycarp flourished in martyrdom, an experience that few pre-Axial worshippers would have been able to recognize as flourishing. Having inherited the Hebrew prophets' Axial turn, Christianity benefited from and radicalized this new religious consciousness. Although Taylor does not devote much space to relating Christianity and pre-Axial religion, this relationship comes to play an important role in his account of ordering modernity to Christianity.

For Girard, the scapegoat mechanism provided the dominant matrix to explain pre-Axial, or what he calls "archaic" religion. This mechanism answered the problem of violence that arose from the rivalry borne of mimetic desire. The widespread ritualized killing in archaic societies released the tensions that resulted from a buildup of rivalry. Without this ritualized killing, as I mentioned in chapter 4, the earliest groups of humans would have found it difficult to survive. Humanity, says Girard, desperately needed to discover a way to de-escalate mimetic crises, and it found one in the scapegoat mechanism and the subsequent ritual repetition of this event. Absent a theory assigning value to ritual, Romantics presupposed the nobility of primitive, preritualized cultures and therefore judged religion to be a perversion from an earlier, pristine natural state.[24] Anthropologists and archaeologists, however, have found abundant evidence of sacrifice and ritual at humanity's origins, but as of yet no social contract. Girard explains:

> All the philosophers locate society's origin in a deliberate decision, but one that, all the same, is born of a sort of constraint: the need to come to an

agreement on certain things. In the end this is even true of Hobbes, who, lacking the scapegoat mechanism, must conclude: violence looms, thus human beings are obliged to collaborate. It's even true of Freud, in *Totem and Taboo*: first there's the murder of the father, and then the brothers fight, and one fine day they decide to make peace. So they sit down at the negotiating table. It's this idea of a well-thought-out starting point that I'm against.[25]

What comes first, the priest or the cult? For Girard, the answer is obvious: "If we simply consider that the clergy cannot really precede the invention of culture, then religion must come first and far from being a derisory force, it appears as the origin of the whole culture."[26]

Although modern society frequently derides primitive sacrificial ritual and taboos, Girard determines that these institutions saved humanity from self-destruction. Unlike other animal societies based on dominance hierarchy, early human societies found another basis for stability: "Human societies are very different from animal dominance patterns. . . . because their rituals, their prohibitions, and their symbolic systems of segmentation replace animal dominance patterns as a means of preserving or moderating—most of the time—the mimetic rivalries that must be held in check."[27]

Religion, in this sense, helps humanity learn to live with itself. Yet influential anthropologists like Claude Lévi-Strauss explained the emergence of human culture through the logic of Enlightenment contract theory. On this point, Girard notes, "[Human] symbolic cultures certainly did not originate in the gentlemanly "social contract" cooked up by eighteenth-century theorists. Lévi-Strauss has revived once again this absurd idea, blithely suggesting that one fine day prehuman groupings decided (after some kind of constitutional referendum no doubt) that cultural differentiations, language, and other cultural institutions would be nice things to have."[28] The scapegoat mechanism, unlike the social contract, presents a mimetic solution to a wholly mimetic problem. From this idea Girard concludes that, although violent and false in its origins, archaic religion paradoxically allows the human species to survive. Under a Girardian lens the apparent irrationality of taboos and rituals become entirely reasonable.

Before he turned his attention to the Bible, Girard offered a pessimistic take on the human quest for peace in *Violence and the Sacred*: "The best men can hope for in their quest for nonviolence is the unanimity-minus-one of the surrogate victim."[29] Later, Girard associated this logic with Caiaphas, who "puts victims to death to save those who live. By reminding us of this John emphasizes that every real cultural *decision* has a sacrificial character (*decidere*, remember, is to cut the victim's throat) that refers back to an unrevealed effect of the scapegoat, the sacred type of representation of persecution."[30] Archaic religion and its subsequent religious myths tell a lie necessary for human survival. Christianity's revelation removes the veil from the mythic fabrications that conceal the scapegoat's innocence.

Compared to Girard, Taylor says comparatively little about the nature of Christianity. Yet three points emerge from his distinction of Christianity from generic Axial religion. First, for Taylor, Christianity produces an advanced sense of inwardness. In *Sources of the Self*, he identifies Augustine as a protomodern figure who, compared to his Greek ancestors, exalted the role of the will in the human psyche. As Augustine attests in his *Confessions*, the Platonic maxim—"the good would be done if it were known"—does not account for the will's radical perversion resulting from original sin and bad habits. Several steps lie between knowing and doing the good. In addition to the elevation of willing over knowing, Taylor's Augustine brings God into the interiority of human consciousness in a way hitherto unseen: "Our principal route to God [for Augustine] is not through the object domain but "in" ourselves. This is because God is not just the transcendent object or just the principle of order of the nearer objects, which we strain to see. God is also and for us primarily the basic support and underlying principle of our knowing activity."[31] Augustine develops this inwardness in his psychological analogy of the Trinity, wherein the pattern of knowing—memory, intellect, and will—functions as a vestige of the Trinitarian persons. Taylor remarks: "Augustine shifts the focus from the field of objects known to the activity itself of knowing; God is to be found here."[32] This emphasis serves as a precursor to the modern self, which accents its inwardness. Taylor connects Augustine to Descartes, thus bypassing the medieval world altogether: "It is hardly an exaggeration to say that it was Augustine who introduces the inwardness of radial reflexivity and bequeathed it to the Western tradition of thought."[33] In Taylor's account, Christianity's greatest mind propelled the West toward modernity like nobody else.

Taylor identifies the second distinguishing feature of Christianity through an examination of Calvinism and its Puritan offshoots. For Taylor, the affirmation of ordinary life comes about primarily due to the reforming efforts that culminated in the sixteenth-century reformations.[34] The old sacramental system of mediation that had undergirded medieval Christianity no longer circumscribed friendship with God. Instead, each individual was responsible for his own faith, and his commitment to God had to be total. Following Max Weber, Taylor posits the importance of the idea that each person's call in life could be carried out with excellence. This idea, when paired with the democratization of discipline and order, made transforming an entire society imaginable.

In the years between *Sources of the Self* and *A Secular Age*, Taylor ceased his strict correlation between this disciplinary movement and the Protestant Reformation. *A Secular Age* emphasized medieval efforts and argued for a more general and less specifically Protestant impulse in Christianity as *semper reformans*. Of the Franciscan emphasis on *haecceitas*, Taylor writes, "Though it couldn't be clear at the time, we with hindsight can recognize this as a major turning point in the history of Western civilization, an important step towards that primacy of the individual which defines our culture."[35] Late medieval and early modern Christians repeatedly attempted to triage the radical separation between sacred and profane so that God could be experienced in everyday life. For Taylor, this reforming spirit constitutes a fundamental tendency or essential quality in Christianity.[36] Modernity expresses this desire for reform, albeit unconsciously, through seemingly secular actions, such as the temperance movement and the fitness studio.

The ethic of *agape*—the selfless love of others so exalted in the New Testament—forms the third and perhaps most central feature of Christianity. Taylor finds this ethic most clearly embodied in the story of the Good Samaritan (Luke 10). Here the unselfish love to which Christians are called extends beyond the basic communal ethic of solidarity. *Agape* can even disrupt that solidarity; an ethic of solidarity alone would not compel the Good Samaritan to help the injured man on the roadside.[37]

Taylor makes two interesting comparative points: first, loving self-renunciation, which Jesus exemplifies on the cross, differs markedly from Stoic renunciation.[38] It does so because Christianity, as opposed to another powerful ethic like Stoicism, does not reject the goodness of ordinary flourishing. Second, Christian *agape* overlaps neatly with the Buddhist doctrines of *anatta* and *karuna*.[39] Taylor's appeal to *agape* and the example of the Good Samaritan, sprinkled throughout *A Secular Age*, anchor this claim about the centrality of *agape* for Christianity. In the incarnation and crucifixion of Christ, Christianity posits an identification of this love with God's own being. Thus the most central doctrines and events in Christianity coalesce with its distinctive ethical emphasis.

As I have recounted in earlier chapters, Girard considers Christianity the great *antimythology*. For the first time, the Hebrew scriptures tell stories of scapegoating from the perspective of the victim. Instead of myths that cover up the founding violence, scripture exposes the real violence underlying mythic superstructure. Besides this negative function, Judaism and Christianity positively reveal both a God who has nothing to do with violence and a God who sides with the victim. The New Testament goes a step further by identifying God with the victim. This is the evangelical truth "hidden since the foundations of the world" (Matt. 13:35). Jesus' cry from the cross—"Forgive them, Father, for they know not what they do" (Luke 23:34)—is not based on a Platonic theory of evil, but instead on the insight revealed to Judaism about the nature of human culture and the origins of human violence.[40] Girard declares, "The Gospels constantly reveal what the texts of historical persecution, and especially mythological persecutors, hide from us: the knowledge that their victim is a scapegoat . . . [The Gospel] indicates more clearly the innocence of this victim, the injustice of the condemnation, and the causelessness of the hatred of which it is the object."[41]

Despite the revolutionary power of the gospel, the strong pull toward archaic religious patterns leads Girard to conclude that the gospel often fails to take root in so-called Christian societies. For Girard, this failure does not delegitimize the gospel or alter its truth—it can still infiltrate society slowly. The radical nature of the Christian *kerygma*, for Girard, has transformed the West, but not necessarily in the most predictable manner.

The Nature and Cause of Modernity

At this point, it is helpful to keep in mind how Girard and Taylor depart from the model of "intellectual deviation" so popular among genealogists of modernity.[42] One such recent manifestation, received with both acclaim and controversy, is Brad Gregory's *The Unintended Reformation*.[43] In his response to critics on *The Immanent Frame* blog, Gregory noted that the book has received more than sixty reviews, including numerous conference panels devoted to the book, and four forums in learned journals.[44] This does not include the ten reviews on the *The Immanent Frame* blog. By drawing a direct line between the Protestant Reformation and the rise of modern secularism, *The Unintended Reformation* perfectly corresponds to Taylor's model of "Intellectual Deviation." In this model, Christianity had progressed splendidly until something threw it off the tracks: For Gregory, this was the Reformation with a nod to Scottish univocity. Such genealogists, as Michael Gillespie rightly notes, have rebutted the claims that modernity represents "a radical break with the past."[45] And they have attempted to trace, in myriad ways, how this tremor first appeared in medieval Christianity. This move produces a twofold effect: first, it shows the lineage of modernity to be Christian; second, it shows modernity to be less menacing, precisely on account of Christianity's relationship to the modern. However one measures the antagonism between secularism and Christianity, one cannot ignore modernity's reliance on Christianity when assessing this antagonism.[46]

Unlike many of these genealogists, Taylor and Girard locate their genetic differentiation in the very essence of Christianity. This move makes intellectual deviation and the corresponding genealogies obsolete because it roots the cause in the Gospels themselves. Such an interpretation has the advantage of permitting a wider scope of analysis. It also raises the stakes in locating essential Christianity. Girard's and Taylor's differences regarding essential Christianity also explain how they part from one another in their etiologies of modernity.

The attempt to understand and explain modernity and secularism has occupied a much greater portion of Taylor's scholarly endeavors than of Girard's. One gets this sense from Taylor's choice of titles—*A Secular Age* speaks for itself. Some form of "modern" also finds its way into most of his books: the subtitle of *Sources* is *The Making of Modern Identity,* his Marian address was called "A Catholic Modernity," and his second book on Hegel is titled *Hegel and Modern Society.* Additionally, one could add his precursor to *A Secular Age,* called *Modern Social Imaginaries,* and even his abbreviated version of *Sources, The Ethics of Authenticity,* was originally titled "The Modern Malaise." Girard can best be described as curious, but Taylor seems positively obsessed with modernity.

A Secular Age opens by countering mistaken conceptions of the secular, such as (1) God is absent from common institutions like the modern state and in its social spaces; (2) the secular entails a more general loss of religious belief and practice marked by such indicators as declining church attendance.[47] Instead, Taylor argues that secularism, optimally conceived as one option among others, removes belief from its presecular status as presupposed: "The shift to secularity in this sense consists, among other things, of a move from a society where belief in God is unchallenged and indeed, unproblematic, to one in which it is understood to be one option among the others, and frequently not the easiest to embrace."[48] Taylor liberates secularism from the subtraction theory, according to which a loss of belief is replaced by something like science. This notion only makes sense if Christian belief is antiquated, like a geocentric model of the universe. Despite widespread misunderstanding, Christianity is not inherently incompatible with modern science. The witness of scores of Christian scientists belies the flaccidity of the subtraction theory. Taylor confirms this point in *Sources of the Self,* "But what is questionable is the thesis that they [scientific rationality and industrialization] are sufficient conditions of the loss of religious belief. . . . If religious faith were like some particulate illusory belief, whose erroneous nature was only masked by a certain set of practices, then it would collapse with the passing of these and their supersession by others; as perhaps certain particular beliefs about magical connections have. This then is the assumption which often underpins the institutional account."[49] For Taylor, here are the more trenchant questions: Why did so many moderns fail to see options that would allow for a greater integration? Or why were these options unappealing to so many people?

A brief recapitulation of the emergence and nature of modernity, according to Taylor, can identify some of modernity's Christian roots.

Modernity's emphasis on ordinary life and human flourishing, for Taylor, derives from late medieval and early Puritan Christianity. These Christian iterations extended to the entire population ascetic disciplines that had been hitherto reserved for the elites. This ascetic ideal could spread to all believers, and thus society could be transformed, not simply by common participation in a ritual but through each individual striving toward holiness and submitting to disciplinary penitence on the occasions of falling short of the ideal.

Taylor connects this movement with modern secularism, but he does not consider it as a deviation from authentic Christianity. It merely identifies the difference between Christianity and secularism as *genetic*. As Taylor argues, the ascetic zeal for perfection dislodged itself from traditional Christianity and mutated into what he calls "exclusive humanism," which "closes the transcendent window, as though there were nothing beyond."[50] A human teleology rooted in the Sermon on the Mount— "Be perfect as your heavenly Father is perfect"—dislodged itself from any divine source. Despite Nietzsche's complaint about modernity ushering in the Last Man, it is undeniable that modernity encourages an intense quest for self-betterment, which manifests itself in a wide array of ascetic practices: dieting, extreme exercise, and eighty-hour workweeks for the wealthy. If Taylor is right, both the law firm and the fitness studio should pay royalties to the monastery.

An account of Taylor's understanding of modernity must include his emphasis on the "buffered" self, which connected the process of "disenchantment" borrowed from Max Weber and Marcel Gauchet.[51] Taylor contrasts this buffered self with the premodern "porous" self, which feels itself seamlessly connected both to its social and natural surroundings.[52] Today we can experience this porous self only through musical concerts, sporting events, or partaking in sports like surfing. These experiences yield a distinct contrast to the experience of the self as buffered. Moderns struggle to grasp just how differently they experience themselves as compared to their premodern ancestors. Taylor uses the example of feeling depressed or melancholy: "A modern is feeling depressed, melancholy. He is told: it's just your body chemistry, you're hungry, or there is a hormone malfunction, or whatever. Straightaway, he feels relieved. . . . But a pre-modern may not be helped by learning that his mood comes from black bile. Because this doesn't permit a distancing. Black bile is melancholy."[53] For premoderns, moods, feelings, and states of awareness inhere in things, just as spirits or fairies might inhabit a wood or forest, or King Richard might embody England.

Modernity replaces the enchanted world with the neutral world of matter and motion, which houses people who imagine themselves originally isolated and only secondarily connected to others. The modern self also construes moods abstractly and as ontologically disconnected to a material substance, such as one of the four humors. Taylor continues: "For the modern, buffered self, the possibility exists of taking a distance from, disengaging from everything outside the mind. My ultimate purposes are those which arise within me, the crucial meanings of things are those defined in my responses to them."[54] Again, this conception of the buffered self arises as a mutation within the imaginative horizon of the long and winding Christian tradition. Therefore, whatever the shortcomings of the buffered self (and one need not see it as deficient in comparison to the porous self), its existence is not intrinsically disordered or sinful in Taylor's account.[55]

A distinct moral feature of modernity is the concern for all human beings and the need to alleviate suffering. Taylor connects this feature with the gospel ethic of *agape* and emphasizes the uniqueness of this quality: "Our age makes higher demands for solidarity and benevolence on people today than ever before. Never before have people been asked to stretch out so far so consistently, so systematically, so as a matter of course, to the stranger at the gates."[56] Responses to such natural disasters as earthquakes and hurricanes, or to human disasters like the Middle Eastern refugee crisis, offer acute examples. The fact that groups of volunteers can consist of both committed atheists and conservative evangelicals surprises nobody. The Christian might be motivated by a modified divine command ethic or might have a particular loyalty to her pastor or parish. The atheist might scoff at the impurity of such motives, given that the same moral grammar justifies any number of moral failings. The atheist thus claims a more rational ethic. Of significance for Taylor is that both share a peculiarly modern concern to alleviate the suffering of those at the margins.

Although modernity has many different "sources" at its disposal, Taylor points to its failure to cobble together a synthesis between its two characteristically modern modes of knowing: instrumental rationality and expressive individualism. A worldview based entirely on varieties of scientism—strictly mechanical or biological accounts that reduce morality to pain/pleasure, and neo-Darwinian renderings that generate (albeit not necessarily) an anthropology and a corresponding ethic based on the laws of evolution—excludes Romantic individualism *tout court*. Romantics attach profound importance to self-given meaning that constitutes the inner depths of being human. As Taylor argues, most people do not want to face the existential or teleological consequences indicated by evolutionary biology: our lives have no meaning, and human flourishing is not the purpose of the universe. Moreover, most moderns distrust accounts that read the self-sacrificial love of a parent for a child out of any valid description of reality, as scientistic accounts do. Modern individuals want to find profound meaning in the depths of their souls, or in nature; the religiously inclined seek to connect this meaning with the divine. Romanticism exclusive of rationality and modern science, however, seems too much like the leap of faith that religion requires. So can it happen that secular worldviews compete for priority without ever arriving at a satisfactory synthesis.

Taylor's genetic horizon of understanding explains the difference between modern secularism and Christianity. He writes: "Secular humanism also has its roots in Judeo-Christian faith; it arises from a *mutation* out of a form of that faith. The question can be put, whether this is more than a matter of historical origin, whether it doesn't also reflect a continuing dependence. . . . My belief, baldly stated here, is that it does."[57] As Taylor describes it, the Christian West made possible a horizon within which secularism was imagined. Although he does not make the case that Christianity "causes" modernity, he does regard it as inconceivable without Christianity—hence the language of *mutation*.[58]

Only after the transcendent, Axial God created a greater distance between earth and heaven could the terrestrial be imagined as autonomous and self-sufficient. In contrast to Milbank and, to a lesser extent, Hart, who both regard secularism as a downward reversal of an upward trajectory, Taylor understands secularism as the third major era in religious development, after the pre-Axial and the Axial. In addition, Taylor's genealogy places modern ideas in a historical setting, generated not from unadulterated mental ether, but rather through the grit and dirt of an intermingling with social and psychological factors that complicate any purely intellectual genealogy of modernity. The difference between secularism and Christianity cannot be encompassed by a dialectical narrative. One needs, in its place, a more genetic account that renders modernity as an iteration or mutation, however unfortunate, wrong-headed, and un-self-conscious that iteration might have been.

This contextualization permits Taylor to present modernity outside the framework of the boosters and knockers mentioned above. Taylor addresses this point head-on: "In modern, secularist culture there are mingled together both authentic developments of the gospel, of an incarnational mode of life, and also a closing off to God that negates the gospel."[59] His argument strongly expresses the genetic difference outlined by Lonergan. Taylor continues, "In relation to the earlier forms of Christian culture, we have to face the humbling realization that the breakout [modern secularism] was a *necessary* condition of the development."[60] Taylor argues that Christianity, even if more accidentally than necessarily, birthed modernity.

Girard's account, although in many ways concordant with Taylor's, offers a more perspicacious reading of modernity. This despite Girard's professed disinterest in elaborating a theory of modernity—Girard declared in an interview that such a theory "is not my main concern."[61] Despite his professed disinterest, an analysis of his corpus reveals three characteristics of modernity: the modern concern for victims, the tendency to self-scrutiny, and the modern belief in the superiority of scientific method. Each of these, according to Girard, is unthinkable without Christianity. Thus Girard connects Christianity to secularism on the basis of the former's break with archaic religion: "I link secularization and Christianity essentially because Christianity caused a break in the cultural history of mankind, in particular the history of mankind's religions."[62] His analysis of modernity is rooted in this insight.

Like Taylor, Girard points out the particular Western concern for victims:

Our society is the most preoccupied with victims of any that ever was. Even if it is insincere, a big show, the phenomenon has no precedent. No historical period, no society we know, has ever spoken of victims as we do.

Examine ancient sources, inquire everywhere . . . and you will not find anything anywhere that even remotely resembles our modern concern for victims. The China of the Mandarins, the Japan of the samurai, the Hindus, the pre-Columbian societies, Athens, republican or imperial Rome—none of these were worried in the least little bit about victims, whom they sacrificed without number to their gods, to the honor of the homeland.[63]

The modern concern for victims begins in Judaism and Christianity, which alter the mythic perspective by telling persecutory tales from the perspective of the victim. Girard undermines modern objections to "Christian" atrocities like the Crusades and the witch hunts by pointing out that such arguments apply a thoroughly Christian moral grammar to the relation between persecutor and victim. Girard does not deny that modernity produces victims; the horrors of the twentieth century would make such a position untenable. He notes, however, that the modern world "also saves more victims than any previous historical moment ever did."[64] Before Christianity, Girard insists, it would have been unthinkable to make a moral argument by identifying with the victim. In mythology, the scapegoat is always guilty. In Judaism and Christianity, it is innocent. Since siding with the victim or the outsider forms a central tenet in both Christianity and modernity, Girard is able to say that the world is becoming, paradoxically, more and more Christian: "We [moderns] are all believers in the innocence of victims, which is at the core of Christianity."[65]

By announcing the victim's innocence, the gospel forces those who live in (post-)Christian cultures to look differently at familiar constellations. Instead of regarding the other as guilty, Christianity forces believers to consider their own sinfulness, either individually or on the level of the group, in order to discern their antagonisms toward others. This level of self-scrutiny aligns with Taylor's buffered self. No society has ever been more self-critical than modern, Western society, and the reason for this scrutiny, according to Girard, stems not from a longer ledger of misdeeds. The secular desire not to be shaped entirely by one's culture arises from Christianity. Girard identifies this attitude with the convert who, by the grace of God, resists the ordinarily forceful mimetic pull: he "is the one who can resist the crowd."[66] Girard shows that secularism uses a

Christian argument to denounce Christianity, a point frequently lost on secular intellectuals like Jonathan Israel.

Another abiding marker of modernity has been the rise of modern sciences, based not in a biblical or theocentric worldview, but rather on evidence, experiment, and trial and error. The Enlightenment narrative insists that this painfully achieved shift happened against the wishes of ecclesial authority. Girard offers an alternative etiology, which overlaps with Michael Buckley's work in this area (treated in greater detail in the following chapter). In his book on the early modern rise of atheism, Buckley writes, "How ironic it is to read in popular histories of the 'antagonisms of religion and the rising science.' That was precisely what the problem was not! These sciences did not oppose religious convictions, they supported them. Indeed, they subsumed theology, and theologians accepted with relief and gratitude this assumption of religious foundations by Cartesian first philosophy and Newtonian mechanics."[67] Though less precise than Buckley, Girard manages to locate the agreement in Christianity's most essential feature. He argues that the scientific zeal depends on the Christian attitude about victims. Since victims are chosen arbitrarily and are usually innocent, the gospel implores its followers to search for alternative reasons. Girard explains: "The scientific spirit cannot come first. It presupposes the renunciation of a former preference for the magical causality of persecution so well defined by the ethnologists. Instead of natural, distant, and inaccessible causes, humanity has always preferred causes that are significant from a social perspective and permit of corrective intervention—victims."[68] Christianity's proclamation of the forgiving victim's resurrection not only shatters religious paradigms but also paves the way for modern science. Just as we are no longer consoled by simple theodicies to explain natural disasters, so we are no longer sated by the older victimology. Girard explains, "The invention of science is not the reason that there are no longer witch-hunts, but the fact that there are no longer witch-hunts is the reason that science has been invented."[69] Those who would scoff at Girard's claim, and reflexively accuse him of blustering overreach, would need to refute his essential claim that Christianity revealed the scapegoat mechanism before jettisoning his explanation for the rise of science.

It is no surprise that the most popular television dramas are now the most scientific. I am referring to the explosion of *CSI* (*Crime Scene*

Investigation) series. Christianity has made us vigilant about the culpability of the accused. Hearsay and verbal testimony no longer convince the modern audience, which wants scientific evidence and DNA. Girard notes, "The successes of science have given rise to an enormous amount of idolatry and have led to its being considered as a group of specific methods, but its success, it seems to me, is due less to method than to the type of object studied by thinking freed from the ancient constraints of the sacred. This success is so intoxicating that the social and human sciences never give up hoping to become "truly scientific" by transporting the methods that work in the hard sciences into their domains."[70] By placing the origin of modernity's relationship to victims in the Gospels, Girard undercuts the coupling of the scientific spirit with a post-Christian ideology. Christianity, Girard reminds his readers, has bred the love of science, the critique of religion, and the suspicion against magic that embody secular, intellectual virtues.

Christianity after Modernity?

The nature and depth of phenomena like secularism, modernity, or the loss of belief present serious challenges: Are they exceptional, passing fads, entirely circumstantial? Or do they signal something bigger, more seismic, and more permanent? It may still be hasty to declare a permanent drop in belief, but one can nonetheless determine that a sizeable majority among educated classes in the West adhere to a secular worldview. Moreover, the old means through which people came to know God may no longer be as effective as they used to be.

Charles Taylor's massive investigation of the cause and nature of modern secularism concludes by examining how Christianity might best respond to this situation. Taylor uses the impasse at which late modern secularism stands in order to carve out a space for Christianity to flourish. The final chapter of *A Secular Age*, "Conversions," recalls how previously unbelieving moderns have found a way to believe within the immanent frame.[71] Beyond reference to the conversions of influential individuals—Walker Percy, T. S. Eliot, Christopher Dawson, Charles Péguy—Taylor points to the Christian attempt to imagine how a Christian civilization persists *without* a return to Christendom. Jacques

Maritain earns a privileged place in Taylor's rendering. After his youthful association with *Action Française*—the monarchist movement that Charles Maurras started and that sought to restore Catholicism as the state religion—Maritain realized that recovery could not mean return. As Taylor explains, "[Maritain] sought a unity of Christian culture on a global scale, but in a dispersed network of Christian lay institutions and centres of intellectual and spiritual life . . . The central feature of this new culture will be 'l'avènement spirituel non pas de l'ego centré sur lui-même, mais de la subjectivité créatrice.'"[72] Taylor admires how converts like Maritain were able to identify what is lost in a world without Christ, while not simply resorting to nostalgia for a better, earlier order. A truly modern Christianity "invites us to a conversation which can reach beyond any one such order. . . . Inevitably and rightly, Christian life today will look for and discover new ways of moving beyond the present orders to God."[73] Precisely as an instance in which people come to see their previous vision as limited, conversion accounts help Taylor to explain how secular citizens can find intelligibility in Christianity.

The examination of different stories of conversion also allows Taylor to introduce the possibility of hope. This hope consists in the discovery that God's self-sacrificial love in Christ can manifest the authenticity so dearly sought by moderns. Moreover, Christianity, especially its Catholic branch, urges its followers to imagine the journey of a wayfaring pilgrim as communal and shared: "The Church was rather meant to be the place in which human beings, in all their difference and disparate itineraries, come together."[74] Taylor's final chapter contains perhaps his most impassioned writing and reveals his concern to articulate the abiding truth of Christianity.

Despite all of the important ground covered by Taylor, Girard's insights into modernity demonstrate the capacity of mimetic theory to enlarge theological interpretation of modern secularism. On this point, my analysis overlaps with the aforementioned Cowdell's *René Girard and Secular Modernity*, which identifies seven distinctive elements of Girard's description and critique. A brief recapitulation is in order: (1) modernity is not so much about a loss of personal faith as a loss in the agreed-upon public function of religion; (2) Christianity is an alternative to traditional (archaic) religion; (3) secular modernity is not rooted so much in late medieval nominalism as in Christianity itself; (4) Girard's account overlaps with Taylor's, with the caveat that mimetic theory shows that even the modern self is more porous than it would seem; (5) modern secularism, since it no longer believes in the power of the scapegoat mechanism—thanks to Christianity—may not be able to constrain violence that erupts; (6) in agreement with Blumenberg, Weber, and Gauchet, the ultimate source of secular modernity is Christianity; (7) modernity deals with disenchantment by finding an enchantment in peculiarly modern entities: the nation-state, political ideology, and market forces.[75] Cowdell considers Girard the more profound reader of modernity: "Girard goes deeper, darker, and further back . . . Girard's version is highly explanatory and predictive—for instance, the return of religion and pseudoreligion."[76] The above comparison supplements and, I hope, complements Cowdell's perspicacious analysis.

Girard makes two relevant historical points about the implications of the scapegoat mechanism. First, Christianity undoes its power, thus paving the way for modernity's unique and singular concern with victims; or, in Taylor's terms, an inclusivist view of humanity. The second is the historical failure of Christianity for so much of its history. The examples of anti-Judaism, witch hunts, and the Crusades suffice. With his evangelical hermeneutic, Girard interprets such modern measures as humanitarian aid, the abolition of slavery and serfdom, and different forms of egalitarianism as evidence for a certain kind of Christian progress. He notes, "We are not Christian enough. The paradox can be put in a different way: Christianity is the only religion that has foreseen its own failure."[77] Girard then offers us his hitherto dormant eschatology. Although he had made a similar comment in *I See Satan Fall Like Lightning*, he did so without the apocalyptic conclusions put forth in *Battling to the End*, where he states, "Christian truth has been making an unrelenting historical advance in our world. Paradoxically, it goes hand in hand with the apparent decline of Christianity." He continues, "The fact that our world has become solidly anti-Christian, at least among elites, does not prevent the concern for victims from flourishing—just the opposite . . . The majestic inauguration of the 'post-Christian era' is a joke. We are living through a caricatural 'ultra-Christianity' that tries to escape from the Judeo-Christian orbit by 'radicalizing' the concern for victims in an anti-Christian manner."[78] Whereas Taylor points to the authenticity of Christian converts, who chart a *better* way to be good moderns, Girard points to an incongruence of modern secularists and post-Christian moralists. This incongruence indicates the kind of dissatisfaction with modernity articulated by the "knockers" in my opening section of this chapter. Yet Girard reads modernity as far too Christian to judge it as a mistake or a reversal of a better Christian past.

This evangelical hermeneutic licenses Girard to understand both modernity and secularism as fundamentally Christian. Secularism is not simply an unfortunate side effect but the logical result of Christianity's efforts at demythologizing. Christianity teaches us how to be secular. And as the next chapter shows, it teaches us how to be atheists.

CHAPTER SEVEN

MIMETIC THEORY AND ATHEISM

The previous chapter recalled how Charles Taylor took issue with the dialectical account of the relationship between Christianity and secularism. In the dialectical retelling, the space formerly occupied by religious institutions was evacuated and replaced by a secular space. One finds a subset of this narrative in accounts of belief in God: as science explains more and more, modern believers will increasingly come to doubt or deny God's existence. Taylor, of course, challenges this narrative by imploring a paradigm shift in the way we order secularism and belief to one another.

Attempted panoramic discussions of atheism often take on the same hue. In contemporary discussions, regardless of the substantive points made for or against God, the press and the public often frame the debate as if belief in God stands for something outdated, while disbelief seems contemporary. Believing has become associated with conservatism and unbelief with progress. Taylor points to the nonnecessity of this arrangement.

The recent spate of discussions and debate about the existence of God and the emergence of modern atheism indicate the urgency of the discussion. Even though Girard lacks the theological and philosophical training to advance the positions already staked in these debates, his work still manages to enter into conversation with the most pressing discussions about the existence of God. Below I demonstrate this capacity by bringing mimetic theory into conversations with two of the leading contemporary theological interpreters of atheism, Michael Buckley and

David Bentley Hart. By pairing Girard's and Buckley's interpretations of the origins of atheism, and then comparing Girard and Hart on modernity's most heralded anti-Christian, Friedrich Nietzsche, I show how mimetic theory allows Christian theology to rethink what the absence of God might mean. Such an exercise can in fact deepen faith in God.

The Buckley Thesis

Buckley's research has substantially revised the accepted narrative that put atheism and belief on a cosmic collision course. One can see this revision when one contrasts Buckley's work with that of Henri de Lubac. In *The Drama of Atheist Humanism*, de Lubac offers a careful reading of Nietzsche, Marx, Comte, and Freud, among others.[1] Although de Lubac does not refrain from critiquing Christian structures and history, he does not analyze atheism genealogically. Instead, de Lubac juxtaposes the atheist worldview to Christianity: "Today it is not one of the bases or one of the consequences of Christianity that is exposed to attack: the stroke is aimed directly at its heart." A page later de Lubac writes, "To the Christian ideal they oppose a pagan ideal. Against the God worshipped by Christians they proudly set up their new deities. In doing so they are conscious of attacking essentials and sweeping everything away at one stroke."[2] These words were written in the middle of World War II, when de Lubac himself was resisting the Nazis and Vichy, and such expressions are not only understandable but commendable. Later in the book, which is a pastiche of various essays, de Lubac asks whether one can best understand Nietzsche as a kind of mystic. This is not to suggest that de Lubac misreads these figures or that he provides a stultified analysis. Mimetic theory identifies similarity, not difference, as the basis of so much conflict. Consequently, slightly tilting the analysis permits a more genetic reading of the difference between atheism and belief. Buckley's analysis provides the key basis for such a reading.

Buckley's research has not only altered the assessment of the history of atheism, but it has also deepened our understanding of modernity's emergence.[3] Early reactions to Buckley's first book, *At the Origins of Modern Atheism*, indicate this impact. James Force, for instance, writes,

"Michael Buckley has gone for broke . . . [The book] will undoubtedly be taken as an indispensable new focus for future discussions about the relation of reason to religious apologetics in the early modern period and about method in the history of ideas."[4] A review by John Milbank adds, "Buckley, however, offers his own reading as a substitute for this oft-told tale of emancipation from religious tutelage: modern atheism is rather the unintended creation of a confused and contradictory theological apologetic which arose in the 17th and 18th centuries." Milbank later calls the book "a splendid, bold endeavor."[5] Taylor even announces that his *A Secular Age* was intended to complement the work done by Buckley, among others. Taylor elsewhere praises Buckley's "penetrating book" and described its thesis as a "striking fact."[6] Gavin Hyman's chapter on the modern development of atheism in *The Cambridge Companion to Atheism* also pays heed to Buckley's work.[7]

Buckley uses the principle of dialectics to guide his historical investigation. He remarks, "The meaning of 'atheism' is inescapably dialectical, its understanding parasitic upon the 'theism' of which it is the denial. This semantic dependence is compounded when one recognizes that 'atheism' has been applied to many different forms of hidden convictions or of systematic thought."[8] The word "atheism," then, has not generated its semantic content independently. Building on this point, Buckley asks: "If the meaning of atheism is shaped by the going theism, is this also true of its *existence*? . . . If theism is responsible for the patterns of atheism, did it also generate its actual birth?"[9] In *At the Origins of Modern Atheism*, Buckley poses the question of generation that animated my previous chapter on modernity: "Does atheism also depend upon theism for its very existence? . . . Does theism not only shape, but generate its corresponding atheism? Does theism not only set the meaning, but also generate the existence of the atheism which emerges in the middle of the eighteenth century? Is the content of god, the idea of the divine, so internally incoherent that it moves dialectically into its denial?"[10]

After covering, among other topics, the religious apologetics of Leonard Lessius and Marin Mersenne, the philosophical system of René Descartes, the mechanics of Isaac Newton, and the atheistic mutations of these systems by Denis Diderot and Baron Paul-Henri d'Holbach, Buckley concludes the book by answering his own question. Arguments made by theists did contain internal contradictions that made possible the emergence of the peculiar form of atheism that arose in the modern West. Buckley writes: "There was a contradiction between this content [of the theists] and the form in which it was advanced. . . . In this process of self-alienation, religion denied itself both a proper form to reflect upon this issue and commensurate evidence by which it could be resolved—and all of this before the question had even been raised by the intellectual culture in which the theologians wrote."[11] For Buckley, the contradictory nature of theological argument helped generate modern atheism. The contradiction consisted in arguing through impersonal means—natural theology—for a personal God.

One offshoot of Buckley's research is manifested in his discussion of the relation between faith and science. In response to the commonly held belief about the conflict between faith and science, Buckley writes: "Popular renditions have presented this relationship as minatory antagonism."[12] But Buckley deems these renditions wildly inaccurate: "It was not the opposition of science to religion; it was much more the endorsement of science that generated modern atheism."[13] Buckley then shows how, in the wake of the monumental scientific discoveries coupled with the split in Western Christianity, theologians felt compelled to locate their apologetic arguments in the purportedly neutral territory of natural philosophy. Starting with Leonard Lessius and Marin Mersenne, "the existence of God was taken primarily as a philosophic question and defended through the evidence provided by new learning [i.e., Newtonian mechanics]."[14] Christian theologians, Buckley shows, stopped using the data generated by Christianity itself. These data include more than just scripture; they encompass the witness of holy people and the lived religious experience of ordinary believers. Instead of appealing to such data, theologians opted for the universal mechanics of Newton. Buckley avers, "Mechanics may not have needed theology, but theology in its apologetics had come to need mechanics, whether in astronomy or biology. Theology had become addicted to it."[15] By the end of the seventeenth century, theology ceased to provide theological arguments that would justify its own existence.

Such an unrelenting reliance on Newtonian mechanics resulted in the apologetic equivalent of keeping a loaded gun in the house. The existence of God now depended on the veracity of Newton's system, at the heart of which lay the conviction that matter was inert. Such an understanding of matter, however, fell from grace in the eighteenth century, especially in France. Buckley identifies Paul-Henri Thiry, Baron d'Holbach, as the key figure in overturning the Newtonian supremacy.[16] Whereas Newton considered gravity a secondary property of matter, d'Holbach determined it primary. This was part of a larger shift that brought motion into matter. Buckley notes, "The merger of motion with matter as the actional principle of universal nature has its correlative expression in the crucial assertion that gravity is an inherent and primary property of matter."[17]

D'Holbach's *Système de la nature* overturned the Cartesian-Newtonian presupposition about matter's inertia and revived Spinoza's vitalist monism, in which the principle of motion inhered in matter. The loaded gun now found itself in the wrong hands; by relying on universal mechanics to prove the existence of God, theology subjected itself to another science for its first principles. D'Holbach himself articulated this thesis: "Doctor [Samuel] Clarke, as well as all other theologians, found the existence of their God upon the necessity of a power that may have the ability to begin motion. But if matter has always existed, it has always had motion, which as we have proved, is as essential to it as extent, and flows from its primitive properties."[18] Clarke, of course, wanted to deploy Newton to rebuff atheists, but he instead shepherded a Trojan horse into Christian apologetics.

The aim of Buckley's inquiry into atheism was to understand what made possible such a sea change in modern thought. Rather than beginning with the atheists themselves, Buckley turned first to the theists, in particular the Christian apologists. Buckley explains how these apologists disseminated the contradiction that the validation of belief in a *personal* god was best confirmed by reliance on *impersonal* evidence, reflected by the cosmos, for God's existence. This internal contradiction could not stand, and his first monograph on the subject, *At the Origins of Modern Atheism*, traced the initial cracks and the dismantling of the foundation upon which the house of theism rested.

Buckley's second book on the subject, *Denying and Disclosing God*, extended his analysis of modern atheism into the last two centuries. It did so with the aim of providing a postsecular response to atheism, offered in the book's final two chapters. If atheism itself results from an "internal contradiction," then can the negation of God be negated? Buckley estimates Feuerbach's theory of projection as the most profound breakthrough in nineteenth-century atheism. Feuerbach's idea proved fundamental to the devastating critiques by Marx and Freud, both of whom relied on his concepts of alienation and projection. Buckley notes, "One must begin with the originating genius of this movement, Ludwig Feuerbach . . . the man whose writings were so successful, so influential that Marx saluted him as the great precursor of dialectical atheism and Freud held him as his favorite philosopher."[19] Buckley recounts how the transposition to Lockean and then Kantian epistemology dictated Feuerbach's decision to begin his famous treatise, *The Essence of Christianity*, with an analysis of the human being. The presumed conflict between God and humanity drove Feuerbach's work. In turn, nineteenth-century atheism achieved the militancy against both Christianity and the very idea of God described by de Lubac. Buckley offers an apt description of this conflict: "Christianity was revealed as a destructively parasitic and decadent hostility to human life."[20] Yet this false opposition between divinity and humanity, between critical thinking and religious faith, does not have the last word.

Feuerbach's theory that humans project anthropic qualities onto a cosmic canvas finds resonance among many theists. The God to whom believers pray expresses a wish fulfillment and a desire that we ourselves ran the universe. Buckley reads the nineteenth-century attack on belief as a critique of a "too-easy" theism, pointing out how it runs parallel to a similar critique by "a movement equally aware of the proclivity of religion to become projection."[21] This movement is the Christian apophatic tradition, marked by such luminaries as Pseudo-Dionysius, Gregory of Nyssa, and John of the Cross.

Buckley centers his retrieval on John of the Cross, the great Carmelite mystic who described the "dark night of the soul." Already in the preface to *Denying and Disclosing God*, Buckley points to the overlap between John's apophaticism and Feuerbach's projection theory: "The negation of these projections comprises the classical night of the soul, moving beyond the negation of God as projection to the further negation of the negation itself in the affirmation of God."[22] Christian mystics had long claimed that one could pass through something like projection on the way to a deeper knowledge of the one, true God. Like Freud and Feuerbach, John of the Cross judges the quotidian experience of God as deeply flawed and problematic. He frequently appeals to the Scholastic maxim: *quidquid recipitur ad modum recipientis recipitur.*[23] Our experience, even the in-breaking of the divine that can occasion prayer, is necessarily conditioned by our own capacity to receive. True religious consciousness does not, however, stop at identifying the fraught nature of ordinary religiosity. Buckley explains: "What we grasp and what we long for is very much shaped and determined by our own preconceptions, appetites, concepts, and personality-set. If these are not disclosed and gradually transformed by grace and by its progressive affirmation within religious faith, working its way into the everyday of human history and choices, then there is no possibility of contemplation of anything but our own projections."[24] John of the Cross's analysis goads believers into recognizing and disavowing the idolatry and the projection that often masquerade for worship of the true God.

Buckley's retrieval of apophatic theology, of course, entails the recognition that some atheist writings offer valuable insights about religious experience. Rather than a more traditional tactic that would cede no ground to atheism, Buckley suggests that the proper aim "should be less to refute Feuerbachian and Freudian analysis than to learn from them what they have to teach about the relentless remolding of the image of God by religious consciousness."[25] Beneath the façade of anti-Christianity, one finds a visage with all the markings of Christianity. Buckley's dialectic does not permit a notion of theism and atheism as static, binary terms. Instead, the very contradiction upon which modern atheism rests logically implies the generation of "its own further negation, the negation of the negation."[26] This process is what Buckley intended to accomplish in his appeal to apophaticism and to the mystical theology of John of the Cross. By offering a genealogy of atheism, Buckley also provides one possible response.

The Girardian Contribution

Girard's own theory of religion seems poised to complement Buckley's daring thesis. Buckley's genealogy destabilizes the purported antagonism between Christianity and atheism. Western atheism necessarily assumes a particularly Christian form of atheism; Christian theology produced the soil from which modern atheism sprouted. If this genealogy is true, then it behooves apologetic theology to adopt a less conflictual mode of engagement. The apologetic task must extend beyond a mere declaration of difference. By showing the kinship between Christianity and atheism, Girard's work helps Christian apologetics to understand the nature of the atheism they want to oppose.

Since Girard writes so infrequently on atheism, it is possible to flesh out the implications of these statements. The New Atheists, whom Girard calls "today's anti-religion," overlook Christianity's role in denuding the world of so much of its religion, as I discussed in chapter 4. Girard responds to this new wave of atheism by highlighting how Christian their anti-Christianity is: "Today's anti-religion combines so much error and nonsense about religion that it can barely be satirized. It serves the cause that it would undermine, and secretly defends the mistakes that it believes it is correcting. . . . By seeking to demystify sacrifice, current demystification does a much worse job than the Christianity that it thinks it is attacking because it still confuses Christianity with archaic religion."[27] A quick perusal of the works of the "four horseman" of the New Atheist apocalypse—Richard Dawkins, Christopher Hitchens, Sam Harris, and Daniel Dennett—demonstrates a conflation of Christianity with archaic religion.[28] For Hitchens, "Religion is scapegoating writ large."[29] If the goal is to demystify religion and to promote reason in place of superstition, then Christianity should be an ally to the New Atheism. Yet prejudice and confusion seem to prevent these figures from realizing how Christian their worldview is. Christianity is the great deconstructor of the archaic, as Girard explains: "By revealing the founding murder, Christianity destroyed the ignorance and superstition that are indispensable to such religions."[30] By locating Christianity between the archaic and the secular, mimetic theory undercuts much of the New Atheist narrative.

Girard's critique of religion leads to a question: If the gospel destroys the archaic sacred and all of the accompanying powers and principalities, then what can prevent the destruction of postarchaic sacred space? This question underlies much of Girard's thought on atheism. From the perspective of mimetic theory, the genesis of atheism makes sense. Yet Girard notes how contemporary atheism confuses Christianity with the powers of archaic mythology instead of with demythologizing forces that cripple it: "At present the 'wise' and the 'discerning,' which I suppose refers to academics, are furiously redoubling their attacks on Christianity and once again congratulating themselves on its forthcoming demise."[31] If Buckley is right and atheism is always parasitic on the regnant theism, then contemporary atheism tells us much about the ambient theism.[32] Modern atheism takes for granted the innocence of the scapegoat and the emptiness of sacred violence. Yet these truths, according to mimetic theory, are the product of the Christian story. In addition, Christianity's love commandment keeps mimetic escalation properly ordered. Danger looms in a post-Christian society that neither believes in *agape* nor fears the power of the sacred. This threat explains the gloomy tone of Girard's last major work, *Battling to the End*. He opines, "Without this [Christian] love, the world would have exploded long ago."[33]

Although it may seem that a mimetic rendering of historical Christianity would give too heroic a portrayal, Girard admits that historical Christianity has not only failed but has also maintained elements of archaic religion.[34] An analysis of Christianity can never stop at the purely theoretical, but it must take seriously its historical manifestations, even those that would be more comfortably elided. Against the New Atheists, Girard does not argue that Christianity has not failed in the past, but only that so many atheist ripostes against Christianity have taken on a *Christian* moral shape. Like Buckley, Girard acknowledges a dialectic wherein modern atheism turns the Christian negation of religion against Christianity itself. Yet unlike Buckley, Girard underscores the *a*-theistic shape of Christianity.

For two centuries, the Roman Empire criminalized Christianity, which promoted *atheism*. Christians denied the Roman pantheon and refused to participate in the variations of pagan sacrifice.[35] Modern and contemporary atheism, unlike the Christian *a*-theism of the first three centuries, concerns itself less with the worship of idols and more with the God of monotheists.[36] Girard's understanding of the relationship between Christianity and archaic religion, however, denudes modern atheism of its moral force. According to Girard, modern critics cannot believe in the innocence of victims while simultaneously denouncing Christianity.

In his analysis of the book of Job, Girard compares it to the Oedipus myth, but he highlights Job's refusal to connect his misfortune with any divine judgment.[37] To the extent that belief in God vouchsafed the guilt of all victims, Job was an atheist. Girard notes in a later interview, "At the beginning of the story, God says to Satan: 'You'll see, Job won't speak against me.' Later he seems to do so, but in fact he is speaking against a god of violence, who is neither the Yahweh of the prophets nor the Father to whom Jesus refers."[38] Girard makes this point even more clearly in the next paragraph: "[Job] resists, and in doing so, he moves—perhaps coming close to atheism—toward a religion in which God has no solidarity with vengeful crowds."[39] Girard finds the difference between the God revealed in the Bible and the gods of archaic religion so extreme that he even shows a willingness to jettison the word "God" when discussing the former God. James Alison makes the same point when discussing the breakthrough of Hebraic monotheism: "And this, of course, is part of the genius of monotheistic Judaism: the realisation that 'one God' is much more like 'no god at all' than like 'one of the gods.' In other words, that atheism, which is untrue, offers a much less inadequate picture of God than theism, which is true."[40] Yet modern atheism, at least as manifested in such collections as *The Cambridge Companion to Atheism, The Portable Atheist*, and the writings of the aforementioned New Atheism's four horsemen, does not take any account of this difference.[41] A real debate between the New Atheists and Christian theology cannot happen, for any debate requires some agreement on the thing about which the two sides disagree.[42]

From mimetic theory's vantage point, the emergence of modern atheism makes sense as a genetic development out of Christianity. In a world stripped of sacred violence, and with a God more like nothing than like one of the gods, it follows that some would believe in a total absence of divinity. As I mentioned in the last chapter, Girard deems Christianity the only religion that has foreseen its own failure.[43] Yet the hostility toward Christianity cannot be explained through appeal to the purported scientific spirit and detached rationality of the New Atheists. Their unlearned vitriol signals something deeper. Here David Hart's commentary on Sam Harris's *The End of Faith* ably captures this point: "If Harris's argument holds any real interest here, it is as an epitome—verging on unintentional parody—of contemporary antireligious rhetoric at its most impassioned and sanctimonious. As such, it gives especially vivid and unalloyed expression to two popular prejudices that one finds also in the work of Dennett, but nowhere in so bracingly simplistic a form. These prejudices are, first, that all religious belief is in essence baseless; and, second, that religion is principally a cause of violence, division, and oppression."[44] The refusal to learn even the most basic metaphysical and doctrinal bases underlying Christianity, and the willful misrepresentation of historical truths, indicates a deeper, more profound issue operating in today's anti-Christianity. Hitchens, for instance, does not believe in the historical existence of Jesus of Nazareth, and he rejects the argument that Christianity motivated Martin Luther King's nonviolence.[45] Irony of ironies, Christianity itself becomes the scapegoat for modern atheism. Its critics closely resemble forces in a mob, eager to believe the worst of their opponents, and thus represent the mirror image of Christian "fundamentalists."[46] As anti-Christianity, contemporary atheism provides ample material for sociological observation, but it does not represent a serious partner for discussion and disagreement because it has failed to say anything about the God that Christians worship. Girard's contribution highlights the internal contradictions in any twenty-first-century atheism that wants to reject Christianity while siding with victims.

Hart's Reading of Nietzsche

Besides highlighting Girard's diffuse comments on atheism, it is possible to give a fuller picture of a mimetic theology of atheism by connecting the above points to Girard's reading of modernity's greatest atheist, Friedrich Nietzsche.[47] For all of his vitriol, Nietzsche, unlike the four horsemen, took Christianity seriously, and Girard certainly noted this point: "It can be said without paradox, or almost, that this text [*The Will to Power*, 1052] is the greatest theological text of the nineteenth century."[48] In a way similar to the first half of this chapter, it will be helpful to align Girard's interpretation with that of a leading theologian. Like Girard, David Hart has gone against the grain of many commentators by focusing on Nietzsche's peculiar concern with Christianity. Although Hart neither admits nor owes a debt to mimetic theory, it is notable that his treatment of Nietzsche depends on an understanding of Christianity very similar to the one offered by Girard.[49]

Like many theologians writing about God in the wake of the New Atheists, Hart has lamented the lack of seriousness of these critics, which is captured in the opening chapter of *Atheist Delusions*:

> My own impatience with such remarks, I should confess, would probably be far smaller if I did not suffer from a melancholy sense that, among Christianity's most fervent detractors, there has been a considerable decline in standards in recent years . . . The extraordinary scientific, philosophical, and political ferment of the nineteenth century provided Christianity with enemies of unparalleled passion and visionary intensity. The greatest of them all, Friedrich Nietzsche, may have had a somewhat limited understanding of the history of Christian thought, but he was nevertheless a man of immense culture who could appreciate the magnitude of the thing against which he had turned his spirit . . . Moreover, he had the good manners to despise Christianity, in large part, for what it actually was— above all, for its devotion to an ethics of compassion—rather than allow himself the soothing, self-righteous fantasy that Christianity's history had been nothing but an interminable pageant of violence, tyranny, and sexual neurosis. He may have hated many Christians for their hypocrisy, but he hated Christianity itself principally on account of its enfeebling solicitude for the weak, the outcast, the infirm, and the diseased . . . By comparison to these men, today's gadflies seem far lazier, less insightful, less subtle, less refined, more emotional, more ethically complacent, and far more interested in facile simplifications of history than in sober and demanding investigations of what Christianity has been or is.[50]

Here and elsewhere, Hart laments the striking inferiority of contemporary critics to Nietzsche. His earlier and more substantial work, *The Beauty of the Infinite*, engages in a lengthy exposition of Nietzsche's reading of Christianity.[51]

Hart centers his treatment on Nietzsche's genealogical reading of Christianity, elaborated most fully in *Beyond Good and Evil* and

Genealogy of Morals. Christianity undermined pagan ethics, and it took a thinker of Nietzsche's training and orientation to expose the impact of Christianity in this matter. Hart notes, "Nietzsche grasped, even more completely than Celsus (the only other significant pagan critic of faith), how audacious, impertinent, and absolute was Christianity's subversion of the values of antiquity: thus allowing theology to glimpse something of its own depths in the mirror of his contempt."[52] Nietzsche's valorization of antiquity led him to read Christianity as a "revaluation of values." Biblical religion, especially Christianity, infected Greco-Roman culture through this revaluation. Christianity replaced the noble morality of antiquity with a herd morality that catered to the poor, the weak, and the outcast. It is, as John Milbank states twice in *Theology and Social Theory*, "a writing of the *City of God* back-to-front from a neo-pagan point of view."[53] Hart adds: "Nietzsche's principal charge against Christianity, in fact, was that it constituted a slave revolt in values: a new and sickly *moral* vision of reality, judging all things, noble or base, according to the same pernicious and vindictive categories of good and evil. It was, Nietzsche claimed, this monstrous sedition against greatness and beauty that ultimately caused both the heroic joy of the Greeks and the stern grandeur of the Romans to sink beneath the flood of Christian spitefulness, pusillanimity, and otherworldliness."[54] The replacement of an earlier, nobler ethic with a later inferior one could have only been brought about through *ressentiment*, which Hart calls "the spite that animates the impotent and incites the mob against its masters."[55] Christianity's slave ethic resulted in a culture that substituted a natural instinct for life with a derived and perverted priestly ethic.

In *The Beauty of the Infinite*, Hart approaches Nietzsche's critique of Christianity and of God from a narrative, aesthetic perspective: Christianity offers a better and more beautiful story than the father of so many postmodern, postmetaphysical, genealogical, and archaeological critiques. Hart's subtitle—*The Aesthetics of Christian Truth*—foretells his approach. For Hart, Nietzsche replaces the gospel of *agape* with the will to power, but such categories fall under narratology: "The will to power is only a story, perhaps, but so is every metaphysics; and even as a story, its plot has often a poignantly dialectical logic."[56] Hart operates within a postmodern discourse and seems willing to play the apologetic game by postmodern rules.[57] Hart approaches the difference between paganism and Christianity through the metaphor of two vintages of wine, one of a coarse, Dionysian vintage, and inducing all kinds of violence and disorder, as it is meant to induce blind intoxication; the other coming from a smoother vintage, meant to enhance friendship, and produce mirth and merriment. Hart continues, "Of course, Nietzsche was a teetotaler and could judge the merit of neither vintage, and so it is perhaps unsurprising that his attempts at oino-theology should betray a somewhat pedestrian palate."[58] Hart concludes this section with an aesthetic argument: "The most potent reply a Christian can make to Nietzsche's critique is to accuse him of a defect of sensibility—of bad taste. And this, in fact, is the last observation that should be made at this point: Nietzsche had atrocious taste."[59]

Hart roots his analysis, as mentioned above, in Milbank's observation that Nietzsche reverses Augustine's ordering of the two cities: "Nietzsche is quite correct: as Celsus understood, Christianity did indeed subvert the language of noble virtue, especially insofar as the latter presupposed the necessity of strife and honored strength for its own sake."[60] Christianity, in other words, challenged the story about creation and humanity that presupposed strength and power as primordial. Nietzsche's seemingly Darwinian account, according to Hart, does not differ descriptively from Augustine's: "When Nietzsche says that every civil state is created and maintained by violence, or that cruelty lies at the base of society and culture, he asserts nothing that is not already present in Augustine's account of the *civitas terrena* as a city founded upon violence, indeed upon fratricide (Rome being the paradigm of all secular polities)."[61] On this point Hart's treatment resembles Girard's; Augustine's comparison between the foundational murders of Abel and of Remus has served as a touchstone in Girard too.[62] Yet for all of Nietzsche's genealogical critique, he does not realize that this presumption of primordial violence is itself part of a story about who we are and where we are going—violence and force play undeniable roles, but Nietzsche's ordering need not be preferred. Hart continues in the same paragraph: "For Augustine, though, this genealogy of culture remains a thoroughly historical observation; another city can be imagined, enacted, even experienced in the midst of a history alien to it, a history known to the church as sin: originally unnecessary and of a secondary order of reality. For Nietzsche, though, it describes . . . the inexorable advance of the ubiquitous will to power."[63] The Augustinian imagination permits a better story, one in which Christian protology—being freely and peacefully created through the sheer gratuity and excess of a benevolent God—foreordains the eschatology, namely, that all human flourishing and goodness brings us closer to a union with God, who makes us for, but does not compel us into, this union.

The undeniable record of malice, greed, violence, and force—what for Augustine constitutes the *libido dominandi*—is, as Hart correctly renders, not ultimately the most truthful or even the most real aspect of created reality; it is only its shadow side. Christianity fits this evidence into a different story about what *is* real. Nietzsche begs to differ: "In Christianity neither morality nor religion come in contact with reality at any point."[64] The story of the will to power is the only real story for Nietzsche; evidence in the natural world attests to this: cells battling other cells, stronger plant life destroying the weaker, and one animal eradicating the other. In the pagan civilizations extolled by Nietzsche, this story and its consequent ethic reigned. And for Nietzsche, if societies need to invent a god, they should have the decency to invent a god that undergirds this indefatigable lust for power. Speaking of like-minded readers, Nietzsche writes, "What sets *us* apart is not that we recognize no God . . . but that we find that which has been reverenced as God not 'godlike' but pitiable, absurd, harmful, not merely an error but a *crime against life*."[65] Hart astutely points out that Nietzsche based his anti-Christianity on a decision to tell a certain story, instead of any kind of empirical observation: "Nietzsche is engaged principally in identifying an aesthetic disposition, a critical vantage, from which to wage a war of stories; he wishes to overcome the Christian narrative but never imagines he has 'proved' it meaningless."[66] Hart engages Nietzsche on the latter's terms, where the true and the beautiful are translatable. In a profoundly perspicacious reading, Hart's aesthetic apologetic demonstrates how Christianity outnarrates the Nietzschean variant of postmodernity.

In the first half of this chapter, Buckley's genealogy of atheism was paired with Girard's interpretation of modern atheism. The intention was not to show a hidden influence, or to force an alignment that distends the reader's generosity; rather, the pairing effected a realization that mimetic theory, somewhat unexpectedly, manages to find its way into the heart of important theological conversations. This claim has been part of the underlying argument of the entire book. The final section of this chapter proceeds with much the same objective.

Girard, the Last Nietzschean

Girard's first serious attempt to grapple with Nietzsche came in a 1976 essay that cites Nietzsche's relationship with Wagner as evidence of the force of *ressentiment* in Nietzsche's personal relationships. Here Girard avoids Nietzsche's relationship to Christianity, and thus his earliest attempt does not carry the same force as later writings. Girard insists, as he does later, that Nietzsche's insanity stemmed not from syphilis or some other physiological origin, but rather from his inability to temper his obsessions. Girard asserts, "The insanity of a Nietzsche and of many others is rooted in an experience with which none of us can be really unfamiliar."[67] By this Girard meant that the sinful proclivities toward envy, resentment, and mimetic reciprocation, which course through the psychic lives of even holy people, also surface in those who, in our Romantic age, are considered above the fray on the basis of their solitary genius.[68] Nietzsche's pathologies, thus, represent only exaggerated normal human tendencies.

Nietzsche's triangular relationship with Richard and Cosima Wagner offers a particularly relevant data point for examining his psychic life and patterns of desire.[69] Girard notes how Nietzsche's relationship with the great composer was rife with mimetic identification and envy. For Girard, *Ecce Homo* can be read as Nietzsche's attempt to transfer to himself the praise that he had lavished on Wagner: "Every time the name of Wagner appears [in Nietzsche's earlier work] the name of Nietzsche must be substituted."[70] Yet Nietzsche's metaphysical desire to become Richard Wagner failed miserably. Cosima's first husband, Hans von Bülow, infamously stated, after Cosima left him for Wagner: "For a woman torn between a man and a god, it is excusable to choose the god."[71] Nietzsche's metaphysical desire for Wagner was, in a mimetic analysis, a sublimated attempt to become a god. In his late period, Nietzsche oscillated between identifying with Dionysus and with Christ. He signed numerous letters, "The Crucified," and wrote to Cosima Wagner: "I too have been hanged on the cross." Additionally, in January 1889, he wrote to Jean Bourdeau, "I am the Christ, Christ in person, Christ crucified."[72]

Wagner's prodigious talent ran in concert with his oversized ego. And, in juxtaposition to Nietzsche, Wagner's contemporaries reckoned him entitled to the eccentricities of genius. Nietzsche, whose genius is now unquestioned, likely accepted the judgments from his contemporaries, many of whom deemed him a failure. In order to expand on Girard's reading, I now turn my attention to a recent mimetic attempt to understand Nietzsche: Giuseppe Fornari's *A God Torn to Pieces*. This work deepens Girard's understanding of Nietzsche's relationship to Wagner and of Nietzsche's madness in general.[73]

Fornari chronicles how Nietzsche's attempts to become Wagner—both the composition of music and the obsession with Cosima—ended in abject failure. Regarding the former attempt, Fornari recalls a response by von Bülow to Nietzsche's 1872 effort to compose music. In his original query to von Bülow, Nietzsche had described his piece as horrible. If he had expected from this show of humility a more generous assessment, he did not get it. Von Bülow described Nietzsche's attempt as "in fact, more horrible than you may credit; that is to say, not ordinarily damaging, but worse: damaging to yourself, who could not have found a worse way of killing even an excess of spare time than to rape Euterpe in this fashion."[74] This blow stung Nietzsche so profoundly that he cited it sixteen years later in *Ecce Homo*: "I composed a counter overture for *Manfred* of which Hans von Bülow said that he had never seen anything like it on paper, and he called it a rape of Euterpe."[75] Fornari chronicles how deeply Nietzsche wanted to rival Wagner as a creator of art, and how deeply he failed in this imitation.

With the aid of letters and other primary documents to which Girard did not have access, Fornari fortifies Girard's claims about Nietzsche's longing for Cosima: "Nietzsche fell in love with Cosima for the same reasons that he wrote his music: to draw close to the idolized and envied model, to dislodge him and take his place."[76] At this, too, Nietzsche failed spectacularly. Cosima never reciprocated Nietzsche's interest. Fornari opines, "Never was a lover less likely to succeed."[77] Cosima's reaction to Nietzsche's composition, for instance, provoked a mix of confusion and pity. Her diary recorded: "We are a bit annoyed by our friend's music-making dalliances."[78] From a nonmimetic perspective, Nietzsche's wild oscillation, pro and contra Wagner, must stem from some change of heart or shift in opinion. From a mimetic perspective, the sycophantic praise that Nietzsche heaped on Wagner, and the bitter scorn of later years, reflect the oscillation that normally results from the fraught relation between imitator and model/rival.

In Girard's 1976 treatment of Nietzsche, this claim was more of a hunch than anything else. After the publication of a more definitive *Sämtliche Werke*, it became possible for Girard to confirm this hunch.[79] In Girard's lecture "Nietzsche and Contradiction," he declared himself "glad to report that I have found the 'smoking gun.'"[80] Girard refers to fragments written by Nietzsche in 1886–87, where Nietzsche admits his profound admiration for Wagner's most Christian opera, *Parsifal*. Every novice reader of Nietzsche knows that Nietzsche's earlier break with Wagner had to do with his disgust at Wagner's late preference for a Christian rather than a pagan theme. Even upon learning of the odd power dynamic in their relationship, devoted Nietzscheans can still hold onto Nietzsche's principled, pagan stand against Wagner's art. Yet in this fragment, Nietzsche declares himself "completely transported and moved." And later, "No artist has ever been able to express as magnificently as Wagner does such a somber and melancholy vision. Not even Dante, not even Leonardo."[81] By 1888, when Nietzsche wrote *The Case of Wagner*, he lambasted Wagner's Christian turn as a negation against life.[82] This fragment confirms for Girard the oscillation, or contradiction, in Nietzsche that he himself tried to suppress.[83] The case of *Parsifal* brings together Nietzsche's tortured relationship with both Wagner and Christianity.

In the 1980s and 1990s, Girard engaged Nietzsche's thought with greater frequency, concentrating more on Nietzsche and Christianity. In addition to the follow-up article on Wagner, Girard published his 1984 article "Dionysus versus the Crucified," and he also gave a paper centering on Nietzsche's famous aphorism 125 from *The Gay Science*, which was included in *Violence and Truth*. Girard's subsequent writings, including the last chapter from *I See Satan Fall Like Lightning*, echo these earlier readings of Nietzsche. Like Hart, Girard largely assents to Nietzsche's interpretation of Christianity.

Both Hart and Girard cite almost the entire final paragraph from aphorism 1052 in *The Will to Power*, which reads:

> Dionysus versus the "Crucified" there you have the antithesis. It is not a difference in regard to their martyrdom—it is a difference in the meaning of it. Life itself, its eternal fruitfulness and recurrence, creates torment, destruction, the will to annihilation. In the other case, suffering—the "Crucified as the innocent one"—counts as an objection to this life, as a formula for its condemnation.—One will see that the problem is that of the meaning of suffering: whether a Christian meaning or a tragic meaning. In the former case, it is supposed to be the path to a holy being; in the latter case, being is counted as *holy enough* to justify even a monstrous amount of suffering. The tragic man affirms even the harshest suffering . . . Dionysus cut to pieces is a *promise* of life: it will be eternally reborn and return again from destruction.[84]

The first line of this famous citation also concludes *Ecce Homo*.[85] Girard notes that, unlike positivists, who looked at the facts and concluded mere continuity between the collective murders of Dionysus torn to pieces by a mob and Jesus nailed to a cross, Nietzsche saw an essential difference. Girard remarks, "Every great book of anthropology of the age tries to demonstrate that Judaism and Christianity are the same as any other religion with a sacrificial origin. Nietzsche alone rejected the conclusion, while accepting the factual insight."[86] Nietzsche's specialization in Greek and Roman literature allowed him to distance himself from the positivism of nineteenth-century anthropology. Girard notes, "He knew too much about pagan mythology not to be revolted by the shallow assimilation of the Judeo-Christian with the pagan" traditions.[87] For Nietzsche, the difference lay not in the event, but in its interpretation. The similarity of the Passion narrative with so many mythic tales enables the difference to emerge so starkly: *the problem is that of the meaning of suffering; whether a Christian meaning or a tragic meaning.* Girard concludes that Nietzsche "knew that the 'facts' mean nothing unless and until they are interpreted."[88] For Girard, Christianity interprets the death of Jesus to mean that the crowd was wrong, the victim was innocent, and God did not demand or require this death.

Other factors help explain why almost nobody had come to this insight before Nietzsche. The nineteenth century, especially Germany, witnessed the rise of a particular form of theological anti-Semitism. With winds of philological speculation and crude phrenology at their backs, theologians and biblical scholars drove a chasm between Judaism and Christianity, insisting that the latter's relation to the former consisted only in repudiation. Nietzsche, however, rejected any essential severance between Judaism and Christianity: "Christianity can be understood only by referring to the soil out of which it grew—it is *not* a counter-movement against the Jewish instinct, it is actually its logical consequence."[89] In place of Judaism, Nietzsche located the true object of Christian scorn: archaic religion. Girard confirms this reading: "The Christian passion is not anti-Jewish, as the vulgar antisemites believe; it is anti-pagan; it reinterprets religious violence in such a negative fashion as to make its perpetrators feel guilty for committing it, even for silently accepting it."[90] The concern for victims makes biblical religion unique and puts it in contrast with pagan religions that consider the murder of innocents *life-giving*.[91] When Nietzsche stated his preference for Dionysus over Jesus, he understood the contrast as fundamental. Such an understanding ran against almost every nineteenth-century trend, a point missed entirely by Nietzsche's most noted twentieth-century interpreters, especially Heidegger.

Although Nietzsche saw the contrast between Christianity and archaic religion more clearly than his contemporaries, and thus brushed against Girard's insight about what is truly revelatory in the Gospels, Nietzsche sided with Dionysus and called for a return to his cult. Girard judges this decision not only tragic, in the sense that it abetted Nietzsche's descent into madness, but also mistaken. Regarding the tragic, Girard writes, "In his later years, Nietzsche kept reviving, glorifying, and modernizing more and more sinister aspects of the primitive sacred. I am convinced that this process became more intolerable as it became more radical and led to his final breakdown."[92] More perspicacious is Girard's later remark, namely, that Nietzsche fundamentally mistook the slave revolt in Christianity. Nietzsche failed to distinguish between a religion that speaks from the perspective of the victim and a religion that inspires the weak. The crowd, notes Girard, is *against* Christ in the Passion: "[Nietzsche] thinks he is against the crowd, but he doesn't realize that the dionysian unanimity *is* the voice of the crowd . . . What Nietzsche doesn't see is the mimetic nature of unanimity. He doesn't seize the meaning of the Christian reflection of the mob phenomenon. He does not see that the dionysiac is the spirit of the crowd, of the mob, and the Christian is the heroic exception."[93] This comment conforms to Hart's judgment that, despite Nietzsche's searing insights into Christianity, he oftentimes exhibited a failure in the matters of taste upon which he so prided himself.

With Nietzsche's interpretation of Christianity in the background, Girard's read on Nietzsche's famous aphorism on the death of God comes into sharper focus. Girard notes, somewhat wistfully, that collective murder is the obvious theme of the aphorism declaring the death of God (*The Gay Science*, sec. 125). This point has been the central focus of Girard's work on archaic societies. Yet even in a passage that many students of Nietzsche can recite verbatim, Girard contends that they have ignored the most obvious meaning: "Perfectly respectable scholars, men who would not touch my own collective murder with a ten foot pole, quote Nietzsche's text in preference to any other, but their comments betray no awareness of the murder theme."[94] Even the great Heidegger's essay on this aphorism opted to relate this killing to the "suprasensory world" rather than to any real human violence.[95] The God that Nietzsche declares dead did not expire from old age, for Nietzsche's text itself belies such a conclusion: "[Nietzsche's aphorism] rejects very pointedly the very notion . . . of God as something childish and meaningless really that men gradually learned to do without in the modern age." The cause of God's death lies elsewhere: "Nietzsche sees the disappearance of God as a horrible murder in which every man is involved: '*We have killed him—*you and I. All of us are his murderers.'"[96]

If every atheism depends for its definition on the theism it opposes, then certainly the manner of God's death conditions the nature of the atheism in question. Girard contrasts the atheism of the Enlightenment, which understood belief in God as otiose, with the atheism of Nietzsche. In aphorism 125, Nietzsche juxtaposes the crowd's attitude with that of the madman. The crowd seems nonplussed by the madman's pleas: "They too were silent and stared at him in astonishment," after initially mocking the madman's search for God.[97] A natural death generates little effect. A collective murder, on the other hand, produces a much larger ripple. Nietzsche seems to recognize this distinction when he relates the madman's insistence that new rituals will result: "What water is there for us to clean ourselves? What festivals of atonement, what sacred games shall we have to invent."[98] This death of God, then, births a new religion. Therefore the kind of death God suffers matters immensely. Post-death-of-God humans can go along merrily living their lives, or they can deal with the blood on their hands. It all depends on the cause of death. Chris Fleming and John O'Carroll's essay establishes this point: "Whatever else might be said of Girard's reading, it contains a valuable point regarding not simply the brute fact of atheism, but its manner of existing. For thinkers allied to the "new atheism," the non-existence of God is simply a proposition which they claim to be correct. For Nietzsche, this is not enough; contrarily, one has to reject God in the *right way*."[99] Nietzsche's madman, according to Girard, embodies a prophetic caution against the kind of "post-Christian" atmosphere that Girard has ridiculed, both in the passages cited above from *Battling to the End* and in his chapter on Nietzsche in *I See Satan Fall Like Lightning*. In agreement with Nietzsche, Girard bemoans the current state of affairs: "The majestic inauguration of the 'post-Christian era' is a joke. We are living through a caricatural 'ultra-Christianity' that tries to escape from the Judeo-Christian orbit by 'radicalizing' the concern for victims in an anti-Christian manner."[100]

Nietzsche detested with his entire being the emergence of such trends. A recent movie, *Easy A*, portrays life in a California high school while retelling Hawthorne's *The Scarlet Letter*. In a hypermodern twist, the protagonist, who is innocent, decides to flaunt her bad reputation by stitching a red "A" into her clothes herself. The movie sheds light on the hypocrisy of scapegoating and embodies what Girard would call an "ultra-Christian" standpoint by telling the story, literally, from the perspective of the victim, who narrates the events into a video recorder. Yet when the plot needs a villain, it finds one in the hypocritical Christians totally bereft of charity. This anecdote does not aim to be part of a larger cultural commentary about Christians as the "real victims." Rather, it is to give an example of what results from the wrong kind of atheism that Girard, through Nietzsche's insight, laments. Echoing Hart, Girard applauds Nietzsche for having the decency to oppose Christianity for what it is, and not for what it is not.

Girard's insights into Nietzsche's reading of Christianity allow for some concluding remarks on mimetic theory's contribution to a "theology of atheism." Atheism has never been a term, like *geocentric* or *cell phone*, that has a stable meaning. Atheism in the twenty-first-century West means a rejection of the monotheistic God, whose acceptance has marked, with the appropriate qualifications, Christian culture. Yet if Girard has correctly identified the breakthrough of Western monotheism with the ethical stance toward victims, then today's atheism faces a dilemma: it can dishonestly or naïvely suppose that the rejection of this God has no impact in our stance toward victims, or it can face this truth, as Nietzsche did, and choose Dionysus over the Crucified. In the penultimate chapter of *Atheist Delusions*, Hart recalls some of the ethical proposals, including infanticide, euthanasia, experimentation on the mentally handicapped, and first-strike nuclear attacks on unenlightened countries, that have been suggested by the post-Christian intellectual elite.[101] To the extent that these ethical positions seem unpalatable to the majority of citizens, their cultures have been infused with biblical worldviews. Yet Hart also foretells, correctly in my view, that Western moral grammar may not always remain Christian.

Something deeper is at stake, however, in any discussion of the options available for a truly post-Christian society. According to Girard, the experience undergone, through which one comes to understand the victim as innocent, happens through revelation; God gives us this graced knowledge, which not only tells us something about ourselves but also about God. In other words, the truth has theological content. Therefore the only option for an honest atheist, who does not believe in any divinely revealed truth, is the Nietzschean version. One of Nietzsche's more provocative aphorisms, from *Twilight of the Idols*, declares, "I fear we have not freed ourselves from God, because we still believe in grammar."[102] Here Nietzsche repeats the madman's concerns about the societal impact of rejecting God. If one substitutes "victims" for "grammar," then the point comes into even greater focus. One can only reject God if one no longer believes in the innocence of victims, or that their suffering should be curtailed, or that their lives matter. A mimetic theology of atheism demonstrates how this position arises from the unveiling of the true nature of the biblical God, and the radical reorientation that underlies the most basic affirmation of this God.

EPILOGUE

One Final Apology

In this book, I have attempted to weave two strands of argument. The first underscores Girard's importance for contemporary fundamental theology. I have demonstrated how Girard's thought, in particular, and mimetic theory, more broadly, offer new, interesting, and unique answers to pressing questions and problems in fundamental theology. The second strand involves an apology for Girard, in the sense of clarifying, reconciling, and supplementing his theological positions, so as to correct confusion and misreadings.

Regarding the first strand, the significance of mimetic theory comes out most strongly in the chapters on religion, revelation, and ecclesiology. The aim in such instances was to highlight the relevance of mimetic theory for understanding a particular theological problem. Part—maybe even the most important part—of the apology undertaken herein is of this sort. Not all of the arguments I offered have proceeded in this way. In some chapters, or sections within chapters, the aim has been more restrained—rather than showing how mimetic theory outstrips earlier theological efforts, the aim has been merely to demonstrate that mimetic theory maps onto the efforts of other leading Christian theologians. Chapter 7, on atheism, for instance, intended only to show how Girard's thought aligns with the research of Michael Buckley or with the interpretation of Nietzsche offered by David Hart. The same judgment applies to chapter 2 on faith and reason, and chapter 6 on modernity. These more modest arguments, although harder to disagree with, also raise a question: Why bother making such modest arguments?

The modest aim in these chapters can be justified. For decades many in the Christian theological community have considered Girard's thought so far outside the theological orbit that they have not bothered to engage his arguments, or the arguments of those theologians intrigued by mimetic theory. Therefore, showing how mimetic theory leads Girard to a position akin to Charles Taylor's in regard to modernity is no small feat; it brings mimetic theory into orbit with more familiar and accepted figures. Building on earlier efforts by such scholars as James Williams and Robert-Hamerton Kelly (biblical studies), James Alison (original sin), Raymund Schwager (soteriology), Brian Robinette (resurrection), and Mark Heim (atonement theory), among others, the preceding chapters have brought Girard into more explicit conversation with the subdiscipline of theology known as fundamental theology.

The second strand of argument concerns itself with clarifying the nature of Girard's thoughts, and the implications of mimetic theory for theology, as exposited by some of its leading proponents. My introduction addressed the nature of theological discourse itself, noting a diversity of "operations" done by Christian theologians. The second of those operations involves borrowing from nontheological discourses, and it is the default operation for fundamental theology. My argument in the book's introduction suggested that some of Girard's writings already qualified as theology, in which Girard himself borrowed from mimetic theory in order to make theological arguments or to explain biblical passages. Rather than demarcating just how Girard's thought qualifies as theology, in the preceding chapters I asserted that Girard was already doing theology, and doing it at a very high level. Taking Kevin Mongrain's qualifications into account—that Girard's work only qualifies as theology if one expands theology beyond the narrowly academic or scholastic (see the introduction)—it was seen that Girard's willingness to engage scripture marked the theological character of his arguments. Chapter 2 clarified some of the consequences of faith-based or biblically inspired arguments in comparison with more properly scientific modes of discourse. The rest of the chapters (excluding chapter 1) were not simply an apology for Girard, but a Girardian apologetic. They examined arguments offered by mimetic theory and—sometimes with almost no labor, at other times with greater labor—demonstrated how these arguments constituted an apology for Christianity, or developed a branch of fundamental theology germane to such arguments.

Returning to the second strand, an apology *for* Girard, perhaps it is unwise to end a book that has attempted to break new ground with a point that may be obvious. Yet the point still needs to be made. Theological critiques of Girard are not new (Balthasar, North, Milbank), nor do they seem to be on the wane (Ormerod, Coakley). Even if it is the case that Girard has been misread or misunderstood, one can still raise the question that Michael Kirwan asked in *Girard and Theology*: Do the sheer number of misinterpretations of mimetic theory raise a red flag?[1] In an earlier article, I suggested that Girard's corpus poses a number of problems for a theological readership and requires at some points a greater hermeneutical generosity than should be reasonably required.[2]

I have applied such a generous hermeneutic because it is required for any orthodox theological appropriation of Girard. As Mathias Moosbrugger has shown in painstaking detail, this was also the primary motive of Girard's first and most important theological commentator, Raymund Schwager.[3] On a number of points, Girard's statements in his earlier work raised troubling questions for traditional Christianity. I have found, almost without exception, that Girard's most problematic statements often find correction in his later work. It is not the case that critics have simply misinterpreted him, but that they have failed to read him widely enough. The hope is that my labors here advance the state of the many questions that theologians have raised about the relevance and the viability of Girard's project for Christian theology.

A great deal is at stake in the role accorded to Girard. It could be that his deepest insights advance Christian apologetics, but that his overall system and worldview stands in contradiction to traditional Christianity, or orthodox Catholic theology. If this assessment gains ascendancy, then Girard will become a figure like Joseph de Maistre or Carl Schmitt: interesting, to be sure, but so fundamentally flawed as to be relegated to the margins of mainstream theological scholarship. Such was the judgment of Hayden White, already in 1978, when he not only compared Girard to de Maistre—a protofascist, according to Isaiah Berlin—but also suggested that Girard preferred Nazi Germany to the modern liberal state.[4] Three and a half decades later, amid consternation that leading Christian intellectuals take him seriously, Sarah Coakley reached a similar judgment (minus the national socialist aspersions) about the incompatibility of mimetic theory with a Christian metaphysics or worldview.[5]

Theologians have engaged mimetic theory since the mid-1970s, and the bibliography and notes herein attest to the breadth and vigor of that engagement. Earlier debate, helpful as it was in initiating discussion about the theological implications of mimetic theory, was of necessity focused around Girard's earlier work, especially *Things Hidden*. Nearly thirty years subsequent to its English translation (1987), it is now imperative that theologians engage the breadth of Girard's corpus, including his work in his final productive decade (2000–2010). The Girardian canon is closed. Although this book is not the first to incorporate the full scope of Girard's writings, it is the first to bring this breadth to bear in dialogue with leading questions in fundamental theology. In the course of doing so, it has treated the relevant arguments and questions in such a way as to advance the discussion between Girard and theology, while staying primarily focused on the broad argument of the book and the particular arguments of the individual chapters. The goal of positioning such an unlikely apologist into the stream of fundamental theology has been not only to understand the nature of Girard's thought but also to carry out the biblical imperative so central to fundamental theology—"Always be ready to make your defense [*apologian*] to anyone who demands from you an accounting for the hope that is in you" (1 Pet. 3:15).

NOTES

Introduction

1. Scott Cowdell, *René Girard and Secular Modernity: Christ, Culture, and Crisis* (Notre Dame, IN: University of Notre Dame Press, 2013); Mathias Moosbrugger, *Die Rehabilitierung des Opfers: Zum Dialog zwischen René Girard und Raymund Schwager um die Angemessenheit der Rede vom Opfer im christlichen Kontext* (Innsbruck: Tyrolia, 2014); John Edwards, "Developing a 'Theology in the Order of Discovery': The Method and Contribution of James Alison" (Ph.D. diss., Boston College, 2014).

2. The October 2014 *Bulletin*, for instance, contains more than one hundred bibliographic entries, the majority of which cover religious and theological themes.

3. Hans Urs von Balthasar, *The Action*, trans. Graham Harrison. Vol. 4 of *Theo-Drama: Theological Dramatic Theory* (San Francisco: Ignatius, 1994), 299. The German edition appeared in 1980.

4. Ibid., 313.

5. Ibid., 308.

6. For this point see Moosbrugger, *Die Rehabilitierung des Opfers*, 144. One juicy morsel from this correspondence is Balthasar's report that Henri de Lubac already recommended Girard's *Violence and the Sacred* to Balthasar in 1977 (ibid., 17). Girard confirmed his friendship with de Lubac in an interview with Giulio Meotti: "I was honored by his friendship. When I had been accused of not being a Christian, de Lubac told me that everything that I was writing was right and there wasn't anything heretical in it" (*Il Foglio*, March 20, 2007). For an English version, see Meotti, "Intellectuals as Castrators of Meaning: An Interview with René Girard," trans. Paul N. Faraone and Christopher S. Morissey, *First Principles*, January 1, 2008, http://www.firstprinciplesjournal.com /print.aspx?article=1656&loc=b&type=cbbp (accessed March 26, 2016).

7. Moosbrugger, *Die Rehabilitierung des Opfers*, 22–23.

8. Kevin Mongrain, *The Systematic Thought of Hans Urs von Balthasar: An Irenaean Retrieval* (New York: Crossroad/Herder, 2002).

9. Kevin Mongrain, "Theologians of Spiritual Transformation: A Proposal for Reading René Girard through the Lenses of Hans Urs von Balthasar and John Cassian," *Modern Theology* 28, no. 1 (2012): 81–111.

10. Ibid., 82.

11. Girard, *The One by Whom Scandal Comes*, trans. Malcolm DeBevoise (East Lansing: Michigan State University Press, 2014), 68; Mongrain, "Theologians of Spiritual Transformation," 94.

12. Mongrain, "Theologians of Spiritual Transformation," 94. Girard's efforts on this front have not wholly alleviated concerns about the gnostic valence in Girard's thought. See Neil Ormerod, "Doran's *The Trinity in History*: The Girardian Connection," in *Method: Journal of Lonergan Studies* 4, no. 1 (2013): 56n25.

13. Mongrain, "Theologians of Spiritual Transformation," 83.

14. Ibid., 84.

15. Ibid., 86.

16. Girard, "Violence Renounced," in *Violence Renounced: René Girard, Biblical Studies, and Peacemaking*, ed. Willard M. Swartley (Telford, PA: Pandora, 2000), 315.

17. All of these works are listed in the book's bibliography. The journal *Method* devoted a recent issue to Doran's book. Two of that issue's essays take up Doran's interaction with Girard: the aforementioned by Ormerod, "Doran's *The Trinity in History*," 47–60, and my own article, Grant Kaplan, "New Paths for a Girard/Lonergan Conversation: An Essay in Light of Robert Doran's *Missions and Processions*," *Method: Journal of Lonergan Studies* 4, no. 1 (2013): 23–38.

18. Earlier analogues for the approach of these later efforts, especially Robinette's and Doran's, would be Miroslav Volf, *Exclusion and Embrace: A Theological Exploration of Identity, Otherness, and Reconciliation* (Nashville, TN: Abingdon, 1996), and Walter Wink, *Engaging the Powers: Discernment and Resistance in a World of Domination* (Minneapolis: Fortress, 1992). Volf and Wink did not write Girardian books, but they instead brought Girard to bear on their theologies of reconciliation and of power.

19. Michael Kirwan, *Girard and Theology* (New York: T & T Clark, 2009).

20. Karl Rahner and Herbert Vorgrimler, eds., "Fundamentaltheologie," in *Kleines Theologisches Wörterbuch*, 10th ed. (Freiburg: Herder, 1976), 131–32. I have translated from the German without consulting the English translation, titled *Dictionary of Theology*.

21. What Rahner and Vorgrimler call *systematische Theologie* and *Dogmatik* in "Fundamentaltheologie," 132.

22. Rahner and Vorgrimler, "Fundamentaltheologie," 132–33.

23. Subsequent citations come from *Pensées/The Provincial Letters*, trans. W. F. Trotter, (New York: Modern Library, 1941). It follows the same groupings as the Brunschvicg edition.

24. In the next paragraph of the aphorism, Pascal asserts, "Let them conclude what they will against deism, they will conclude nothing against the Christian religion, which properly consists in the mystery of the Redeemer."

25. No less an apologist than John Henry Newman makes a similar claim in his thirteenth "Oxford Sermon" when he writes, "What, then, is the safeguard [of faith] if Reason is not? . . . The safeguard of Faith is a right state of heart. This it is that gives it birth; it also disciplines it. This is what protects it from bigotry, credulity, and fanaticism. It is holiness"; see Newman, *Fifteen Sermons Preached before the University of Oxford* (Notre Dame, IN: University of Notre Dame Press, 1997), 234.

26. Avery Dulles, *A History of Apologetics*, 2nd ed. (San Francisco: Ignatius, 2005), 332; here Dulles evokes *Gaudium et spes*, sec. 22.

27. Wolfgang Palaver, *René Girard's Mimetic Theory*, trans. Gabriel Borrud (East Lansing: Michigan State University Press, 2013), 224.

28. Ibid., 228. Tobin Siebers makes these claims in "Language, Violence, and the Sacred: A Polemical Survey of Critical Theories," in *To Honor René Girard: Presented on the Occasion of His Sixtieth Birthday by Colleagues, Students, and Friends*, ed. Alphonse Juilland (Saratoga, CA: Anma Libri, 1986), 203–19.

29. Palaver, *René Girard's Mimetic Theory*, 228–29.

30. I make this point in an entirely different context in Grant Kaplan, *Answering the Enlightenment: The Catholic Recovery of Historical Revelation* (New York: Crossroad/Herder, 2006), esp. 34–36, 176n61.

31. Palaver, *René Girard's Mimetic Theory*, 229.

32. Ibid.

33. Girard, *I See Satan Fall Like Lightning*, trans. James G. Williams (Maryknoll, NY: Orbis, 2001), 188–89.

34. Mongrain, "Theologians of Spiritual Transformation," 96. He later adds, "It is also fair to say that [Girard] has been increasingly clear and consistent in the past decade (ibid., 96–97).

35. Rebecca Adams, "Violence, Difference, Sacrifice: A Conversation with René Girard," *Religion and Literature* 25, no. 2 (1993): 25.

36. In his preface, Palaver thanks Raymund Schwager for the suggestion "to incorporate Augustine into my presentation and analysis of mimetic theory" (Palaver, *René Girard's Mimetic Theory*, x). Although himself a leading Balthasarian, Cyril O'Regan also tries to connect Girard to Augustine, albeit with much greater reservations; see O'Regan, "Girard and the Spaces of Apocalyptic," *Modern Theology* 28, no. 1 (2012): 125–31.

37. Girard, *When These Things Begin: Conversations with Michel Treguer*, trans. Trevor Cribben Merrill (East Lansing: Michigan State University Press, 2014), 133.

38. Palaver, *René Girard's Mimetic Theory*, 222.

39. Grant Kaplan, "Renewing the Tradition: The Theological Project of James Alison," *America Magazine*, May 19, 2014, 25–27.

40. Palaver, *René Girard's Mimetic Theory*, 230. Earlier in the paragraph, Palaver uses the same metaphor absent the modifier "outer" (ibid., 229).

41. Ibid., 230.

42. René Girard, *Battling to the End: Conversations with Benoît Chantre*, trans. Mary Baker (East Lansing: Michigan State University Press, 2010), xv.

43. In his comparison of Alison and Girard, John Edwards helpfully distinguishes between *fides quae* and *fides qua* in order to organize different mimetic theological modes; see Edwards, "From a 'Revealed' Psychology to Theological Inquiry: James Alison's Theological Appropriation of Girard," *Contagion* 21 (2014): 121–30.

44. René Girard, *The Girard Reader*, trans. James Williams (New York: Crossroad, 1996), 268.

45. Girard, *When These Things Begin*, 2. Later in the same set of interviews, Girard notes, "To truly repent the way Peter and Paul do is to understand one's personal participation in the expulsion of God" (ibid., 98).

Chapter One

1. Aristotle, *Poetics*, bk. 4, 1448b. The passage comes from *Aristotle's Poetics*, trans. S. H. Butcher (New York: Hill and Wang, 1961), 15.

2. Erich Auerbach, *Mimesis: The Representation of Reality in Western Literature*, trans. Willard Trask (New York: Doubleday Anchor, 1953).

3. René Girard, *Things Hidden Since the Foundation of the* World, trans. Stephen Bann and Michael Metteer (Stanford, CA: Stanford University Press, 1987), 7.

4. See Scott Garrels: "Imitation, Mirror Neurons, and Mimetic Desire: Convergences between the Mimetic Theory of René Girard and Empirical Research on Imitation," *Contagion* 12 (2006): 47–86; and Garrels, ed., *Mimesis and Science: Empirical Research on Imitation and the Mimetic Theory of Culture and Religion* (East Lansing: Michigan State University Press, 2011).

5. Garrels, "Imitation, Mirror Neurons, and Mimetic Desire," 56.

6. James Alison, *Broken Hearts and New Creations: Intimations of a Great Reversal* (New York: Continuum, 2010), 161.

7. Garrels, "Imitation, Mirror Neurons, and Mimetic Desire," 58.

8. A recent article from *The New Yorker* confirms the ape/toddler comparison; see Elizabeth Kolbert, "Sleeping with the Enemy: What Happened between the Neanderthals and Us?" *The New Yorker*, August 15 & 22, 2011, 64–75. Kolbert writes, "When researchers from Leipzig performed a battery of tests on chimpanzees, orangutans, and two-and-a-half-year-old children, they found that the chimps, the orangutans and the kids performed comparably on a wide range of tasks that involved understanding of the physical world. . . . They were equally skillful at manipulating simple tools.

Where the kids routinely outscored the apes was in tasks that involved reading social cues. . . . In general, apes seem to lack the impulse toward collective problem-solving that's so central to human society" (ibid., 71).

9. Scott Garrels, "Human Imitation: Historical, Philosophical, and Scientific Perspectives," in *Mimesis and Science*, 3.

10. Alison, *Broken Hearts*, 162.

11. Only a reductionist would conclude that recent neuroscience "proves" mimetic theory. Like reductionism, determinism narrows the complexity of human action. Girard makes his opinion about such worldviews explicit: "I have never said that the mimetic mechanism is deterministic"; Girard, *Evolution and Conversion: Dialogues on the Origin of Culture* (London: T & T Clark, 2007), 67.

12. Girard, *Things Hidden*, 359.

13. I explore more deeply Girard's disagreement with Romanticism in Grant Kaplan, "Saint vs. Hero: René Girard's Undoing of Romantic Hagiology," in *Postmodern Saints of France: Refiguring "the Holy" in Contemporary French Philosophy*, ed. Colby Dickinson (London: T & T Clark, 2013), 153–67.

14. René Girard, *A Theater of Envy: William Shakespeare* (South Bend, IN: St. Augustine's Press, 1991), 24.

15. René Girard, *Deceit, Desire, and the Novel: Self and Other in Literary Structure*, trans. Yvonne Freccero (Baltimore: Johns Hopkins University Press, 1965), 14–15.

16. Ibid., 294.

17. Girard, *A Theater of Envy*, 3. Similar articulations of this point are found throughout Girard's work.

18. Peter Thiel made this point during his talk on July 9 at the 2015 Colloquium on Violence & Religion.

19. Girard, *Theater of Envy*, 9.

20. Girard, *Things Hidden*, 9.

21. In René Girard, *Violence and the Sacred* (Baltimore: Johns Hopkins University Press, 1977), Girard did not make the link between mimetic desire and the scapegoat mechanism as clear as it could have been. He later noted: "My first

book was on mimetic desire and rivalry in modern literature, my second was the extension of the theses on mimetic desire to archaic religion, but I deliberately put mimetic desire only in the sixth chapter. Eric Gans was the only person who really questioned the composition of that book. He asked me: 'Why only in the sixth chapter? It should be the first, because you have to start from the beginning, from mimetic desire'" (*Evolution and Conversion*, 38).

22. Girard, *Violence and the Sacred*, 146.

23. The lecture has been published as *Wissenschaft und christlicher Glaube* (Tübingen: Mohr Siebeck, 2007), esp. 12–16. Although the title is in German, the text reproduces Girard's English with a facing German translation.

24. Girard, *"To Double Business Bound": Essays on Literature, Mimesis, and Anthropology* (Baltimore: Johns Hopkins University Press, 1978), 201.

25. Ibid.

26. Girard, *Evolution and Conversion*, 56.

27. Ibid., 57.

28. Girard, *Things Hidden*, 302.

29. My account has been recollected from visits to Cahokia and has been cross-checked by the official website: http://cahokiamounds.org/, and by *Wikipedia*: http://en.wikipedia.org/wiki/Cahokia (both accessed on October 16, 2011).

30. See Jared Diamond, *Collapse: How Societies Choose to Fail or Survive* (New York: Viking, 2005).

31. Girard, *Things Hidden*, 27.

32. René Girard, *Battling to the End: Conversations with Benoît Chantre*, trans. Mary Baker (East Lansing: Michigan State University Press, 2010), 19. Unless otherwise indicated, all italics in quoted material throughout this book appear in the original.

33. Girard, *Things Hidden*, 63.

34. Girard, *Evolution and Conversion*, 72.

35. Girard, *Violence and the Sacred*, 259.

36. Jared Diamond, "Vengeance Is Ours," *The New Yorker*, April 21, 2008, 74–87. The article generated intense scrutiny and backlash, but of the numerous criticisms I have read, none dismantles the claims germane to the points made below. For a collection of critiques against Diamond and his purported lack of journalistic integrity, see: http://www.imediaethics.org/special-investigations/jared-diamonds-factual-collapse/ (accessed March 27, 2016).

37. Ibid., 76.

38. Ibid. The legal claims against Diamond revolved around the number of people killed, the number of pigs slaughtered, and his overreliance on a single source.

39. Ibid., 84.

40. Paul Sillitoe and Mako John Kuwimb, "Rebutting Jared Diamond's Savage Portrait: What Tribal Societies Can Tell Us about Justice and Liberty," April 28, 2010, http://www.imediaethics.org/rebutting-jared-diamonds-savage -portrait/ (accessed March 27, 2016).

41. The two also mention the positive impact of Christianity: "In the Wola region, Christianity has had a considerable influence in prompting old enemies to forgive and forget old scores and live in peace" (Sillitoe and Kuwimb, "Rebutting Jared Diamond's Savage Portrait," 17). It should be noted that Diamond entirely ignores the role of religion in determining the success or failure of various groups.

42. Girard, *Things Hidden*, 11.

43. Girard, *Violence and the Sacred*, 33–38.

44. Ibid., 56–67. He explains: "In some primitive societies twins inspire a particular terror. It is not unusual for one of the twins, and often both, to be put to death. The origin of this terror has long puzzled ethnologists. . . . It is only natural that twins should awaken fear, for they are harbingers of indiscriminate violence, the greatest menace to primitive societies" (ibid., 56–57).

45. Girard, *Things Hidden*, 12.

46. Ibid., 13.

47. Girard, *Violence and the Sacred*, 221.

48. Girard, *Things Hidden*, 26. Later he writes: "We know that the ineradicable character of mimetic rivalry means that the importance of any object as a stake in conflict will ultimately be annulled and surpassed and that acquisitive mimesis, which sets members of the community against one another, will give way to antagonistic mimesis, which eventually unites and reconciles all members of a community at the expense of a victim" (ibid., 95).

49. Examples include Michael Kirwan, *Discovering Girard* (London: Darton, Longman and Todd, 2004), esp. 48–49, and James Alison, *Raising Abel: The Recovery of the Eschatological Imagination* (New York: Crossroad, 1996), 21; Raymund Schwager demonstrates the conflation perfectly: "In this way mutual violence and confusing animosities can very quickly, almost instantaneously even, turn into a unified violence of all against one. Girard calls this the scapegoat mechanism or the collective transfer of diffuse violence upon a chance victim"; see Schwager, *Must There Be Scapegoats? Violence and Redemption in the Bible*, trans. Maria Assad (New York: Crossroad, 1987), 18–19.

50. Girard, *Evolution and Conversion*, 67.

51. Girard, *Things Hidden*, 24.

52. Girard, *Violence and the Sacred*, 4; he continues, "The sacrifice serves to protect the entire community from *its own* violence; it prompts the entire community to choose victims from outside itself" (ibid., 8).

53. For an account of these events, see the documentary film *Steve Bartman: Catching Hell*, directed by Alex Gibney (ESPN Films, 2011), DVD.

54. For the alleged "Curse of the Billy Goat," see http://en.wikipedia.org /wiki/Curse_of_the_Billy_Goat (accessed August 8, 2011).

55. See Bill Simmons, "Interview with Alex Gibney," ESPN Radio, September 27, 2011, http://espn.go.com/espnradio/play?id=7025837 (accessed October 23, 2011). Gibney also says the same thing in his article on the film, "Alex Gibney on Catching Hell," September 27, 2011, http://www.grantland.com /blog/hollywood-prospectus/post/_/id/34295/alex-gibney-on-catching-hell (accessed October 24, 2011).

56. Girard, *Violence and the Sacred*, 90.

57. Ibid., 92.

58. For the Dinka, see Godfrey Lienhardt, *Divinity and Experience: The Religion of the Dinka* (Oxford: Clarendon, 1961).

59. Girard, *Violence and the Sacred*, 97–98.

60. Ibid., 98.

61. Ibid. The *pharmakos* represented both the problem and the solution to the problem. He is like the *pharmakon*, which "in classical Greek means both poison and antidote for poison, both sickness and cure" (ibid., 95).

62. Ibid., 95.

63. Michelle Obama notoriously broke protocol by patting the queen's back. See Howard Chua-Eoan, "The Queen and Mrs. Obama: A Breach in Protocol," *Time*, April 1, 2009, http://www.time.com/time/world/article/0,8599,1888962 ,00.html (accessed October 24, 2011). At the end of this piece, Chua-Eoan's explanation of the taboo's origin leads to a question that the article, of course, does not ask: Whence this taboo?

64. Girard, *Things Hidden*, 53.

65. In *Things Hidden* (56–68), Girard cites E. E. Evans-Pritchard as an example of an ethnologist who gathers the evidence but fails to connect coronation ceremonies and the founding murder. See E. E. Evans-Pritchard, *Social Anthropology and Other Essays* (New York: Free Press, 1964).

66. Girard, *Violence and the Sacred*, 99.

67. Ibid., 302.

68. Chapter 2 treats the topic of falsifiability in greater detail.

69. Girard, *Violence and the Sacred*, 316.

70. René Girard, *The Scapegoat*, trans. Yvonne Freccero (Baltimore: Johns Hopkins University Press, 1986), 25.

71. Jane Harrison, *Themis* (Cambridge: Cambridge University Press, 1912), 14–16.

72. Girard, *Scapegoat*, 70.

73. One sees this pattern in Girard's comparison of Plutarch's and Livy's accounts of the founding of Rome. Plutarch notes the older versions of Romulus's death, many of which describe a collective murder. The older versions become less communal and less explicit, to the point where even the translators conceal the collectivity by translating *turba* ("crowd") as "scuffle" (see Girard, *Scapegoat*, 89–94). Girard makes the same point in his treatment of non-Western myths in Girard, "Generative Scapegoating," in *Violent Origins: Walter Burkert, René Girard, and Jonathan Z. Smith on Ritual Killing and Cultural Formation*, ed. Robert Hamerton-Kelly (Stanford, CA: Stanford University Press, 1987), 101.

74. Guillaume de Machaut, *Le Jugement du Roy de Navarre* (Paris: Ernest Hoeppfner, 1908).

75. Cited in Girard, *Scapegoat*, 2.

76. Girard, *Things Hidden*, 115.

77. Girard, *Scapegoat*, 37.

78. Ibid., 41; see also Girard, *Job: The Victim of His People*, trans. Yvonne Freccero (Stanford, CA: Stanford University Press, 1987), 31: "The friends [of Job] cannot be expected to recognize their own injustice. As with all those who create scapegoats, they consider their victim to be guilty. Therefore, for them, there is no scapegoat."

79. Girard, *Scapegoat*, 40.

80. Rebecca Adams, "Violence, Difference, Sacrifice: A Conversation with René Girard," *Religion & Literature* 25, no. 2 (1993): 18.

81. Kirwan, *Discovering Girard*, 69.

82. Girard, *Job*, 38.

83. Ibid., 35.

84. Girard's most insightful take on Nietzsche comes in his article "Dionysus versus the Crucified," *Modern Language Notes* 99 (1984): 816–35, which I cover in chapter 7.

85. Girard, *Job*, 37. Chapter 6 on Girard and secular modernity fleshes out the genetic relation of Christianity to modernity in greater detail.

Chapter Two

1. The most famous magisterial affirmation of this claim comes from the Fifth Lateran Council: "Cumque verum vero minime contradicat" ["since truth cannot contradict truth in any way"], Heinrich Denzinger and Peter Hünermann, eds., *Enchiridion Symbolorum: definitionum et declarationum de rebus fidei et morum*, 41st ed. (Freiburg: Herder, 2007), sec. 1441.

2. Tertullian, *De praescriptione haereticorum*, chap. 7, in *Ante-Nicene Fathers*, Vol. 3: *Latin Christianity: Its Founder, Tertullian*, ed. Alexander Roberts and James Donaldson (New York: Christian Literature Publishing, 1885), 17–60.

3. On Luther's use of this term and his more nuanced theology of reason, see Denis Janz, "Whore or Handmaid? Luther and Aquinas on the Function of Reason in Theology," in *The Devil's Whore: Reason and Philosophy in the Lutheran Tradition*, ed. Jennifer Hockenbery Dragseth (Minneapolis: Fortress, 2011), 47–52.

4. *Summa Theologiae* I, q. 1, a. 8. For the history of the axiom, see Johann Beumer, "Gratia supponit naturam: Zur Gesichichte eines theologischen Prinzips," *Gregorianum* 20 (1939): 381–406, 535–52.

5. Nobody has insisted on this point more emphatically than Henri de Lubac. See *The Mystery of the Supernatural*, trans. David L. Schindler (New York: Crossroad Herder, 1998), esp. chap. 4, "Toward a Real Gratuitousness," 53–74.

6. Anselm, *Proslogion*, chap. 1.

7. Girard, *When These Things Begin*, 98.

8. The story is complicated, but Immanuel Kant's 1798 *Conflict of the Faculties* marks the decisive realignment of thinking on this matter.

9. *Dei Filius*, ch. 2. The full phrase reads, "Eadem sancta mater Ecclesia tenet et docet, Deum, rerum omnium principium et finem, naturali humanae rationis lumine e rebus creatis certo cognosci posse" (Denzinger and Hünermann, *Enchiridion Symbolorum*, 3004).

10. Sarah Coakley, *Sacrifice Regained: Reconsidering the Rationality of Religious Belief* (Cambridge: Cambridge University Press, 2012), esp. 12–15, quote at 12.

11. Coakley makes note of these changes, but does not seem to have grasped their consequence. See Coakley, *Sacrifice Regained*, 13–14. For a nuanced Girardian response to her position, see Chelsea King, "Girard Reclaimed: Finding Common Ground between Sarah Coakley and René Girard on Sacrifice," *Contagion* 23 (2016) (forthcoming).

12. Kirwan, *Discovering Girard*, 94. Of the combiners, the most helpful metaphor comes from Cyril O'Regan, who writes of "the bifocal diagnostic apparatus of Girard, with one lens being anthropological, the other biblical" (O'Regan, "Girard and the Spaces of Apocalyptic," 113).

13. John Milbank, *Theology and Social Theory: Beyond Secular Reason* (Oxford: Blackwell, 1990), 3.

14. Girard, *Things Hidden*, 263–74.

15. Milbank, *Theology and Social Theory*, 392–98; for an extended argument against Girard's application of the scientific study of religion, see Milbank, "Stories of Sacrifice," *Modern Theology* 12, no. 1 (1996): 27–56.

16. Milbank, *Theology and Social Theory*, 394.

17. Ibid.

18. Fergus Kerr has already done so in Kerr, "Rescuing Girard's Argument," *Modern Theology* 8, no. 4 (1992): 385–99. It is noteworthy that Kerr's critique does not argue that Milbank should revise his position in light of Girard's later writings. Instead, Kerr demonstrates how Milbank misread Girard, especially *Things Hidden*, quite egregiously. For a less direct correction, see O'Regan, "Girard and the Spaces of Apocalyptic," 125–31.

19. Recent books of note: Jared Diamond, *Collapse: How Societies Choose to Fail or Survive* (New York: Viking, 2005); Robert Bellah, *Religion in Human Evolution: From the Paleolithic to the Axial Age* (Cambridge, MA: Belknap, 2011); Steven Pinker, *The Better Angels of Our Nature: Why Violence Has Declined* (New York: Viking, 2011).

20. For a sample of these critiques, see Girard, *Evolution and Conversion*, 136–52.

21. North, "Violence and the Bible: The Girard Connection," *Catholic Biblical Quarterly* 47 (1985): 2. North cites Richard Hecht, "Studies on Sacrifice, 1970–80," *Religious Studies Review* 8 (1982): 253–59.

22. Herzog, "Religionstheorie und Theologie René Girards," in *Kerygma und Dogma* 38, no. 2 (1992): 131–33, esp. 131: "Sein System verschliesst sich kritischer Prüfung; kein empirisch fundierter Einwand kann es je widerlege.—Aber wenn es zu den Minimalbedingungen wissenschaftlicher Theoriebildung gehört, dass sie an den Gegebenheiten, die zu ihrem Gegenstandsbereich gehören, überprüft, modifiziert und auch widerlegt werden kann, dann ist dies Unangreifbarkeit teuer, eben um den Preis der Unwissenschaftlichkeit, erkauft worden." See also Hayden White, "Ethnological 'Lie' and Mythical 'Truth,'" *Diacritics* 8, no. 1 (1978): 7: "Like Freud and Levi-Strauss, Girard explains too much. What is lacking, in his work as in theirs, are any criteria of falsifiability, any specification of the kind of data one would have to produce in order to disprove his contentions about the nature of religion, society, sacrifice, myths, and so forth. There is nothing about culture and society that Girard's theories cannot predict. In this respect, they are exactly like any religious system or any metaphysical one. This does not make them useless, but it is fatal to the claim of scientificity."

23. Charles K. Bellinger, *The Genealogy of Violence. Reflections on Creation, Freedom and Evil* (Oxford: Oxford University Press, 2001), 73.

24. Ibid., 88.

25. Girard, *Battling to the End*, 195.

26. Ibid., 196.

27. Grant Kaplan, "An Interview with René Girard," *First Things* online, November 2011, http://www.firstthings.com/onthesquare/2008/11/an-interview-with-rene-girard.

28. Girard, *The One by Whom Scandal Comes*, 86.

29. Girard, *Battling to the End*, 196; earlier, he says, "Since the beginning of the 'novelistic conversion' in *Deceit, Desire, and the Novel*, all of my books have been more or less explicit apologies of Christianity" (ibid., xv).

30. Girard, *The Girard Reader*, 288.

31. Bernard Lonergan, *Insight: A Study of Human Understanding*, ed. Frederick Crowe and Robert Doran (Toronto: University of Toronto Press, 1992), 600.

32. Girard, *Evolution and Conversion*, 144.

33. Michel Serres, *Atlas* (Paris: Julliard, 1994), 219–20.

34. Girard's later writings and interviews reveal two influences previously unknown: Friedrich Hölderlin and Charles Darwin. For this point, see James Williams, *Girardians: The Colloquium on Violence and Religion, 1990–2010* (Münster: Lit Verlag, 2012), 21–22.

35. Girard, *Evolution and Conversion*, 96; the italicized quotation comes from Charles Darwin, *The Autobiography of Charles Darwin*, ed. Francis Darwin (New York: Norton, 1958), 140.

36. Kant, *Critique of Pure Reason*, B xiii; italics are mine.

37. Darwin, *Autobiography of Charles Darwin*, 124.

38. Although he has not done fieldwork as an anthropologist, Girard considers it perfectly legitimate as a scientist to trust the work of others: "I have to trust my peers' research in their archeological or paleontological findings and interpretations" (*Evolution and Conversion*, 144).

39. Girard, *Evolution and Conversion*, 160.

40. Ibid., 165.

41. Ibid., 143.

42. Ibid., 165.

43. Arthur Maurice Hocart, *Kings and Counselors: An Essay in the Comparative Anatomy of Human Society* (Chicago: University of Chicago Press, 1970 [1936]).

44. See *The Girard Reader*, 277.

45. Girard, *Evolution and Conversion*, 164.

46. "Discussion," in Girard, *Violent Origins*, 250.

47. Girard, "Foreword," in Robert Hamerton-Kelly, *The Gospel and the Sacred: Poetics of Violence in Mark* (Minneapolis: Fortress, 1994), xi.

48. Girard, *Evolution and Conversion*, 150.

49. Girard, *I See Satan Fall Like Lightning*, 88. Girard repeats this claim in his book on Shakespeare: "In spite of its loudly professed respect for 'all cultural differences,' contemporary rationalism still dismisses primitive religion as totally meaningless, 'pure' superstition, unintelligible mumbo-jumbo" (Girard, *A Theater of Envy*, 208).

50. Girard, *I See Satan Fall Like Lightning*, 88–89; *Evolution and Conversion* echoes these claims: "The expulsion of religion from the field of knowledge . . . continues to take place whenever an anthropologist denies the actual existence of the scapegoat mechanism . . . Modern scholars, who have been trained to be programmatically anti-religious, are continuously scapegoating religion" (139).

51. Girard, "Generative Scapegoating," in *Violent Origins*, 117.

52. Ibid.

53. Girard, *I See Satan Fall Like Lightning*, 89.

54. Ibid., 93.

55. Girard, *Evolution and Conversion*, 170.

56. The text exists in multiple English translations. For the official translation, see Benedict XVI, "Regensburg Lecture," http://www.vatican.va/holy _father/benedict_xvi/speeches/2006/september/documents/hf_ben-xvi_spe _20060912_university-regensburg_en.html.

57. To my knowledge, the two locations where Girard discusses this text are Girard, "Ratzinger Is Right," *New Perspectives Quarterly* 22, no. 3 (2005): 42– 48; and *Battling to the End*, 195–210.

58. In the third footnote of the lecture, which was amended after the controversy, Benedict added, "In the Muslim world, this quotation has unfortunately been taken as an expression of my personal position, thus arousing understandable indignation. I hope that the reader of my text can see immediately that this sentence does not express my personal view of the Qur'an, for which I have the respect due to the holy book of a great religion."

59. For a summary of the talk and its effects, one can consult the *Wikipedia* entry: http://en.wikipedia.org/wiki/Regensburg_lecture (accessed July 25, 2012).

60. Girard, *Battling to the End*, 209.

61. Ibid., 206.

62. Ibid., 207.

63. Ibid., 209.

64. Pope Benedict XVI, "Regensburg Lecture"; emphasis is mine.

65. It should be pointed out that Cyril O'Regan also noted the overlap between Girard and Pascal, particularly in *Battling to the End*; see O'Regan, "Girard and the Spaces of Apocalyptic," 114.

66. This philosophical dead end forms the conclusion of John Ranieri's book, *Disturbing Revelation: Leo Strauss, Eric Voegelin, and the Bible* (Columbia: University of Missouri Press, 2009). Ranieri uses Girard to show the shortcomings of Strauss and Voegelin, who, despite their theoretical openness to religion, believed too strongly in the mythic power of philosophy.

67. René Girard and Gianni Vattimo, *Christianity, Truth, and Weakening Faith* (New York: Columbia University Press, 2010), 89.

68. Ibid., 46.

69. Ibid., 37.

70. Girard, *Things Hidden*, 263–80.

71. Ibid., 263.

72. Ibid., 272.

73. Ibid., 273.

74. I owe this observation to Wolfgang Palaver, who has made the point to me in numerous conversations.

75. Girard, *The Girard Reader*, 288.

76. For Girard's own account of his conversion, see *The Girard Reader*, 283–86, and *Quand ces choses commenceront—: Entretiens avec Michel Treguer* (Paris: Arléa, 1994), 189–95.

77. The biblical focus only confirms Mongrain's claim that Girard is a theologian, so long as one uses a wider definition: "In short, Girard writes theology like someone who respects the Biblical narrative in all its messy imprecision as the source of truth about God and history" (Mongrain, "Theologians of Spiritual Transformation," 84).

78. Girard, *Evolution and Conversion*, 159–60.

79. Ibid., 60.

80. Ibid., 136.

81. Girard, *The Girard Reader*, 266.

82. Girard, *Evolution and Conversion*, 170.

83. Girard, *Battling to the End*, 196.

84. Girard, *I See Satan Fall Like Lightning*, 7–18.

85. Ibid., 7.

86. Ibid., 9.

87. Recall here the critique of Robert North, "Violence and the Bible," 1–27. It should be noted that the new Girardian lectionary, assembled by Paul Nuechterlein, offers tremendous promise for renewed engagement. The lectionary gives a Girardian interpretation for each Sunday's readings; see http://girardianlectionary .net/instructions.html (accessed August 21, 2012).

88. Girard, *I See Satan Fall Like Lightning*, 12.

89. Girard, *The Scapegoat*, 125–65.

90. This famous *memorial* was supposedly found sown inside Pascal's coat when he died, and it corresponded with a profound religious experience he had in 1654. This translation is taken from A. J. Krailsheimer's edition of the *Pensées* (New York: Penguin Books, 1995), 285.

91. Girard, *When These Things Begin*, 93.

92. Girard, *Evolution and Conversion*, 173.

93. Girard, *The Girard Reader*, 284; see also *Deceit, Desire, and the Novel*, esp. 249, 258, 294.

94. He connects this hesitancy with the problem of "ne veux pas tomber dans le narcissisme auquel nous sommes tous enclins" (*Quand ces choses commenceront*, 190).

95. Girard, *The Girard Reader*, 285.

96. Girard, *Quand ces choses commenceront*, 191.

97. Girard, *The Girard Reader*, 285; in *Quand ces choses commenceront*, Girard identifies the latter as his "vraie conversion" (ibid., 194).

98. Ibid., 285.

99. This quotation comes from my 2008 interview, and it was omitted from the edited version that *First Things* published.

100. Girard, *Battling to the End*, 132.

101. Girard, *The Girard Reader*, 268.

102. Girard, *When These Things Begin*, 98.

103. Girard, *The Girard Reader*, 286.

Chapter Three

1. Prominent exceptions include N. T. Wright, *Jesus and the Victory of God* (Minneapolis: Augsburg Fortress, 1996); Sandra Schneiders, *The Revelatory Text: Interpreting the New Testament as Sacred Scripture* (New York: Harper-Collins, 1991).

2. Charles Hefling, "Revelation and/as Insight," in *The Importance of Insight: Essays in Honor of Michael Vertin*, ed. John J. Liptay and David S. Liptay (Toronto: University of Toronto Press, 2007), 109.

3. Ibid., 110.

4. René Latourelle, *Theology of Revelation* (Staten Island, NY: Alba House, 1966); the French original, *Théologie de la révélation* (Bruges: Brouwer, 1963), did not include the commentary on *Dei verbum* added to the English translation.

5. Patrick W. Carey, "Cardinal Avery Dulles, S.J., among the Theologians: A Memorial Reflection," *Theological Studies* 71 (2010): 79; Dulles himself pays heed to Latourelle in the preface to Avery Dulles, *Models of Revelation* (New York: Double Day, 1985): "Latourelle's monumental monograph of 1963 was the first major Catholic contribution to these theological questions, and it remains to this day one of the best" (xvii). This repeats his assertion in Dulles, *Revelation and the Quest for Unity* (Washington, DC: Corpus, 1968), 50: "It will presumably remain the standard Catholic work on the subject for some years to come."

6. Avery Dulles, "Review Article," *Theological Studies* 25 (1964): 43–58.

7. Avery Dulles, *Revelation Theology: A History* (New York: Herder and Herder, 1969).

8. Ibid., 183–87. This by no means implies that Dulles agreed with Latourelle on how best to present a theology of revelation. For his critique, see Dulles, *Revelation and the Quest for Unity*, 58–64.

9. See Gabriel Fackre, *The Doctrine of Revelation: A Narrative Interpretation* (Grand Rapids, MI: Eerdmans, 1997), 16–19; Neil Ormerod, *Meaning, Method, and Revelation: The Meaning and Function of Revelation in Bernard Lonergan's Method in Theology* (Lanham, MD: University Press of America, 2000), 7–19; John Montag, S.J., "Revelation: The False Legacy of Suarez," in *Radical Orthodoxy: A New Theology*, ed. John Milbank et al. (London: Routledge, 1999), 38–39, 49. It should be noted here that although they rely on Dulles, these authors disagree with Dulles at key points.

10. Thomas Hughson, "Dulles and Aquinas on Revelation," *The Thomist* 52 (1988): 445–71; and Montag, "Revelation," 38–63.

11. For another account that fails to see a "subjective" approach as the flip side of the "objective," see Thomas O'Meara, "Toward a Subjective Theology of Revelation," *Theological Studies* 36, no. 3 (1975): 401–27.

12. Latourelle, *Theology of Revelation*, 212.

13. Ibid., 195: "The Protestants . . . sacrifice everything before the concept of subjectivity and interiority." Latourelle later writes, "The principles which led to the corruption and dissolution of the concept of revelation were already at work in the birth of Protestantism" (ibid., 248).

14. Dulles, *Models of Revelation*, 36.

15. Ibid., 48.

16. Ibid., 48–49.

17. See Wolfhart Pannenberg, *Revelation as History*, trans. David Granskou (New York: Macmillan, 1960), 135–39.

18. Dulles, *Models of Revelation*, 69.

19. Auguste Sabatier, *Outlines of a Philosophy of Religion Based on Psychology and History* (London: Hodder and Stoughton, 1897), 54; cited in Dulles, *Models of Revelation*, 71–72.

20. Karl Rahner, "Mysticism," in *Encyclopedia of Theology: The Concise "Sacramentum Mundi"* (New York: Seabury, 1975), 1010.

21. Flannery O'Connor, "A Good Man Is Hard to Find," in *The Complete Stories* (New York: Farrar, Straus and Giroux, 1973), 131.

22. Karl Barth, *The Epistle to the Romans*, trans. Edwyn C. Hoskyns (Oxford: Oxford University Press, 1933), 35. It is worth remarking that of all of the models, the dialectical one is the hardest to fit within the conceptual framework of objective and subjective.

23. Dulles, *Models of Revelation*, 98.

24. Teilhard de Chardin, *Christianity and Evolution* (New York: Harcourt Brace Jovanovich, 1971), 143; cited in Dulles, *Models of Revelation*, 99.

25. This heuristic might explain why he views the dialectical model with such consternation.

26. Latourelle, *Theology of Revelation*, 244; Latourelle begins his conclusion by distinguishing "*four* essential aspects of revelation: it is activity of God, event of history, knowledge, encounter" (ibid., 443).

27. Ibid., 195.

28. Ibid., 158.

29. Ibid., 171.

30. Ibid., 195.

31. Ibid., 201.

32. Ibid., 243. His discussion of *Dei filius* is more distinct: "Faith is religious adherence to the word of God under the combined activity of the external word and the inner activity of the Holy Spirit" (ibid., 264).

33. Ibid., 324.

34. Ibid., 349.

35. Ibid., 447.

36. Latourelle even declares the need for a more hermeneutical approach (see *Theology of Revelation*, 229–32). Latourelle writes, "Not only is history the place of revelation, not only does revelation make history, not only does revelation have its own history, but history, *divinely interpreted*, is the medium of revelation. . . . What is needed is to consider the implications of a revelation so completely incorporated in history, implications which affect both its nature and its progress" (ibid., 232; emphasis is mine).

37. Dulles, *Models of Revelation*, 146, 153; see also the penultimate chapter, "The Acceptance of Revelation," esp. 258, and the final chapter, "Revelation at its Present Value," esp. 280.

38. Dulles, *Models of Revelation*, 164.

39. Ibid., 157, 166.

40. Ibid., 268.

41. Francis Fiorenza, *Foundational Theology: Jesus and the Church* (New York: Crossroad, 1984), 296.

42. Ibid., 299.

43. In addition to Fiorenza, the contemporary theologian who takes an approach most similar to the one below is Ormond Rush. He applies this approach deftly towards an ecclesiology of the *sensus fidei*; see Rush, "*Sensus fidei*: Faith 'Making Sense' of Revelation," *Theological Studies* 62 (2001): 231–61; see also Rush: *The Eyes of Faith: The Sense of the Faithful and the Church's Reception of Revelation* (Washington, DC: Catholic University of America Press, 2009).

44. Martin Heidegger, *Being and Time*, trans. John Macquarrie and Edward Robinson (San Francisco: Harper & Row, 1962), 48n1 (26). Here and below the first number indicates the pagination in the Macquarrie translation

and the second number is from *Sein und Zeit*, 7th ed. (Tübingen: Max Niemeyer, 1993).

45. Frederick Lawrence, "The Nominalist Prejudgment," in "Believing to Understand: The Hermeneutic Circle in Gadamer and Lonergan" (Ph.D. diss., University of Basel, 1976), 11; Heidegger, *Nietzsche* II (Pflulingen: Neske, 1961), 223; Heidegger, *Being and Time*, 414 (363n1), 85–89 (59–62), 187 (147).

46. Lawrence, "Believing to Understand," 25.

47. Ibid., 35.

48. Gadamer writes: "In view of this situation it must be admitted that knowledge in the human sciences is not the same as in the inductive sciences, but has quite a different kind of objectivity and is acquired in a quite different way"; see Hans-Georg Gadamer, *Truth and Method*, 2nd rev. ed., trans. Joel Weinsheimer and Donald G. Marshall (New York: Crossroad, 1989). This translation represents a much-improved version from the earlier translation by William Glen-Doepel (New York: Seabury Press, 1975). Since the original translation is the more popular, both the Weinsheimer first and the Glen-Doepel pagination will be given in parentheses: 241 (215).

49. Gadamer, *Truth and Method*, 328 (293).

50. Lawrence, "Believing to Understand," 38–39: "[Kant] thought, in a conceptualist way, that the judgment so central to that knowledge is constituted by a representation of a representation, or a regulated employment of abstract, general, and discursive concepts mediating a representation of a multiplicity given in sensation. He too conceived experience in terms of that 'pure' perception, which Scheler, for one, conclusively demonstrated to be illusory." Lawrence continues, "Kant's portrayal of the judge or physicist, therefore, seems to be that of a detached knowing subject who does not so much question—although the expression is used—as apply its *idées fixes* to sense immediacy: 'Thoughts without content are empty, intuitions without concepts are blind. It is just as necessary to make one's concepts sensible (that is, to add the object to them in intuition) as to make our intuitions intelligible (that is, to bring them under concepts).' Indeed the irony of Kant's lapidary formulation of his own most authentic insight is the absence of the function of questioning" (ibid., 42–43; for Kant, see *Critique of Pure Reason*, B 75).

51. For Gadamer on Schleiermacher, see *Truth and Method*, part II/1: "The Questionableness of Romantic Hermeneutics and of its Application to the Study of History." According to Gadamer, Schleiermacher's goal of divination—getting into the mind of the author—exemplifies the mistaken framework of knowing as bridging the gap between subject and object by entering into another's mind. Recent scholarship on Schleiermacher, it should be noted, points to a disparity between Schleiermacher's actual position and the caricature of it that Gadamer made normative. For one example, see Kristin Gjesdal, "Hermeneutics and

Philology: A Reconsideration of Gadamer's Critique of Schleiermacher," *British Journal for the History of Philosophy* 14, no. 1 (2006): 133–56. I am indebted to Kevin Vander Schel for this reference.

52. Gadamer, *Truth and Method*, 308 (275).

53. For the most succinct account of Gadamer's appropriation of Heidegger, see *Truth and Method*, part II/1/3/b: "Heidegger's Project of a Hermeneutical Phenomenology." Gadamer writes, "Heidegger's thesis was that being itself is time. This burst asunder the whole subjectivism of modern philosophy, and, in fact, as was soon to appear, the whole horizon of questions asked by metaphysics, which tended to define being as what is present" (ibid., 257 [228]).

54. Gadamer, *Truth and Method*, 311 (277–78); italics are mine.

55. Walter Ong, *Orality and Literacy: The Technologizing of the Word* (New York: Routledge, 1982); Ong, *The Presence of the Word: Some Prolegomena for Cultural and Religious History* (New Haven, CT: Yale University Press, 1967).

56. Marshall McLuhan, *The Gutenberg Galaxy: The Making of Typographic Man* (Toronto: University of Toronto Press, 1962).

57. Ong, *Orality and Literacy*, 31.

58. Ong, *Presence of the Word*, 112.

59. Ibid., 12; Ong later writes that in an oral culture, "The expression of truth is felt as itself always an event" (ibid., 33).

60. Ibid., 33ff.; see also Eric Havelock, *A Preface to Plato* (Cambridge, MA: Belknap, 1963).

61. Ong, *Presence of the Word*, 34–35. Ong qualifies this description of Plato by discussing Plato's trepidation about the written text. See also Ong, *Orality and Literacy*, 78–80.

62. Ong, *Presence of the Word*, 3.

63. Although Peter Ramus has been omitted from these pages, it should be mentioned that Ong gives a central role to Ramus (*Presence of the Word*, 221). See also Walter Ong, *Ramus, Method, and the Decay of Dialogue* (Cambridge, MA: Harvard University Press, 1958).

64. Ong, *Presence of the Word*, 66–67.

65. Ibid., 73.

66. Ibid., 171.

67. Ibid., 308.

68. Ong, *Orality and Literacy*, 172–73.

69. Ong, *Presence of the Word*, 317.

70. Ibid.

71. The only attempt to bring Gadamer and Girard together, to my knowledge, is William Schweiker's "Sacrifice, Interpretation, and the Sacred: The Import of Gadamer and Girard for Religious Studies," *Journal of the American*

Academy of Religion 55, no. 4 (1987): 791–810. Schweiker limits his comparison to the use of mimesis in both thinkers.

72. Girard, *The Scapegoat*, 189.

73. See the contrast of the two cities in Augustine, *City of God*, 14.28. Augustine even noted, when comparing the founding of Rome with Cain's founding of the first city (Gen. 4:17), that a murder underlay the founding of both cities (*City of God*, 15.5).

74. Girard, *Evolution and Conversion*, 170.

75. Girard, "Peter's Denial," in *The Scapegoat*, 149–64.

76. Girard, *The Scapegoat*, 156. There is a lot more Peter (and Pilate) in each of us that we like to admit: "Close up, the same elements can be recognized in our own lives and are, to tell the truth, scarcely amusing" (ibid.).

77. Ibid., 154–55. To Girard's interpretation of Peter, Wolfgang Palaver adds: "This systematic insight, that the Resurrection of Jesus is prerequisite to Peter's conversion, is rooted deeply in the Christian tradition. El Greco, for instance, illustrates this idea at the end of the sixteenth century with 'The Repentant Peter,' a painting that depicts Peter shedding tears of regret"; Palaver, *René Girard's Mimetic Theory*, 230–31.

78. Girard and Vattimo, *Christianity, Truth, and Weakening Faith*, 43.

79. Ibid., 107: "A proper application of the mimetic and scapegoating insights provided by the gospels can, so to speak, probe all these texts with X rays."

80. Girard, *The Scapegoat*, 101.

81. Girard, *Things Hidden Since the Foundation of the World*, trans. Stephen Bann and Michael Metteer (Stanford, CA: Stanford University Press, 1987), 154.

82. For the most succinct account, see Girard, "Are the Gospels Mythical?" *First Things* 62 (April 1996): 27–31. For the definitive treatment of Girard and myth, see Richard J. Golsan, *René Girard and Myth: An Introduction* (New York: Routledge, 2002).

83. Girard, *Things Hidden*, 158–63. He gave a fuller explication in his 2004 address to the Colloquium on Violence & Religion, which appeared as "The Evangelical Subversion of Myth," in *Politics and Apocalypse*, ed. Robert Hamerton-Kelly (East Lansing: Michigan State University Press, 2007), 29–49.

84. In Benedict Viviano's "The Gospel according to Matthew," in *The New Jerome Biblical Commentary*, ed. Brown, Fitzmeyer, and Murphy (Englewood Cliffs, NJ: Prentice Hall, 1990), 630–74, Viviano notes, "[The passage] is of historical interest . . . because it shows us the Matthean community in polemical dialogue with the rival academy in Jamnia" (ibid., 666).

85. Girard, *Things Hidden*, 159.

86. Girard, "Evangelical Subversion of Myth," 38; elsewhere, "In order for the Gospels to have the universal significance Christians claim for them, it is

necessary for there to be nothing on earth that is superior to the Jewish religion and the sect of the Pharisees" (*Things Hidden*, 175).

87. Girard references Nils Dahl's work (*Things Hidden*, 161; 452n53); see Dahl, "Der Erstgeborene Satans und der Vater des Teufels (Oolyk. 7:1 und John 8:44)," in *Apophoreta: Festschrift für Ernst Haenchen*, ed. Walther Eltester (Berlin: Töpelmann, 1964), 70–84. Dahl notes that a Jewish Targum had already called Satan the father of Cain (ibid., 72).

88. Girard, *Things Hidden*, 161.

89. See Girard, "Evangelical Subversion of Myth," 42.

90. For an insightful Girardian treatment of this paradox, see S. Mark Heim, *Saved from Sacrifice: A Theology of the Cross* (Grand Rapids, MI: Eerdmans, 2005), 192–215.

91. Girard, "Evangelical Subversion of Myth," 38; see also *Things Hidden*, 175: "There is one last trick, one last victim and this is the text itself, which is chained to a fallacious reading and dragged before the tribunal of public opinion."

92. It should be noted that this phrase is not found in the earliest Lukan manuscripts.

93. Girard, *Things Hidden*, 277.

94. *Dei verbum*, sec. 2 (Vatican II).

95. Girard, *Evolution and Conversion*, 219.

96. Girard, *Anorexia and Mimetic Desire*, trans. Mark Anspach (East Lansing: Michigan State University Press, 2013), 63–64.

97. James Alison's distinction between acquisition and undergoing underscores Girard's point. In an essay on Alison, I described this feature as follows: "If God's gift is always a self-gift, then Alison correctly deduces that any real encounter entails a kind of passivity. Like the jolt of falling in love, it happens to us"; Kaplan, "Renewing the Tradition: The Theological Project of James Alison," *America Magazine*, May 19, 2014, 26.

98. Girard, *The Scapegoat*, 114.

99. Ibid., 212. This is the penultimate paragraph of the book. The last sentences of the book read, "The time has come for us to forgive one another. If we wait any longer there will not be time enough" (ibid.).

100. James Alison, *Knowing Jesus* (Springfield, IL: Templegate, 1993), 45.

101. See, for instance, what David Tracy says about a "classic." Tracy argues that classic texts challenge the notion of our autonomy because instead of experiencing ourselves as subjects before a text, or a work of art, we experience the opposite, and this experience deconstructs the very framework in which subject and object relate. When we encounter a truly beautiful text, "We find ourselves in the grip of an event, a happening, a disclosure, a claim to truth which we cannot deny"; Tracy, *The Analogical Imagination: Christian Theology in the Culture*

of Pluralism (New York: Crossroad, 1981), 114. Tracy's description mirrors that of a conversion. Like the more hermeneutical notion of revelation in Heidegger and Gadamer (upon whom Tracy depends), and in Girard and Alison, Tracy describes a profound transformation brought about by the text: "When a work of art so captures a paradigmatic experience of that event of truth, it becomes in that moment normative. Its memory enters as a catalyst into all our other memories and, now subtly, now compellingly, transforms our perceptions of the real. It becomes a classic" (ibid., 115). If one substitutes "art" for "Jesus," it is easy to imagine the kind of transformation that can take place within a person who undergoes this encounter.

102. James Alison, *The Joy of Being Wrong: Original Sin through Easter Eyes* (New York: Crossroad, 1998), 69.

103. Girard, *I See Satan Fall Like Lightning*, trans. James G. Williams (Maryknoll, NY: Orbis, 2001), 139.

104. Girard, *Things Hidden*, 271.

105. Girard, *Job: The Victim of his People*, trans. Yvonne Freccero (Stanford, CA: Stanford University Press, 1987), 159.

106. In his dialogue with Vattimo, Girard declared: "It is finally time to give Christian theology the anthropology it deserves to have" (Girard and Vattimo, *Christianity, Truth, and Weakening Faith*, 47).

107. Girard, *Things Hidden*, 401.

108. Ibid., 138.

109. Girard, *The Scapegoat*, 163. In his commentary on this passage, Alison notes that the original French—*qui domine*—indicates an even stronger sense that "controlled"; see Alison, *The Joy of Being Wrong*, 25n8.

110. Palaver, *René Girard's Mimetic Theory*, 229–30.

111. Alison, *The Joy of Being Wrong*, 68.

112. Girard, "Evangelical Subversion of Myth," 42.

113. The 2011 English translation of this phrase is truer to the Latin from the third Eucharistic prayer—*agnoscens Hostiam, cuius voluisti immolatione placari*—but far less pithy: "Recognizing the sacrificial Victim by whose death you willed to reconcile us to yourself."

114. Girard, *Job*, 163.

115. Schneiders, *The Revelatory Text*, 171.

116. Alison radicalizes Girard's take on the verse: "This is not just a particular commandment. It is a reading instruction, a hermeneutical key. Whenever you interpret anything, you can read it two ways: in such a way that your interpretation creates mercy, and in such a way that it creates sacrifice"; see Alison, *Jesus the Forgiving Victim: Listening for the Unheard Voice* (Glenview, IL: Doers, 2013), 380.

117. Steve Moyise, "Quotations," in *New Interpreter's Dictionary of the Bible* (Nashville, TN: Abingdon, 2009), 4:709–10.

118. Girard writes, "The parallel between Oedipus and Job reveals the superiority of the biblical text, for the Bible achieves a truly radical demystification . . . that amounts to the resolution of the enigma that mythology presents to us" (Girard, *Job*, 39).

119. Girard, *Job*, 162.

120. Here it is worth recalling Cyril O'Regan's helpful metaphor of Girard's "bifocal diagnostic apparatus . . . with one lens being anthropological, the other biblical"; O'Regan, "Girard and the Spaces of Apocalyptic," *Modern Theology* 28, no. 1 (2012): 113.

121. Girard, *Things Hidden*, 177. I have slightly amended a mistake in the English translation.

122. Alison returns to this passage repeatedly. For his most detailed exegesis, see Alison, *Jesus the Forgiving Victim*, 43–79.

123. Alison, *Jesus the Forgiving Victim*, 65.

124. Girard, *Things Hidden*, 278.

125. Girard, *I See Satan Fall Like Lightning*, 184.

126. Girard, *Job*, 37.

127. James Alison, *Broken Hearts and New Creations: Intimations of a Great Reversal* (New York: Continuum, 2010), 236. Subsequent pages in Alison's text are extremely instructive on this point.

128. Alison, *Jesus the Forgiving Victim*, esp. 43–79, 135–73.

129. For a negative assessment of the application of mimetic theory to biblical studies, see Robert North, "Violence and the Bible: The Girard Connection," *Catholic Biblical Quarterly* 47 (1985): 1–27; see also several essays in the William Swartley, ed., *Violence Renounced: René Girard's Biblical Studies and Peacemaking* (Telford: Pandora, 2000).

130. Bernard Lonergan, *Method in Theology* (Toronto: University of Toronto Press, 1971), 77.

131. Although this chapter has not explored the phenomenological avenue, the work of Michel Henry and of Jean-Luc Marion, in particular, creates possibilities in this direction. Karl Hefty, a student of Marion's at the University of Chicago, has completed a promising dissertation on the subject. See Hefty, "The God of Appearance" (Ph.D. diss., University of Chicago, 2012).

132. Chris Lawn makes this point in his helpful introduction to Gadamer. See Lawn, *Gadamer: A Guide for the Perplexed* (New York: Continuum, 2006).

Chapter Four

1. Girard, *Things Hidden*, 219.
2. Girard, "Ratzinger Is Right," 42–48.

3. Lucien Scubla, "The Christianity of René Girard and the Nature of Religion," in *Violence and Truth*, ed. Paul Dumouchel (Stanford, CA: Stanford University Press, 1988), 160.

4. Kirwan, *Girard and Theology*, 120.

5. Ninian Smart, "René Girard: Violence and the Sacred," *Religious Studies Review* 63 (1980): 174.

6. Herzog, "Religionstheorie und Theologie René Girards," 121: "Es ist eigenartig, dass Girard die Vorzüge des Christentums anhand der Unterschiede zu den Religionen 'ethnologischer' Gesellschaften exemplifieziert, einem Vergleich mit anderen Hochreligionen jedoch aus dem Wege geht."

7. Jean-Claude Dussault, "René Girard: La revelation évangélique et le bouddhisme," *Sciences Religieuses/Studies in Religion* 10, no. 1 (1981): 59–66.

8. Ibid., 60.

9. Leo Lefebure, *Revelation, the Religions, and Violence* (New York: Orbis, 2000), 162–64.

10. Ibid., 22.

11. See Leo Lefebure, "Buddhism and Mimetic Theory: A Response to Christopher Ives," *Contagion* 9 (2002): 177. For Lefebure's earliest engagement with Girard, see Lefebure, "Mimesis, Violence and Socially Engaged Buddhism: Overture to a Dialogue," *Contagion* 3 (1996): 122–40; Lefebure repeats the second half of this quotation in *Revelation, the Religions, and Violence*, 162.

12. Mark I. Wallace, "Postmodern Biblicism: The Challenge of René Girard for Contemporary Theology," *Modern Theology* 5, no. 4 (1989): 318.

13. The proceedings have been published in *Contagion* 9 (2002) under the editorship of Robert J. Daly.

14. Robert Daly generously shared with me his unpublished paper from the Berkeley conference, which summarized the central points made at the Boston College COV&R.

15. Kirwan, "Chapter 11: Girard and the Religions," in *Girard and Theology*, 120–31.

16. See Wolfgang Palaver, "A Letter from the President," *Bulletin of the Colloquium on Violence & Religion* 38 (May 2011): 4 (hereafter *Bulletin*); cited in Goodhart, "Letter from the President: 'Navigating Fateful Passages,'" *Bulletin* 30 (2007): 5.

17. "Discussion Summary," *Contagion* 9 (2002): 149.

18. Robert Hamerton-Kelly, "Response to Qamar-ul Huda," *Contagion* 9 (2002): 99.

19. Girard, *Evolution and Conversion*, 212.

20. Ibid., 213–14.

21. Its translation appeared in 2011: Girard, *Sacrifice*, trans. Matthew Pattillo and David Dawson (East Lansing: Michigan State University Press, 2011).

22. Girard, *Sacrifice*, 9–10. Girard uses the selective anthology of these texts edited by Sylvian Lévi, *La Doctrine du sacrifice dans les Brâhmanas* (Paris: Presses Universitaires de France, 1966 [1898]).

23. Ibid., 23.

24. Ibid., 28–29.

25. Lévi, *La Doctrine du sacrifice*, 1301; cited in Girard, *Sacrifice*, 56.

26. Girard, *Sacrifice*, 56.

27. Ibid., 57.

28. Ibid., 92; Girard cites Micah 6:6–7.

29. Grant Kaplan, "Getting History into *Religion*? Appropriating *Nostra Aetate* for the 21st Century," *Heythrop Journal* 52 (2011): 802–21.

30. Pope Benedict XVI used this phrase at the end of the 2006 "Regensburg Lecture."

31. Charles Mabee, "Dispatch from the Girardian Boundary," in *For René Girard: Essays in Friendship and Truth*, ed. Sandor Goodhart et al. (East Lansing: Michigan State University Press, 2009), 212.

32. Girard, *Evolution and Conversion*, 97.

33. Girard, *Sacrifice*, 33.

34. See Bellah, *Religion in Human Evolution*. This book extends his earlier reflections, first given as a lecture at the University of Chicago in 1963, which was published as "Religious Evolution," in Bellah, *Beyond Belief: Essays on Religion in a Post-Traditional World* (New York: Harper & Row, 1970), 20–50. Bellah's biological history of religion does not include a theological analysis.

35. Girard, *Sacrifice*, 33.

36. Girard, *Evolution and Conversion*, 67.

37. Diamond, *Collapse: How Societies Choose to Fail or Succeed*.

38. Girard, *Battling to the End*, xv. He states later, "Humans cannot control reciprocity because they imitate one another too much and their resemblance to one another increases and accelerates. We have to imagine that *for these very reasons* the first human groups self-destructed" (ibid., 19).

39. Bellah specifically rejects the scapegoat mechanism and sees "ganging up" as a result of weaker males making sure that bullies do not subject them to a domination system (*Religion in Human Evolution*, 175–82). Bellah echoes Johan Huizenga by deriving religious ritual from the "play" instinct. See Huizenga, *Homo Ludens: A Study of the Play Element in Culture* (Boston: Beacon, 1938). Bellah adds, "I think ritual is the primordial form of serious play in human evolutionary history" (*Religion in Human Evolution*, 92).

40. Girard, *Evolution and Conversion*, 72; later Girard writes, "Human culture and humanity itself are religion's children" (ibid., 117); and further, "Humanity results from sacrifice; we are thus the children of religion" (*Battling to the End*, ix).

41. Wilfred Cantwell Smith, *The Meaning and End of Religion* (Minneapolis: Fortress, 1991 [1962]), 18–19.

42. Ibid., 120.

43. For the exception proving the rule, see Brent Nongbri, *Before Religion: A History of a Modern Concept* (New Haven, CT: Yale University Press, 2013).

44. Smith, *Meaning and End of Religion*, 64, 70.

45. Ibid., 124.

46. William Cavanaugh, *The Myth of Religious Violence* (Oxford: Oxford University Press, 2009), esp. chap. 2: "The Invention of Religion." Cavanaugh's treatment of Smith is not uncritical (see ibid., 101–2). For my previous appropriation of Cavanaugh's work, see "Getting History into *Religion*?"; and my "Review," *Theological Studies* 71 (June 2010): 479–81.

47. Cavanaugh, *Myth of Religious Violence*, 81.

48. John Milbank makes the same point: "Once, there was no 'secular.' . . . The *saeculum*, in the medieval era, was not a space, a domain, but a time—the interval between fall and eschaton . . . The secular as a domain had to be instituted or *imagined*, both in theory and in practice"; Milbank, *Theology and Social Theory*, 9.

49. One admiring critic of Smith thinks such a question should have been more at the forefront of Smith's classic. See Talal Asad, "Reading a Modern Classic: W. C. Smith's *The Meaning and End of Religion*," *History of Religions* 40, no. 3 (2001): 205–22, esp. 220–22.

50. For an attempt to align Girard with those theorists of the secular, mainly Hans Blumenberg, Max Weber, Marcel Gauchet, and Charles Taylor, who posit a genetic connection between Christianity and modernity, see Scott Cowdell, *René Girard and Secular Modernity*, 6–14. See also my chapter 6 herein.

51. Indeed, this is one possible (and certainly anticlimactic) conclusion to be drawn from Charles Taylor's magisterial *A Secular Age* (Cambridge, MA: Belknap, 2007).

52. The connection between the Axial and the secular age runs throughout Taylor, *A Secular Age*. It is notable that Taylor and Bellah participated in the same 2008 conference in Erfurt, Germany, on the Axial Age: http://www2.uni-erfurt.de/maxwe/aktuelles/ss08/axial_age_tagung/participants.html (accessed May 7, 2012).

53. Nietzsche continues this understanding. See *Der Antichrist*, secs. 26–27.

54. Girard, *Evolution and Conversion*, 72.

55. Schmidt, "Zuerst kam der Tempel, dann die Stadt. Vorläufiger Bericht zu den Grabungen am Göbekli Tepe und am Gürcütepe 1995–1999," *Istanbuler Mitteilungen* 50 (2000): 5–41.

56. Girard, *Evolution and Conversion*, 97.

57. Ibid., 108.

58. Ibid., 127.

59. Ibid., 83.

60. Girard, *Battling to the End*, x.

61. Ibid., xv.

62. Ibid., 198. The English translation has "The Revelation," which implies the book of Revelation. From the context of the paragraph, this translation makes no sense. After consulting the French original, *Achever Clausewitz: Entretiens avec Benoît Chantre* (Paris: Carnets Nord, 2007), 334, I took the liberty to alter the translation.

63. For a critical appraisal of Girard's relationship to the abovementioned theorists of religion, see John Milbank, "Stories of Sacrifice," 27–56.

64. Girard, *Evolution and Conversion*, 170.

65. Girard, *Battling to the End*, 25.

66. Girard makes this point in several texts. He does so with particular force in *Sacrifice*: "Wherever the Gospels take root, blood sacrifices disappear forever" (*Sacrifice*, 87); and, "Nietzsche's colossal error was not to have seen what the unconscious nature of the scapegoat phenomenon implies for the relation between the mythic and the Biblical. It is sacrificial religions that embody slavery in all its forms, whereas the Biblical and Christian attain a truth and freedom that humans may put to very bad use, certainly, but that frees them from the mythological domination forever" (ibid., 81).

67. Balthasar, *The Action*, 308.

68. Balthasar, "Die neue Theorie von Jesus als dem 'Sündenbock,'" *Communio* 9 (1980): 184–85. The German reads, "einer extremen protestantischen These."

69. Rowan Williams, *Wrestling with Angels: Conversations in Modern Theology*, ed. Mike Higton (Grand Rapids, MI: Eerdmans, 2007), 182.

70. Herzog, "Religionstheorie und Theologie René Girards," 113n33.

71. Roch Kereszty, "A Response to Gil Bailie's 'Girard's Contribution to the Church of the 21st Century,'" *Communio* 26, no. 1 (1999): 216.

72. Karl Barth, "§17: The Revelation of God as the Abolition of Religion," in *Church Dogmatics I/2: The Doctrine of the Word of God* (London: T & T Clark, 2004 [1956]), 299–300.

73. Dietrich Bonhoeffer, *Letters and Papers from Prison: The Enlarged Edition*, ed. Eberhard Bethge (New York: Touchstone, 1953), 280. For the full context, see the April 30, 1944, letter to Bethge, which clarifies Bonhoeffer's debt to Barth. For Smith on dialectical theology, see Smith, *Meaning and End of Religion*, 125.

74. Girard, "Chapter 2: A Non-Sacrificial Reading of the Gospel Text," in *Things Hidden*, 180–223.

75. Girard, *Things Hidden*, 227–31.

76. On this point see Robert Daly, *Sacrifice Unveiled* (New York: T & T Clark, 2010).

77. The definitive treatment of this topic has been given by Mathias Moosbrugger, *Die Rehabilitierung des Opfers*, esp. 13–37, 219–66, 289–342. Girard's first published self-correction came in his interview with Rebecca Adams, "Violence, Difference, Sacrifice," 28. Girard offered a fuller explanation for his shift in his article "Mimetische Theorie und Theologie," in *Vom Fluch und Segen der Sündenböcke: Raymund Schwager zum 60. Geburtstag*, ed. Józef Niewiadomski and Wolfgang Palaver (Vienna: Thaur, 1995), 15–29. See also *Evolution and Conversion*, 215.

78. Girard, *Evolution and Conversion*, 211.

79. Ibid., 215. See also Girard, *Sacrifice*, xi: "If the term *sacrifice* is used for the death of Jesus, it is in a sense absolutely contrary to the archaic sense. Jesus consents to die in order to reveal the lie of blood sacrifices and to render them henceforth impossible."

80. Girard, *Evolution and Conversion*, 216–17.

81. Girard and Vattimo, *Christianity, Truth, and Weakening Faith*, 29.

82. Girard, *Battling to the End*, 173.

83. Girard and Vattimo, *Christianity, Truth, and Weakening Faith*, 23–24.

84. Girard, *Battling to the End*, 21.

85. Girard and Vattimo, *Christianity, Truth, and Weakening Faith*, 25.

86. Kirwan, *Girard and Theology*, 140–41.

87. Paul Valadier, "Bouc émissaire et revelation chrétienne selon René Girard," *Études* 357 (1982): 259.

88. Girard, *Battling to the End*, 35.

89. This referent is clearly the last section of Hegel's *Phenomenology of Spirit*, "Das absolute Wissen."

90. Girard, *Battling to the End*, 35.

91. Ibid., 44.

92. Although known more as a follower of Lonergan and Ernest Becker than as a disciple of Girard, Moore's final book, *The Contagion of Jesus*, ed. Stephen McCarthy (Maryknoll, NY: Orbis, 2007), makes explicit his debt and devotion to Girard, especially as filtered through James Alison. Of a piece written in 2003, the editor McCarthy notes, "By this time [Moore] had discovered the enormous contribution of René Girard" (ibid., 20). In the introduction, Moore himself writes, "Then there is James Alison, to whom I owe so much of my present mind inspired by the genius of Girard. . . . When I get depressed about the Church, I have only to think of James" (ibid., xii).

93. Sebastian Moore, *The Crucified Jesus Is No Stranger* (New York: Paulist, 1977).

94. Moore, *The Fire and the Rose Are One* (New York: Seabury, 1980), 141.

95. Ibid., 141–42. What Moore says can also be found in James Alison, *Broken Hearts and New Creations*, 56: "By our preaching or teaching we are not merely supposed to be passing on ideas, or information. We are attempting to get across that a Happening has irrupted into our world; that It matters; that we are at last beginning to find ourselves altered by exposure to this Happening; and that therefore at least part of the truth of what we are talking about should be able to be detected in the way we are undergoing something." See also Alison, *Undergoing God* (New York: Continuum, 2007).

96. As Moosbrugger shows, such a reconciliation was the driving force behind the theological project of Raymund Schwager, especially in *Jesus in the Drama of Salvation: Toward a Biblical Doctrine of Redemption*, trans. James Williams and Paul Haddon (New York: Herder & Herder, 1999). See Moosbrugger, *Die Rehabilitierung des Opfers*, esp. 318–54.

97. Girard, *Evolution and Conversion*, 214. This citation helps reconcile more recent remarks by Girard, which seem to contradict his "evolved" theology of religion and would indicate no advance at all from his "early" intolerant-sounding position.

98. Fr. Francis Clooney generously shared with me his notes from the meeting, whose proceedings are not published.

99. I come to a similar conclusion in Kaplan, "Getting History into *Religion?*" 820–21.

100. Girard, *Battling to the End*, 206.

101. This point deepens Cyril O'Regan's insight that Girard's eschatology shares its greatest overlap with the underrated eschatology of Pope Benedict. See O'Regan, "Girard and the Spaces of Apocalyptic," 125–31.

102. Girard, *Battling to the End*, 207; emphasis mine.

Chapter Five

1. Although only anecdotal, Jeffrey Bethke's "spoken word" that contrasts religion and Jesus, had received more than 29 million views and 195,000 since it was uploaded to YouTube in 2012. See Bethke, "Why I Hate Religion, but Love Jesus," at https://www.youtube.com/watch?v=1IAhDGYlpqY (accessed April 13, 2015). The popularity of this video attests to a strong objection to ecclesial institutions among people not necessarily opposed to religious truth.

2. For this point, see Hermann Josef Pottmeyer, "Die Frage nach der wahren Kirche," in *Handbuch der Fundamentaltheologie. 3 Traktat: Kirche* (Freiburg: Herder, 1985), 214, 223.

3. Many of the authors cited in this section refer to the syllogistic logic behind the *via notarum*. Pottmeyer provides the clearest exposition ("Die Frage nach der wahren Kirche," 224).

4. Francis A. Sullivan, "Church V: Notes of the Church," in *Dictionary of Fundamental Theology*, ed. René Latourelle and Rino Fisichella (New York: Crossroad, 1994), 172.

5. Salvador Pié-Ninot, "Church I: Fundamental Ecclesiology," in Latourelle and Fisichella, *Dictionary of Fundamental Theology*, 143.

6. Dulles, "The Church: Sacrament and Ground of Faith," in *Problems and Perspectives of Fundamental Theology*,259.

7. See, for instance, Hermann Dieckmann's *De Ecclesia* (Freiburg im Breisgau: Herder, 1925). The reference to Dieckmann comes from Pié-Ninot, "Church IV: Via Empirica," in *Dictionary of Fundamental Theology*, 170. Pottmeyer too connects the moral miracle (*moralisches Wunder*) with the *demonstratio christiana* ("Die Frage nach der wahren Kirche," 214).

8. Pié-Ninot, "Church I: Fundamental Ecclesiology," 143.

9. Cited from Heinrich Denzinger and Peter Hünermann, eds., *Enchiridion Symbolorum: definitionum et declarationum de rebus fidei et morum*, sec. 3009.

10. Ibid., secs. 3013–14.

11. The Latin reads "*quasi concreta divina revelatio*"; see *Sacrorum conciliorum nova et amplissima collectio*, ed. Mansi (Paris: H. Welter, 1901–1927), 51:314; cited in Pottmeyer, "Die Frage nach der wahren Kirche," 226.

12. Denzinger and Hünermann, *Enchiridion Symbolorum*, sec. 3014. Canon 6 of chapter 3 follows this claim more forcefully and redoubles its critique of those who have received the faith yet choose doubt over belief.

13. Dulles, "The Church: Sacrament and Ground of Faith," 260. To this point Francis Sullivan contributes, "The far-reaching advances made in biblical, patristic, and historical studies have led to increasing dissatisfaction with the use of the sources that was characteristic of the apologetic method. As more light came to be shed on the early church, it became increasingly evident that Catholic apologists had only too easily been finding in those sources what they wanted to find rather than what was objectively there. The weakness of the 'proof-text' use of the sources became more and more apparent" ("Church V: Notes of the Church," 173).

14. Dulles, "The Church: Sacrament and Ground of Faith," 261.

15. René Latourelle, "Church III: Motive of Credibility," in *Dictionary of Fundamental Theology*, 155.

16. Ibid., 155–56.

17. Grant Kaplan, "What Has Ethics to Do with Rhetoric? Prolegomena to Any Future Just War Theory," *Political Theology* 6, no. 1 (2005): 44.

18. Sullivan, "Church V: Notes of the Church," 171–72.

19. Fries, *Fundamental Theology*, 618.

20. Pottmeyer, "Die Frage nach der wahren Kirche," 212.

21. Fries, *Fundamental Theology*, 619.

22. *Lumen gentium*, sec. 1. The Latin reads, "*Ecclesia sit in Christo veluti sacramentum seu signum et instrumentum.*"

23. See *Lumen gentium*, secs. 9, 48; *Gaudium et spes*, secs. 42, 45; *Sacrosanctum concilium*, secs. 5, 26; *Ad gentes*, secs. 1, 5. This list derives from Walter Kasper, *Theology and Church*, trans. Margaret Kohl (New York: Crossroad, 1989), 113.

24. Kasper, *Theology and Church*, 117–18. Kasper here relies on Karl Rahner (ibid., 219n21; see Rahner, "The Concept of Mystery in Catholic Theology," in *Theological Investigations*, 4:36–73.

25. Pié-Ninot, "Church IV: Via Empirica," 170.

26. Sullivan, "Church V: Notes of the Church," 174.

27. Ibid.

28. Dulles, "The Church: Sacrament and Ground of Faith," 270.

29. Latourelle, "Church III: Motive of Credibility," 167.

30. Ibid. Dulles adds that certain apologetic styles "have left unexplained the presence of sin and weakness in the Church, and its capacity to become, in many respects, a *countersign*" ("The Church: Sacrament and Ground of Faith," 269; emphasis mine).

31. Latourelle, "Church III: Motive of Credibility," 169.

32. Ibid., 169.

33. Many people experience this countersign when hearing arguments from Church officials that come across more as untruth than truth.

34. Dulles, "The Church: Sacrament and Ground of Faith," 268.

35. Ibid., 270.

36. John Dadosky develops this idea most explicitly in three articles: Dadosky, "The Church and the Other: Mediation and Friendship in Post-Vatican II Roman Catholic Ecclesiology," *Pacifica* 18 (2005): 302–22; Dadosky, "Towards a Fundamental Theological RE-Interpretation of Vatican II," *Heythrop Journal* 49 (2008): 742–63; Dadosky, "Has Vatican II Been *Hermeneutered*? Recovering and Developing Its Theological Achievements following Rahner and Lonergan," *Irish Theological Quarterly* 79, no. 4 (2014): 327–49.

37. On this convergence see Richard Gaillardetz, "The 'Francis Moment': A New Kairos for Catholic Ecclesiology," *Catholic Theological Society of America Proceedings* 69 (2014): 64. Dadosky makes the same point about the Extraordinary Synod in "Has Vatican II Been *Hermeneutered*?" 328; "Towards a RE-Interpretation of Vatican II," 745.

38. Dadosky, "Towards a RE-Interpretation of Vatican II," 745.

39. Ibid., 746. All of Dadosky's articles on this topic reflect the difference between the Church and the Other. For Dadosky's most extended meditation on the nature of friendship, see Dadosky, "The Church and the Other," 316.

40. Dadosky, "Has Vatican II Been *Hermeneutered?*" 337.

41. Gaillardetz, "The 'Francis Moment,'" 65.

42. For an accessible collection of these speeches, see Pope Francis, *The Church of Mercy: A Vision for the Church* (Chicago: Loyola Press, 2014). The section titled "To Be a Pastor" relates: "In the homily in the Chrism Mass this year, I said that pastors must have 'the odor of sheep.' Be pastors with the odor of the sheep . . . Your presence is not secondary; it is indispensable." In his apostolic exhortation *Evangelii gaudium*, Pope Francis declared: "Evangelizers thus take on the 'smell of the sheep'" (sec. 24).

43. See Pope Francis, *Evangelii gaudium*, secs. 40–49; this summary comes from Walter Kasper, *Pope Francis' Revolution of Tenderness and Love*, trans. William Madges (New York: Paulist, 2015), 44.

44. Gaillardetz, "The 'Francis Moment,'" 69; Kasper, *Pope Francis' Revolution of Tenderness and Love*, 41.

45. Girard, *The One by Whom Scandal Comes*, 78.

46. Moore, *The Crucified Jesus Is No Stranger*, 8–9.

47. Alison, *Faith beyond Resentment: Fragments Catholic and Gay* (New York: Crossroad, 2001), 32.

48. Alison, *Knowing Jesus*, 82.

49. Ibid., 16.

50. The difference between being loved and being liked forms the central theme of Alison's *On Being Liked* (New York: Crossroad, 2004). Alison also concludes *Jesus the Forgiving Victim* with this distinction (563–64).

51. Alison, *Knowing Jesus*, 90–91; emphasis mine.

52. Which is not to say that one must name it as a grace; Paul describes this very reality when he writes: "We have not received the spirit of the world but the Spirit of God, so that we may understand the things freely given us by God" (1 Cor. 2:12).

53. Alison, *Knowing Jesus*, 91.

54. Alison, *Jesus the Forgiving Victim*, 308–9. Later in the same essay he bemoans the decoupling of soteriology and ecclesiology: "So many of us think of belonging to the Church and being forgiven as two quite separate things" (ibid., 337–38).

55. James Alison, *Raising Abel: The Recovery of the Eschatological Imagination* (New York: Crossroad, 1996), 96.

56. Alison, *The Joy of Being Wrong*, 88.

57. Alison, *Knowing Jesus*, 82.

58. Ibid., 90.

59. Alison, *Undergoing God*, 170.

60. Alison, *Knowing Jesus*, 78–80; Alison, *Raising Abel*, 100–109; Alison, *Jesus the Forgiving Victim*, 317–27.

61. Alison, *Raising Abel*, 101; Alison, *Jesus the Forgiving Victim*, 317.

62. Alison, *Raising Abel*, 108. See also Alison, *The Joy of Being Wrong*, 178–81.

63. Alison, *On Being Liked*, 114–30.

64. Ibid., 25.

65. Ibid., 125; emphasis mine.

66. Ibid., 126.

67. Ibid., 115.

68. Alison, *Undergoing God*, 44.

69. Alison, *Faith beyond Resentment*, 121.

70. Ibid., 122.

71. Ibid.

72. Ibid.

73. Alison, *On Being Liked*, 79, 83. Since the 2001 publication of *Faith beyond Resentment*, Alison has identified as gay in his theological writings.

74. Ibid., 84.

75. *Faith beyond Resentment*, 45.

76. Ibid., 46.

77. Ibid., 47.

78. Ibid., 49.

79. Alison, *Broken Hearts*, 260.

80. Alison, *Undergoing God*, 38.

81. Ibid., 39. Elsewhere Alison uses the phrase "creative protagonism," which we can learn from Jesus (*Broken Hearts*, 258).

82. It is also clear for St. Paul that reconciliation possesses incredible power to form community. See 2 Cor. 5:16–21, especially the phrases "ministry of reconciliation" and "message of reconciliation" (5:18, 19).

Chapter Six

1. Let me take a stab at this canon: Karl Löwith, *Meaning in History: The Theological Implications of the Modern Age* (Chicago: University of Chicago Press, 1949), Hans Blumenberg, *The Legitimacy of the Modern Age*, trans. Robert Wallace (Cambridge: MIT Press, 1983; German orig. in 1966), Stephen Toulmin, *Cosmopolis: The Hidden Agenda of Modernity* (Chicago: University of Chicago

Press, 1990), John Milbank, *Theology and Social Theory*, Louis Dupré, *Passage to Modernity: An Essay in the Hermeneutics of Nature and Culture* (New Haven, CT: Yale University Press, 1993), Michael Allen Gillespie, *The Theological Origins of Modernity* (Chicago: University of Chicago Press, 2008), and, of course, Charles Taylor, *A Secular Age*. More recent entries come from Thomas Pfau, *Minding the Modern: Human Agency, Intellectual Tradition, and Responsible Knowledge* (Notre Dame, IN: University of Notre Dame Press, 2013), and Brad Gregory, *The Unintended Reformation* (treated herein). For a recent critique of the genealogical genre, I recommend Frederick C. Bauerschmidt, "Shaving Ockham," *Commonweal* 142, no. 3 (2015): 32–35.

2. For an influential twentieth-century account, see Hans Urs von Balthasar, *A Theology of History* (San Francisco: Ignatius, 1994).

3. The classic juxtaposition of Augustine and Eusebius can be found in Erik Peterson, "Monotheism as a Political Problem," in *Theological Tractates*, trans. Michael J. Hollerich (Stanford, CA: Stanford University Press, 2011), 68–105, 203–34. See also Chad Pecknold, *Christianity and Politics: A Brief Guide to the History* (Eugene, OR: Cascade, 2010), 37–50.

4. See Charles Taylor, "A Catholic Modernity?" in *A Catholic Modernity? Charles Taylor's Marianist Award Lecture*, ed. James L. Heft (Oxford: Oxford University Press, 1999), 36. He uses the same language of "boosters" and "knockers" in Taylor, *The Ethics of Authenticity* (Cambridge, MA: Harvard University Press, 1991), 11. Taylor returns to this theme in the epilogue to *A Secular Age*, where he argues, not surprisingly, that his own account, though compatible with Milbank's story of modernity as "Intellectual Deviation," is able to explain the rise of modern secularism more comprehensively (*A Secular Age*, 773–76). See also, *A Secular Age*, 637: "Some think that the whole move to secular humanism was just a mistake, which needs to be undone. We need to return to an earlier view of things. Others, in which I place myself, think that . . . there is some truth in the self-narrative of the Enlightenment: this gain was in fact unlikely to come about without some breach with established religion."

5. Jonathan Israel, *Radical Enlightenment: Philosophy and the Making of Modernity 1650–1750* (Oxford: Oxford University Press, 2001); Israel, *Enlightenment Contested: Philosophy, Modernity, and the Emancipation of Man 1670–1752* (Oxford: Oxford University Press, 2006); Israel, *Democratic Enlightenment: Philosophy, Revolution, and Human Rights, 1750–1790* (Oxford: Oxford University Press, 2011); for a more manageable, one-volume overview of the project, see Israel, *A Revolution of the Mind: Radical Enlightenment and the Intellectual Origins of Modern Democracy* (Oxford: Oxford University Press, 2010).

6. Israel, *Enlightenment Contested*, 10.

7. Ibid.

8. Ibid., 870; the reference is to Bernard Williams, *Truth and Truthfulness* (Princeton, NJ: Princeton University Press, 2002), 254.

9. See Alasdair MacIntyre, *After Virtue: A Study in Moral Theory* (Notre Dame, IN: University of Notre Dame Press, 1981).

10. See Leo Strauss, *Natural Right and History* (Chicago: University of Chicago Press, 1953). One could also include Eric Voegelin in this group. See, in particular, the collection of essays in Voegelin, *Modernity without Restraint*, ed. Manfred Henningson (Columbia: University of Missouri Press, 2000). For a helpful effort to bring Strauss and Voegelin into conversation with Girard, see John Ranieri, *Disturbing Revelation: Leo Strauss, Eric Voegelin, and the Bible*.

11. John Milbank, "Knowledge: The Theological Critique of Philosophy in Hamann and Jacobi," in *Radical Orthodoxy: A New Theology*, ed. John Milbank, Catherine Pickstock, and Graham Ward (London: Routledge, 1999), 23–24. Scotists, not surprisingly, have attempted to correct Milbank and his followers. For a recent effort at correction, see Dan Horan, *Postmodernity and Univocity: A Critical Account of Radical Orthodoxy and John Duns Scotus* (Minneapolis: Fortress, 2014).

12. Milbank, "Knowledge," 32.

13. David Bentley Hart, "Christ and Nothing," *First Things* 136 (October 2003): 55.

14. Lonergan, *Method in Theology*, 236. For a fuller development of this theme, see the essay, Lonergan, "Sacralization and Secularization," in *Philosophical and Theological Papers: 1965–1980* (Toronto: University of Toronto Press, 2004), 259–81. I owe this reference to an essay, which in many ways overlaps with the themes in this chapter, by Randy Rosenberg, "The Catholic Imagination and Modernity: William Cavanaugh's Theopolitical Imagination and Charles Taylor's Modern Social Imagination," *Heythrop Journal* 48 (2007): 912.

15. Lonergan, *Method in Theology*, 236.

16. Cowdell, *René Girard and Secular Modernity*, 169.

17. Taylor, *A Secular Age*, 146–58; Taylor, *Modern Social Imaginaries* (Durham, NC: Duke University Press, 2004), 49–67.

18. Taylor, *A Secular Age*, 792. See Karl Jaspers, *Vom Ursprung und Ziel der Geschichte* (Zürich: Artemis, 1949). Taylor also relies on Robert Bellah in regard to pre-Axial religion; see Bellah's essay, "Religious Evolution," in *Beyond Belief*, 25–32.

19. Taylor, *A Secular Age*, 147.

20. Taylor, *Modern Social Imaginaries*, 54.

21. Ibid., 150.

22. Taylor does not adopt Jaspers wholesale (see *A Secular Age*, 792). What matters is not so much the dating, but the break between the two religious systems. For Taylor's qualifications, see *A Secular Age*, 438–45.

23. Taylor, *Modern Social Imaginaries*, 151.

24. For Girard on Rousseau, see Girard, *Evolution and Conversion*, 187–88.

25. Girard, *When These Things Begin*, 25.

26. Girard, *Evolution and Conversion*, 72.

27. Girard, "Discussion," in *Violent Origins*, 125.

28. Ibid.

29. Girard, *Violence and the Sacred*, 259.

30. Girard, *The Scapegoat*, 114.

31. Charles Taylor, *Sources of the Self: The Making of the Modern Identity* (Cambridge, MA: Harvard University Press, 1989), 129.

32. Ibid., 230.

33. Ibid., 231.

34. For his treatment of the Christian reform efforts in *A Secular Age*, see chap. 2, "The Rise of the Disciplinary Society," 90–145.

35. Ibid., 94.

36. This spirit of "making all things new" forms the central organizing theme of a delightful and underappreciated book by George Herring, *Introduction to the History of Christianity* (New York: New York University Press, 2006).

37. Taylor, *A Secular Age*, 158; 739–42.

38. Ibid., 17.

39. Ibid.; see also Taylor, "A Catholic Modernity?" 30.

40. In this respect Girard's account seems incompatible with the more inclusive Axial approach of Taylor.

41. Girard, *The Scapegoat*, 117.

42. For Taylor on "intellectual deviation," see *A Secular Age*, 773–76.

43. Gregory, *The Unintended Reformation*.

44. See Brad Gregory, "Genre, Method, and Assumptions," *The Imminent Frame*, January 21, 2014, http://blogs.ssrc.org/tif/2014/01/21/genre-method -and-assumptions/ (accessed February 8, 2014). The journals that have sponsored these forums are *Historically Speaking*, *Church History*, *The Catholic Historical Review*, and *Pro Ecclesia*.

45. Gillespie, *Theological Origins of Modernity*, 11.

46. Of the prominent genealogists, Blumenberg seems most inclined to take this path.

47. Taylor, *A Secular Age*, 1–3.

48. Ibid., 3.

49. Taylor, *Sources of the Self*, 402–3.

50. Taylor, "A Catholic Modernity?" 26.

51. Taylor, *A Secular Age*, 816n6; Max Weber, *The Protestant Ethic and the Spirit of Capitalism*, trans. Talcott Parsons (New York: Scribner, 1958), esp. 105; Marcel Gauchet, *Le désenchantement du monde* (Paris: Gallimard, 1985).

52. Taylor, *A Secular Age*, 38.

53. Ibid., 37.

54. Ibid., 38.

55. It should be pointed out that mimetic theory offers some pushback on the buffered self, precisely because of human interdividuality. Scott Cowdell's brief comparison of Taylor and Girard makes this point; see Cowdell, *René Girard and Secular Modernity*, 11.

56. Taylor, "A Catholic Modernity?" 31.

57. Taylor, *Sources of the Self*, 319; emphasis mine.

58. It should be noted that Taylor's take on modernity is more dialectical in the final, twentieth chapter of *A Secular Age*, "Conversions." Although it is not clear whether he speaks from his own voice, or for Ivan Illich, Taylor declares, "Corrupted Christianity gives rise to the modern" (740).

59. Taylor, "A Catholic Modernity?" 16.

60. Ibid.

61. This concession comes in response to a point raised by Gianni Vattimo. See Girard, *Evolution and Conversion*, 234, 262n1. In their published dialogue, Vattimo stated: "The key term that I began using after having read Girard is just that: *secularization*, which I take to mean the effective realization of Christianity as a nonsacrificial religion . . . Ultimately, Christianity is the religion that opens the way to an existence not strictly religious" (Girard and Vattimo, *Christianity, Truth, and Weakening Faith*, 28).

62. Girard and Vattimo, *Christianity, Truth, and Weakening Faith*, 22–23.

63. See Girard, "The Modern Concern for Victims," in *I See Satan Fall Like Lightning*, 161.

64. Girard, *Evolution and Conversion*, 246.

65. Ibid., 258.

66. Ibid., 239.

67. Michael Buckley, *At the Origins of Modern Atheism* (New Haven, CT: Yale University Press, 1987), 347.

68. Girard, *The Scapegoat*, 204.

69. Ibid.

70. Girard, *When These Things Begin*, 52.

71. Taylor defines the immanent frame as a set of preconditions or unchallenged framework, a "sensed context in which we develop our beliefs." In the case of modernity, it is an immanent order made possible by such factors as disenchantment (*A Secular Age*, 539–93, esp. 549).

72. Taylor, *A Secular Age*, 744: "The spiritual advent, not of the self-centered ego, but of the creative subjectivity." The French comes from Jean-Luc Barré, *Jacques et Raïssa Maritain* (Paris: Stock, 1997), 398.

73. Taylor, *A Secular Age*, 755.

74. Ibid., 772.

75. Cowdell, *René Girard and Secular Modernity*, 10–14.

76. Ibid., 12.

77. Girard, *Battling to the End*, x.

78. Girard, *I See Satan Fall Like Lightning*, 178, 179.

Chapter Seven

1. Henri de Lubac, *The Drama of Atheist Humanism* (San Francisco: Ignatius, 1995; French original, 1944).

2. De Lubac, "The Spiritual Battle," in *Drama of Atheist Humanism*, 113, 114.

3. See Buckley, *At the Origins of Modern Atheism*; Buckley, *Denying and Disclosing God: The Ambiguous Progress and Modern Atheism* (New Haven, CT: Yale University Press, 2004); Buckley, "The Study of Religion and the Rise of Atheism: Conflict or Confirmation?" in *Fields of Faith: Theology and Religious Studies for the Twenty-first Century*, ed. David Ford, Ben Quash, and Janet Soskice (Cambridge: Cambridge University Press, 2005), 3–24; Buckley, "Modernity and the Satanic Face of God," in *Christian Spirituality and the Culture of Modernity: The Thought of Louis Dupré*, ed. Peter Casarella and George Schner (Grand Rapids, MI: Eerdmans, 1998), 100–122; Buckley, "The Rise of Modern Atheism and the Religious Époche," *CTSA Proceedings* 47 (1992): 69–93; Buckley, "Experience and Culture: A Point of Departure for American Atheism," *Theological Studies* 50 (1989): 443–65; Buckley, "Atheism and Contemplation," *Theological Studies* 40 (1979): 680–99.

4. James Force, "The Origins of Modern Atheism," *Journal of the History of Ideas* 50, no. 4 (1989): 153.

5. John Milbank, "Review," *Modern Theology* 8, no. 1 (1992): 90, 92.

6. Taylor, *A Secular Age*, 295, 225, 328.

7. Gavin Hyman, "Atheism in Modern History," in *The Cambridge Companion to Atheism*, ed. Michael Martin (Cambridge: Cambridge University Press, 2007), 27–46.

8. Buckley, "Atheism: I. Origins," in *Dictionary of Fundamental Theology*, 49. George H. Smith makes the same point: "Since an atheist is a person who does not believe in any god or number of gods, how we define atheist will depend on how we define the word *god*"; Smith, *Why Atheism* (Amherst, NY: Prometheus, 2000), 19.

9. Buckley, *At the Origins of Modern Atheism*, 338.

10. Ibid., 16.

11. Ibid., 346.

12. Buckley, *Denying and Disclosing God*, 1.

13. Ibid., 2.

14. Ibid., 33.

15. Ibid., 36.

16. Buckley, "Chapter 5: Atheism as the System of Nature," in *At the Origins*, 251–321.

17. Buckley, *At the Origins*, 286.

18. Paul d'Holbach, *Système de nature, ou Des lois du monde Physique et du monde moral* (London, 1771), 143; cited in Buckley, *At the Origins*, 304.

19. Buckley, *Denying and Disclosing God*, 84.

20. Ibid., 84.

21. Ibid., 109.

22. Ibid., xv.

23. Ibid., 160n46.

24. Ibid., 114.

25. Ibid., 119.

26. Ibid., 121.

27. Girard, *Battling to the End*, 198.

28. For a treatment focusing on the New Atheism and mimetic theory, see my chapter, "The New Atheism: Dawkins, Harris, Hitchens," in *Handbook of Mimetic Theory and Religion*, ed. Wolfgang Palaver and James Alison (Palgrave Macmillan, forthcoming).

29. Christopher Hitchens, *God Is Not Great: How Religion Poisons Everything* (New York: Twelve, 2007), 211.

30. Girard, *Battling to the End*, xiii–xiv.

31. Ibid., xvi.

32. Buckley, *At the Origins*, 15.

33. Girard, *Battling to the End*, 131.

34. Girard and Vattimo, *Christianity, Truth, and Weakening Faith*, 29.

35. See, for just one example, Justin Martyr's *First Apology*, chap. 6: "Thus we are even called atheists"; see Saint Justin Martyr, *The First Apology, the Second Apology, Dialogue with Trypho, Exhortation to the Greeks, Discourse to the Greeks, the Monarchy, or the Rule of God*, ed. Thomas Falls (Washington, DC: Catholic University of America Press, 1948), 38.

36. Thus among the "four horseman" one finds nary a concern that one could come to worship science, in the sense of placing one's hopes and dreams in the hands of scientists and scientific ideology. On this danger, see Mary Midgley, *Science as Salvation: A Modern Myth and Its Meaning* (London: Routledge, 1992).

37. Girard, *Job: The Victim of His People*, trans. Yvonne Freccero (Stanford, CA: Stanford University Press, 1987).

38. Girard, *When These Things Begin: Conversations with Michel Treguer*, trans. Trevor Cribben Merrill (East Lansing: Michigan State University Press, 2014), 30.

39. Ibid., 30.

40. James Alison, *Undergoing God: Dispatches from the Scene of a Break-in* (New York: Continuum, 2006), 18.

41. No reference to Girard, or any similar defense of Christianity, is found in *The Portable Atheist: Essential Readings for the Nonbeliever*, ed. Christopher Hitchens (Philadelphia: De Capo, 2007). John Caputo's chapter, "Atheism, A/theology, and the Postmodern Condition," in *The Cambridge Companion to Atheism*, 267–82, is the only essay in the collection that comes close to doing so by pointing out the common ground shared by Christianity and atheism.

42. David Hart makes this point when discussing contemporary debates about God: "I have come to the conclusion that, while there has been a great deal of public debate about belief in God in recent years, the concept of God around which the arguments have run their seemingly interminable courses has remained strangely obscure the whole time. The more scrutiny one accords these debates, moreover, the more evident it becomes that often the contending parties are not even talking about the same thing; and I would go as far as to say that on most occasions none of them is talking about God in any coherent sense at all. It is not obvious to me, therefore, that their differences really amount to a meaningful disagreement, as one cannot really have a disagreement without some prior agreement as to what the basic issue of contention is"; see Hart, *The Experience of God: Being, Consciousness, Bliss* (New Haven, CT: Yale University Press, 2013), 1–2.

43. Girard, *Battling to the End*, x.

44. Hart, *Atheist Delusions: The Christian Revolution and Its Fashionable Enemies* (New Haven, CT: Yale University Press, 2009), 9–10.

45. Hitchens, *God Is Not Great*, 114, 173–76.

46. This point is not at all original, and the major theological responses to the New Atheism noted as much. Besides Hart's *Atheist Delusions*, see John Haught, *God and the New Atheism: A Critical Response to Dawkins, Harris, and Hitchens* (Louisville, KY: Westminster John Knox, 2008); Alister McGrath, *The Dawkins Delusion: Atheist Fundamentalism and the Denial of the Divine* (Downers Grove, IL: Intervarsity, 2008).

47. Girard's first extensive engagement with Nietzsche came in "Strategies of Madness—Nietzsche, Wagner, and Dostoevski," *Modern Language Notes* 91 (1976): 1161–85. The essay was reprinted in *"To Double Business Bound": Essays*

on Literature, Mimesis, and Anthropology (Baltimore: Johns Hopkins University Press, 1978), 61–83. Girard, "Dionysus versus the Crucified," 816–35; reprinted as "Nietzsche versus the Crucified," in *The Girard Reader*, ed. James G. Williams (New York: Crossroad, 1996), 243–61; Girard, "Nietzsche and Contradiction," *Stanford Italian Review* 1 (1986): 53–65; Girard, "The Founding Murder in the Philosophy of Nietzsche," in *Violence and Truth*, ed. Paul Dumouchel (Stanford, CA: Stanford University Press, 1988), 227–46; Girard, "The Twofold Nietzschean Heritage," in *I See Satan Fall Like Lightning*, trans. James G. Williams (Maryknoll, NY: Orbis, 2001), 170–81. References to Nietzsche appear frequently in Girard's corpus. For a recent overview of Girard on Nietzsche, see Chris Fleming and John O'Carroll, "Nietzsche, the Last Atheist," in *Violence, Desire, and the Sacred: Girard's Mimetic Theory across the Disciplines*, ed. Cowdell, Fleming, and Hodge (New York: Continuum, 2012), 227–50.

48. Girard, *When These Things Begin*, 134. Girard is referring to the aphorism that begins, "Dionysus versus the 'Crucified': there you have the antithesis."

49. It should be noted that at the "Theological Roundtable" at the July 2015 Colloquium on Violence & Religion, Hart declared, in the context of affirming his appreciation for Girard, that his debt might be greater than admitted in his writings.

50. Hart, *Atheist Delusions*, 5–6.

51. Hart, *The Beauty of the Infinite: The Aesthetics of Christian Truth* (Grand Rapids, MI: Eerdmans, 2003), 93–125; for a more condensed version of his treatment of Nietzsche, see Hart, "Christ and Nothing," *First Things* 136 (October 2003): 47–57.

52. Hart, *Beauty of the Infinite*, 94.

53. Milbank, *Theology and Social Theory: Beyond Secular Reason* (Oxford: Blackwell, 1990), 288, 389. Hart cites this phrase, calling it "one of Milbank's more tersely epigrammatic points" (Hart, *Beauty of the Infinite*, 116n134).

54. Hart, *Atheist Delusions*, 130.

55. Hart, *Beauty of the Infinite*, 98.

56. Ibid., 115.

57. It is also obvious that he plays it well, as evidenced by his surging popularity. When I checked in 2014, *The Experience of God* was the number one seller in two different categories on Amazon.com.

58. Hart, *Beauty of the Infinite*, 108–9.

59. Ibid., 125.

60. Ibid., 116.

61. Ibid.

62. Girard notes, "Three quarters of what I say is in Saint Augustine" (*When These Things Begin*, 133).

63. Hart, *Beauty of the Infinite*, 116.

64. Nietzsche, *The Antichrist*, sec. 15. Here and below I cite the Hollingdale translation: *Twilight of the Idols and The Anti-Christ* (New York: Penguin Classics, 1990).

65. Ibid., sec. 47.

66. Hart, *Beauty of the Infinite*, 117.

67. Girard, "Strategies of Madness," in *"To Double Business Bound,"* 80; see also Girard, "Nietzsche and Contradiction," 64.

68. For Girard, Nietzsche is the epitome of the "Romantic" writer: "Nietzsche is fundamentally what I would call a 'romantic' writer, and writing for him is an instrument of repression" (Girard, "Nietzsche and Contradiction," 59).

69. Giuseppe Fornari also performs a mimetic reading of Nietzsche, including a chapter on Nietzsche's relationship with Wagner within the framework of mimetic theory; see Fornari, *A God Torn to Pieces: The Nietzsche Case*, trans. Keith Buck (East Lansing: Michigan State University Press, 2013), esp. 25–51.

70. Girard, "Strategies of Madness," 63.

71. Ibid., 64.

72. Cited from Fornari, *A God Torn to Pieces*, 111.

73. By aligning Girard with Fornari, I rebut a recent effort that puts the two in greater contrast: Martino Pesenti Gritti, "Nietzsche's Double Binds: Giuseppe Fornari and René Girard on Nietzsche's Thought," *Contagion* 20, no. 1 (2013): 141–62. Gritti, for instance, contrasts Fornari's appeal to a more Oedipal approach, with Girard's disavowal of such an approach (ibid., 151–52).

74. Fornari, *A God Torn to Pieces*, 30.

75. Nietzsche, "Why I Am So Clever," sec. 4 in *Ecce Homo*. Here and below I have used Kaufmann's translation in *Basic Writings of Nietzsche* (New York: Modern Library, 1992), 701–2.

76. Fornari, *A God Torn to Pieces*, 34.

77. Ibid.

78. Cited in Fornari, *A God Torn to Pieces*, 29; translation is mine.

79. See Friedrich Nietzsche, *Sämtliche Werke. Kritische Studienausgabe in 15 Bänden*, ed. Giorgio Colli and Mazzino Montinari (Berlin: Walter de Gruyter, 1967–77). The French translation cited by Girard appeared in 1978.

80. Girard, "Nietzsche and Contradiction," 54.

81. Ibid., 60. The original German is found in *Sämtliche Werke*, 12:198–99. Although Girard apologizes "for my poor English version twice removed from the original," I have kept his translation, which accurately renders the German original.

82. See *The Portable Nietzsche*, trans. Walter Kaufmann (New York: Penguin, 1968), 670.

83. Girard, "Nietzsche and Contradiction," 65: "Between the two antipodes the oscillation is frantic throughout his whole career, even though Nietzsche tries to fiercely suppress it, and his writings, being the instrument of that suppression, almost always record a needle firmly planted at the same extremity of the dial."

84. Girard, "Dionysus versus the Crucified," 820; checking the Kaufmann translation against the German, I have only swapped one word: *being* [*Sein*] for *existence*.

85. See Nietzsche, "Why I Am Destiny," sec. 9: "Have I been understood?—*Dionysus versus the Crucified.*—" (*Basic Writings*, 791).

86. Girard, "Nietzsche and Contradiction," 63.

87. Girard, "Dionysus versus the Crucified," 821.

88. Ibid.; Girard also makes this point in *I See Satan Fall Like Lightning*, 171–72.

89. Nietzsche, *The Antichrist*, sec. 24.

90. Girard, "Dionysus versus the Crucified," 823.

91. Elsewhere Girard declares that Nietzsche "discovered the anthropological key to Christianity: its vocation of concern for victims" (*I See Satan Fall Like Lightning*, 171).

92. Girard, "Dionysus versus the Crucified," 827. Girard later notes, "He wanted to side with Dionysus, against Christ, and by doing so he condemned himself to hell, because Dionysus and Satan are the same thing" (*Evolution and Conversion*, 221). Fornari's *The Case of Nietzsche* only strengthens Girard's intuition. Fornari persuasively debunks the claim that syphilis caused Nietzsche's collapse, and his access to the hospital records paint a frighteningly sad picture of Nietzsche.

93. Girard, *Evolution and Conversion*, 197; elsewhere Girard writes, "He opposes, so he believes, the crowd mentality, but he does not recognize his Dionysian stance as the supreme expression of the mob in its most brutal and its most stupid tendencies" (*I See Satan Fall Like Lightning*, 173).

94. Girard, "Dionysus versus the Crucified," 831.

95. See Martin Heidegger, "The Word of Nietzsche: 'God Is Dead,'" in *The Question Concerning Technology and Other Essays*, trans. William Lovitt (New York: Harper & Row, 1977), 53–112. The essay was originally published in *Holzwege* and stems from a 1943 lecture. Although Heidegger does address the murder of God, he downplays its meaning: "The killing means the act of doing away with the suprasensory world that *is* in itself" (ibid., 107).

96. Girard, "Dionysus versus the Crucified," 830.

97. Cited from *The Portable Nietzsche*, 96.

98. Ibid.

99. Fleming and O'Carroll, "Nietzsche, the Last Atheist," 241.

100. Girard, *I See Satan Fall Like Lightning*, 178–79.

101. Hart, *Atheist Delusions*, 219–28.

102. *The Portable Nietzsche*, 483. I have slightly amended the Kaufmann translation to adhere more closely to the German. The aphorism is the fifth under the subheading "'Reason' in Philosophy."

Epilogue

1. Kirwan, *Girard and Theology*, 133.

2. Grant Kaplan, "New Paths for a Girard/Lonergan Conversation: An Essay in Light of Robert Doran's *The Trinity in History*," *Method: Journal of Lonergan Studies* 4, no. 1 (2013): 24.

3. Moosbrugger, *Die Rehabilitierung des Opfers*.

4. White, "Ethnological 'Lie' and Mythical 'Truth,'" 9.

5. Coakley, *Sacrifice Regained*, esp. 12–16.

BIBLIOGRAPHY

My bibliographic proclivities require some explanation. When referencing works more known for a universal notation than for specific pagination—Aquinas's *Summa*, Kant's *Critique of Pure Reason*—I have omitted cumbersome bibliographic addenda. For the Bible I have generally used the Revised Standard Version. In most cases, I have checked translations of French and German against the original, and have indicated where I massaged a given translation. Certain books by Girard I had read in French before the English translation appeared. In the infrequent instances where I worked with the French before the English was available, I have not gone back and substituted the English for the French.

Adams, Rebecca. "Violence, Difference, Sacrifice: A Conversation with René Girard." *Religion & Literature* 25, no. 2 (1993): 9–33.

Alison, James. *Broken Hearts and New Creations: Intimations of a Great Reversal.* New York: Continuum, 2010.

———. *Faith beyond Resentment: Fragments Catholic and Gay.* New York: Crossroad, 2001.

———. *Jesus the Forgiving Victim: Listening for the Unheard Voice.* Glenview, IL: Doers, 2013.

———. *The Joy of Being Wrong: Original Sin through Easter Eyes.* New York: Crossroad, 1998.

———. *Knowing Jesus.* Springfield, IL: Templegate, 1993.

———. *On Being Liked.* New York: Crossroad, 2004.

———. *Raising Abel: The Recovery of the Eschatological Imagination.* New York: Crossroad, 1996.

———. *Undergoing God: Dispatches from the Scene of a Break-in.* New York: Continuum, 2006.

Aristotle. *Aristotle's Poetics.* Translated by S. H. Butcher. New York: Hill and Wang, 1961.

Asad, Talal. "Reading a Modern Classic: W. C. Smith's *The Meaning and End of Religion*." *History of Religions* 40, no. 3 (2001): 205–22.

Auerbach, Eric. *Mimesis: The Representation of Reality in Western Literature.* Translated by Willard Trask. New York: Doubleday Anchor, 1953.

Balthasar, Hans Urs von. *The Action.* Translated by Graham Harrison. Vol. 4 of *Theo-Drama: Theological Dramatic Theory.* San Francisco: Ignatius, 1994.

———. "Die neue Theorie von Jesus als dem 'Sündenbock.'" *Communio* 9 (1980): 184–85.

———. *A Theology of History.* San Francisco: Ignatius, 1994.

Barth, Karl. *Church Dogmatics I/2: The Doctrine of the Word of God.* London: T & T Clark, 2004.

———. *The Epistle to the Romans.* Translated by Edwyn C. Hoskyns. Oxford: Oxford University Press, 1933.

Bauerschmidt, Frederick C. "Shaving Ockham." *Commonweal* 142, no. 3 (2015): 32–35.

Bellah, Robert N. *Beyond Belief: Essays on Religion in a Post-Traditional World.* New York: Harper & Row, 1970.

———. *Religion in Human Evolution: From the Paleolithic to the Axial Age.* Cambridge, MA: Belknap, 2011.

Bellinger, Charles K. *The Genealogy of Violence: Reflections on Creation, Freedom and Evil.* Oxford: Oxford University Press, 2001.

Beumer, Johann. "Gratia supponit naturam. Zur Gesichichte eines theologischen Prinzips." *Gregorianum* 20 (1939): 381–406, 535–52.

Blumenberg, Hans. *The Legitimacy of the Modern Age.* Translated by Robert Wallace. Cambridge, MA: MIT Press, 1983.

Bonhoeffer, Dietrich. *Letters and Papers from Prison.* Enlarged ed. Edited by Eberhard Bethge. New York: Touchstone, 1953.

Buckley, Michael. *At the Origins of Modern Atheism.* New Haven, CT: Yale University Press, 1987.

———. "Atheism and Contemplation." *Theological Studies* 40 (1979): 680–99.

———. *Denying and Disclosing God: The Ambiguous Progress and Modern Atheism.* New Haven, CT: Yale University Press, 2004.

———. "Experience and Culture: A Point of Departure for American Atheism." *Theological Studies* 50 (1989): 443–65.

———. "Modernity and the Satanic Face of God." In *Christian Spirituality and the Culture of Modernity: The Thought of Louis Dupré,* edited by Peter Casarella and George Schner, 100–122. Grand Rapids, MI: Eerdmans, 1998.

———. "The Rise of Modern Atheism and the Religious Époche." *CTSA Proceedings* 47 (1992): 69–93.

―――. "The Study of Religion and the Rise of Atheism: Conflict or Confirmation?" In *Fields of Faith: Theology and Religious Studies for the Twenty-first Century*, edited by David Ford, Ben Quash, and Janet Soskice, 3–24. Cambridge: Cambridge University Press, 2005.

Caputo, John. "Atheism, A/theology, and the Postmodern Condition." In *The Cambridge Companion to Atheism*, edited by Michael Martin, 267–82. Cambridge: Cambridge University Press, 2007.

Carey, Patrick W. "Cardinal Avery Dulles, S.J., Among the Theologians: A Memorial Reflection." *Theological Studies* 71 (2010): 773–91.

Cavanaugh, William. *The Myth of Religious Violence.* Oxford: Oxford University Press, 2009.

Chardin, Pierre Teilhard de. *Christianity and Evolution.* New York: Harcourt Brace Jovanovich, 1971.

Chua-Eoan, Howard. "The Queen and Mrs. Obama: A Breach in Protocol." *Time*, April 1, 2009. Accessed October 24, 2011. http://www.time.com /time/world/article/0,8599,1888962,00.html.

Coakley, Sarah. *Sacrifice Regained: Reconsidering the Rationality of Religious Belief.* Cambridge: Cambridge University Press, 2012.

Cowdell, Scott. *René Girard and Secular Modernity: Christ, Culture, and Crisis.* Notre Dame, IN: University of Notre Dame Press, 2013.

Dadosky, John. "The Church and the Other: Mediation and Friendship in Post-Vatican II Roman Catholic Ecclesiology." *Pacifica* 18 (2005): 302–22.

―――. "Has Vatican II Been *Hermeneutered*? Recovering and Developing its Theological Achievements following Rahner and Lonergan." *Irish Theological Quarterly* 79, no. 4 (2014): 327–49.

―――. "Towards a Fundamental Theological RE-Interpretation of Vatican II." *Heythrop Journal* 49 (2008): 742–63.

Dahl, Nils. "Der Erstgeborene Satans und der Vater des Teufels (Oolyk. 7:1 und John 8:44)." In *Apophoreta: Festschrift für Ernst Haenchen*, edited by Walther Eltester, 70–84. Berlin: Töpelmann, 1964.

Daly, Robert J. *Sacrifice Unveiled: The True Meaning of Christian Sacrifice.* New York: T & T Clark, 2010.

Darwin, Charles. *The Autobiography of Charles Darwin.* Edited by Francis Darwin. New York: Norton, 1958.

Denzinger, Heinrich, and Peter Hünermann, eds. *Enchiridion Symbolorum: definitionum et declarationum de rebus fidei et morum.* 41st ed. Freiburg: Herder, 2007.

Diamond, Jared. *Collapse: How Societies Choose to Fail or Survive.* New York: Viking, 2005.

―――. "Vengeance Is Ours." *The New Yorker*, April 21, 2008, 74–87.

Dulles, Avery. "Apologetics I: History." In *Dictionary of Fundamental Theology*, edited by René Latourelle and Rino Fisichella, 28–35. New York: Crossroad, 1994.

———. "The Church: Sacrament and Ground of Faith." In *Problems and Perspectives of Fundamental Theology*, translated by Matthew J. O'Connell; edited by René Latourelle, and Gerald O'Collins, 259–73. New York: Paulist, 1982.

———. *A History of Apologetics*. 2nd ed. San Francisco: Ignatius, 2005.

———. *Models of Revelation*. New York: Double Day, 1985.

———. "Revelation." In *New Catholic Encyclopedia*, edited at Catholic University of America, 12:441–44. New York: McGraw-Hill, 1967–96.

———. *Revelation and the Quest for Unity*. Washington, DC: Corpus, 1968.

———. *Revelation Theology: A History*. New York: Herder and Herder, 1969.

———. "Review Article." *Theological Studies* 25 (1964): 43–58.

Dupré, Louis. *Passage to Modernity: An Essay in the Hermeneutics of Nature and Culture*. New Haven, CT: Yale University Press, 1993.

Dussault, Jean-Claude. "René Girard: La revelation évangélique et le bouddhisme." *Sciences Religieuses* [*Studies in Religion*] 10, no. 1 (1981): 59–66.

Edwards, John. "Developing a 'Theology in the Order of Discovery': The Method and Contribution of James Alison." Ph.D. diss., Boston College, 2014.

———. "From a 'Revealed' Psychology to Theological Inquiry: James Alison's Theological Appropriation of Girard." *Contagion* 21 (2014): 121–30.

Evans-Pritchard, E. E. *Social Anthropology and Other Essays*. New York: Free Press, 1964.

Fackre, Gabriel. *The Doctrine of Revelation: A Narrative Interpretation*. Grand Rapids, MI: Eerdmans, 1997.

Fiorenza, Francis. *Foundational Theology: Jesus and the Church*. New York: Crossroad, 1984.

Fleming, Chris, and John O'Carroll. "Nietzsche, the Last Atheist." In *Violence, Desire, and the Sacred: Girard's Mimetic Theory across the Disciplines*, edited by Scott Cowdell, Chris Fleming, and Joel Hodge, 227–50. New York: Continuum, 2012.

Force, James. "The Origins of Modern Atheism." *Journal of the History of Ideas* 50, no. 1 (1989): 153–62.

Fornari, Giuseppe. *A God Torn to Pieces: The Nietzsche Case*. Translated by Keith Buck. East Lansing: Michigan State University Press, 2013.

Fries, Heinrich. *Fundamental Theology*. Translated by Robert Daly. Washington, DC: Catholic University of America Press, 1996.

Gadamer, Hans-Georg. *Truth and Method*. Translated by William Glen-Doepels. New York: Seabury, 1975.

———. *Truth and Method*. 2nd rev. ed. Translated by Joel Weinsheimer and Donald G. Marshall. New York: Crossroad, 1989.

Gaillardetz, Richard. "The 'Francis Moment': A New Kairos for Catholic Ecclesiology." *Catholic Theological Society of America Proceedings* 69 (2014):
63–80.

Garrels, Scott. "Imitation, Mirror Neurons, and Mimetic Desire: Convergences
between the Mimetic Theory of René Girard and Empirical Research on
Imitation." *Contagion* 12 (2006): 47–86.

———, ed. *Mimesis and Science: Empirical Research on Imitation and the Mimetic Theory of Culture and Religion*. East Lansing: Michigan State University Press, 2011.

Gauchet, Marcel. *Le désenchantement du monde*. Paris: Gallimard, 1985.

Gibney, Alex. "Alex Gibney on Catching Hell." Grantland. September 27, 2011.
Accessed October 24, 2011. http://grantland.com/hollywood-prospectus
/alex-gibney-on-catching-hell/.

Gillespie, Michael Allen. *The Theological Origins of Modernity*. Chicago: University of Chicago Press, 2008.

Girard Lectionary. http://girardianlectionary.net/instructions.html.

Girard, René. *Achever Clausewitz: Entretiens avec Benoît Chantre*. Paris: Carnets
Nord, 2007.

———. *Anorexia and Mimetic Desire*. Translated by Mark Anspach. East Lansing: Michigan State University Press, 2013.

———. "Are the Gospels Mythical?" *First Things* 62 (April 1996): 27–31.

———. *Battling to the End: Conversations with Benoît Chantre*. Translated by
Mary Baker. East Lansing: Michigan State University Press, 2010.

———. *Deceit, Desire, and the Novel: Self and Other in Literary Structure*. Translated by Yvonne Freccero. Baltimore: Johns Hopkins University Press, 1965.

———. "Dionysus versus the Crucified." *Modern Language Notes* 99 (1984):
816–35.

———. "The Evangelical Subversion of Myth." In *Politics and Apocalypse*, edited by Robert Hamerton-Kelly, 29–49. East Lansing: Michigan State University Press, 2007.

———. *Evolution and Conversion: Dialogues on the Origin of Culture*. London:
T & T Clark, 2007.

———. "The Founding Murder in the Philosophy of Nietzsche." In *Violence
and Truth*, edited by Paul Dumouchel, 227–46. Stanford, CA: Stanford
University Press, 1988.

———. "Generative Scapegoating." In *Violent Origins: Walter Burkert, René
Girard, and Jonathan Z. Smith on Ritual Killing and Cultural Formation*,
edited by Robert Hamerton-Kelly, 73–105. Stanford, CA: Stanford University Press, 1987.

———. *The Girard Reader*. Edited by James G. Williams. New York: Crossroad, 1996.

————. *I See Satan Fall Like Lightning.* Translated by James G. Williams. Maryknoll, NY: Orbis, 2001.

————. *Job: The Victim of His People.* Translated by Yvonne Freccero. Stanford, CA: Stanford University Press, 1987.

————. "Mimetische Theorie und Theologie." In *Vom Fluch und Segen der Sündenböcke: Raymund Schwager zum 60. Geburtstag,* edited by Józef Niewiadomski and Wolfgang Palaver, 15–29. Vienna: Thaur, 1995.

————. "Nietzsche and Contradiction." *Stanford Italian Review* 1 (1986): 53–65.

————. *The One by Whom Scandal Comes.* Translated by Malcolm DeBevoise. East Lansing: Michigan State University Press, 2014.

————. *Quand ces choses commenceront—: Entretiens avec Michel Treguer.* Paris: Arléa, 1994.

————. "Ratzinger Is Right." *New Perspectives Quarterly* 22, no. 3 (2005): 42–48.

————. *Sacrifice.* Translated by Matthew Pattillo and David Dawson. East Lansing: Michigan State University Press, 2011.

————. *The Scapegoat.* Translated by Yvonne Freccero. Baltimore: Johns Hopkins University Press, 1986.

————. "Strategies of Madness—Nietzsche, Wagner, and Dostoevski." *Modern Language Notes* 91 (1976): 1161–85.

————. *A Theater of Envy: William Shakespeare.* South Bend, IN: St. Augustine's Press, 1991.

————. *Things Hidden Since the Foundation of the World.* Translated by Stephen Bann and Michael Metteer. Stanford, CA: Stanford University Press, 1987.

————. *"To Double Business Bound": Essays on Literature, Mimesis, and Anthropology.* Baltimore: Johns Hopkins University Press, 1978.

————. *Violence and the Sacred.* Baltimore: Johns Hopkins University Press, 1977.

————. *When These Things Begin: Conversations with Michel Treguer.* Translated by Trevor Cribben Merrill. East Lansing: Michigan State University Press, 2014.

————. *Wissenschaft und christlicher Glaube.* Tübingen: Mohr Siebeck, 2007.

Girard, René, and Gianni Vattimo. *Christianity, Truth, and Weakening Faith.* New York: Columbia University Press, 2010.

Gjesdal, Kristin. "Hermeneutics and Philology: A Reconsideration of Gadamer's Critique of Schleiermacher." *British Journal for the History of Philosophy* 14, no. 1 (2006): 133–56.

Golsan, Richard. *René Girard and Myth: An Introduction.* New York: Routledge, 1993.

Goodhart, Sandor. "Letter from the President: 'Navigating Fateful Passages.'" *Bulletin* 30 (May 2007): 4–6.

Gregory, Brad. "Genre, Method, and Assumptions." *The Immanent Frame*, January 21, 2014. http://blogs.ssrc.org/tif/2014/01/21/genre-method-and -assumptions/.

———. *The Unintended Reformation: How a Religious Revolution Secularized Society.* Cambridge, MA: Belknap, 2012.

Gritti, Martino Pesenti. "Nietzsche's Double Binds: Giuseppe Fornari and René Girard on Nietzsche's Thought." *Contagion* 20, no. 1 (2013): 141–62.

Hamerton-Kelly, Robert. *The Gospel and the Sacred: The Politics of Violence in Mark.* Minneapolis: Fortress, 1994.

———. "Response to Qamar-ul Huda." *Contagion* 9 (2002): 99–104.

Hart, David Bentley. *Atheist Delusions: The Christian Revolution and its Fashionable Enemies.* New Haven, CT: Yale University Press, 2009.

———. *The Beauty of the Infinite: The Aesthetics of Christian Truth.* Grand Rapids, MI: Eerdmans, 2003.

———. "Christ and Nothing." *First Things* 136 (October 2003): 47–57.

———. *The Experience of God: Being, Consciousness, Bliss.* New Haven, CT: Yale University Press, 2013.

Haught, John. *God and the New Atheism: A Critical Response to Dawkins, Harris, and Hitchens.* Louisville, KY: Westminster John Knox, 2008.

Havelock, Eric. *A Preface to Plato.* Cambridge, MA: Belknap, 1963.

Hecht, Richard. "Studies on Sacrifice, 1970–1980." *Religious Studies Review* 8 (1982): 253–59.

Hefling, Charles. "Revelation and/as Insight." In *The Importance of Insight: Essays in Honor of Michael Vertin,* edited by John J. Liptay and David S. Liptay, 97–115. Toronto: University of Toronto Press, 2007.

Hefty, Karl. "The God of Appearance." Ph.D. diss., University of Chicago, 2012.

Heidegger, Martin. *Being and Time.* Translated by John Macquarrie and Edward Robinson. San Francisco: Harper & Row, 1962.

———. *Nietzsche II.* Pflulingen: Neske, 1961.

———. *The Question Concerning Technology and Other Essays.* Translated by William Lovitt. New York: Harper & Row, 1977.

———. *Sein und Zeit.* 7th ed. Tübingen: Max Niemeyer, 1993.

Heim, S. Mark. *Saved from Sacrifice: A Theology of the Cross.* Grand Rapids, MI: Eerdmans, 2006.

Herring, George. *Introduction to the History of Christianity.* New York: New York University Press, 2006.

Herzog, Markwart. "Religionstheorie und Theologie René Girards." *Kerygma und Dogma* 38, no. 2 (1992): 105–37.

Hitchens, Christopher. *God Is Not Great: How Religion Poisons Everything.* New York: Twelve, 2007.

———, ed. *The Portable Atheist: Essential Readings for the Nonbeliever.* Philadelphia: De Capo, 2007.

Hocart, A. M. *Kings and Counselors: An Essay in the Comparative Anatomy of Human Society.* Chicago: University of Chicago Press, 1970.

d'Holbach, Baron Paul. *Système de nature, ou Des lois du monde Physique et du monde moral.* London, 1771.

Horan, Dan. *Postmodernity and Univocity: A Critical Account of Radical Orthodoxy and John Duns Scotus.* Minneapolis: Fortress, 2014.

Hughson, Thomas. "Dulles and Aquinas on Revelation." *The Thomist* 52 (1988): 445–71.

Huizenga, Johan. *Homo Ludens: A Study of the Play Element in Culture.* Boston: Beacon, 1938.

Hyman, Gavin. "Atheism in Modern History." In *The Cambridge Companion to Atheism,* edited by Michael Martin, 27–46. Cambridge: Cambridge University Press, 2007.

Israel, Jonathan. *Democratic Enlightenment: Philosophy, Revolution, and Human Rights, 1750–1790.* Oxford: Oxford University Press, 2011.

———. *Enlightenment Contested: Philosophy, Modernity, and the Emancipation of Man 1670–1752.* Oxford: Oxford University Press, 2006.

———. *Radical Enlightenment: Philosophy and Making Modernity 1960–1750.* Oxford: Oxford University Press, 2001.

———. *A Revolution of the Mind: Radical Enlightenment and the Intellectual Origins of Modern Democracy.* Oxford: Oxford University Press, 2010.

Janz, Denis. "Whore or Handmaid? Luther and Aquinas on the Function of Reason in Theology." In *The Devil's Whore: Reason and Philosophy in the Lutheran Tradition,* edited by Jennifer Hockenbery Dragseth, 47–52. Minneapolis: Fortress, 2011.

Jaspers, Karl. *Vom Ursprung und Ziel der Geschichte.* Zürich: Artemis, 1949.

Justin Martyr. *The First Apology, the Second Apology, Dialogue with Trypho, Exhortation to the Greeks, Discourse to the Greeks, the Monarchy, or the Rule of God.* Edited by Thomas Falls. Washington, DC: Catholic University of America Press, 1948.

Kaplan, Grant. *Answering the Enlightenment: The Catholic Recovery of Historical Revelation.* New York: Crossroad, 2006.

———. "Getting History into *Religion*? Appropriating *Nostra Aetate* for the 21st Century." *Heythrop Journal* 52 (2011): 802–21.

———. "An Interview with René Girard." *First Things* online, November 2011. http://www.firstthings.com/onthesquare/2008/11/an-interview-with-rene-girard.

———. "The New Atheism: Dawkins, Harris, Hitchens." In *Handbook of Mimetic Theory and Religion*, edited by Wolfgang Palaver and James Alison. New York: Palgrave Macmillan, forthcoming.

———. "New Paths for a Girard/Lonergan Conversation: An Essay in Light of Robert Doran's *The Trinity in History*." *Method: Journal of Lonergan Studies* 4, no. 1 (2013): 23–38.

———. "Renewing the Tradition: The Theological Project of James Alison." *America Magazine*, May 19, 2014, 25–27.

———. "Review." *Theological Studies* 71 (2010): 479–81.

———. "Saint vs. Hero: René Girard's Undoing of Romantic Hagiology." In *Postmodern Saints of France*, edited by Colby Dickinson, 153–67. New York: T & T Clark/Continuum, 2013.

———. "What Has Ethics to Do with Rhetoric? Prolegomena to Any Future Just War Theory." *Political Theology* 6, no. 1 (2005): 31–49.

Kasper, Walter. *Pope Francis' Revolution of Tenderness and Love*. Translated by William Madges. New York: Paulist, 2015.

———. *Theology and Church*. Translated by Margaret Kohl. New York: Crossroad, 1989.

Kereszty, Roch. "A Response to Gil Bailie's 'Girard's Contribution to the Church of the 21st Century.'" *Communio: International Catholic Review* 26, no. 1 (1999): 212–16.

Kerr, Fergus. "Rescuing Girard's Argument." *Modern Theology* 8, no. 4 (1992): 385–99.

King, Chelsea. "Girard Reclaimed: Finding Common Ground between Sarah Coakley and René Girard on Sacrifice." *Contagion* 23 (2016) (forthcoming).

Kirwan, Michael. *Discovering Girard*. London: Darton, Longman and Todd, 2004.

———. *Girard and Theology*. New York: T & T Clark, 2009.

Kolbert, Elizabeth. "Sleeping with the Enemy: What Happened between the Neanderthals and Us?" *The New Yorker*, August 15 & 22, 2011, 64–75.

Latourelle, René. "Church III. Motive of Credibility," and "Fundamental Theology I. History and Specific Character." In *Dictionary of Fundamental Theology*, edited by René Latourelle and Rino Fisichella, 154–70; 324–32. New York: Crossroad, 1994.

———. *Theology of Revelation*. Staten Island, NY: Alba House, 1966.

Lawn, Chris. *Gadamer: A Guide for the Perplexed*. New York: Continuum, 2006.

Lawrence, Fred. "Believing to Understand: The Hermeneutic Circle in Gadamer and Lonergan." Ph.D. diss., University of Basel, 1976.

Lefebure, Leo. "Mimesis, Violence and Socially Engaged Buddhism: Overture to a Dialogue." *Contagion* 3 (1996): 122–40.

———. *Revelation, the Religions, and Violence*. New York: Orbis, 2000.

Lévi, Sylvian. *La Doctrine du sacrifice dans les Brahmanas*. Paris: Presses Universitaires de France, 1966 [1898].

Lienhardt, Godfrey. *Divinity and Experience: The Religion of the Dinka*. Oxford: Clarendon, 1961.

Lonergan, Bernard. *Insight: A Study of Human Understanding*. Edited by Frederick Crowe and Robert Doran. Toronto: University of Toronto Press, 1992.

———. *Method in Theology*. New York: Herder and Herder, 1971.

———. "Sacralization and Secularization." In *Philosophical and Theological Papers: 1965–1980*, 250–81. Toronto: University of Toronto Press, 2004.

Löwith, Karl. *Meaning in History: The Theological Implications of the Modern Age*. Chicago: University of Chicago Press, 1949.

Lubac, Henri de. *The Drama of Atheist Humanism*. San Francisco: Ignatius, 1995.

———. *Mystery of the Supernatural*. Translated by David L. Schindler. New York: Crossroad, 1998.

Mabee, Charles. "Dispatch from the Girardian Boundary." In *For René Girard: Essays in Friendship and Truth*, edited by Sandor Goodhart, 211–21. East Lansing: Michigan State University Press, 2009.

Machaut, Guillaume de. *Le Jugement du Roy de Navarre*. Paris: Ernest Hoeppfner, 1908.

MacIntyre, Alasdair. *After Virtue: A Study in Moral Theory*. Notre Dame, IN: University of Notre Dame Press, 1981.

McGrath, Alister. *The Dawkins Delusion: Atheist Fundamentalism and the Denial of the Divine*. Downers Grove, IL: Intervarsity, 2008.

McLuhan, Marshall. *The Gutenberg Galaxy: The Making of Typographic Man*. Toronto: University of Toronto Press, 1962.

Midgley, Mary. *Science as Salvation: A Modern Myth and Its Meaning*. London: Routledge, 1992.

Milbank, John. "Knowledge: The Theological Critique of Philosophy in Hamann and Jacobi." In *Radical Orthodoxy: A New Theology*, edited by John Milbank, Catherine Pickstock, and Graham Ward, 21–37. London: Routledge, 1999.

———. "Review." *Modern Theology* 8, no. 1 (1992): 89–92.

———. "Stories of Sacrifice." *Modern Theology* 12, no. 1 (1996): 27–56.

———. *Theology and Social Theory: Beyond Secular Reason*. Oxford: Blackwell, 1990.

Mongrain, Kevin. *The Systematic Thought of Hans Urs von Balthasar: An Irenaean Retrieval*. New York: Crossroad/Herder, 2002.

———. "Theologians of Spiritual Transformation: A Proposal for Reading René Girard through the Lenses of Hans Urs von Balthasar and John Cassian." *Modern Theology* 28, no. 1 (2012): 81–111.

Montag, John, S.J. "Revelation: The False Legacy of Suarez." In *Radical Orthodoxy: A New Theology*, edited by John Milbank et al., 38–63. London: Routledge, 1999.

Moore, Sebastian. *The Contagion of Jesus*. Edited by Stephen McCarthy. Maryknoll, New York: Orbis, 2007.

———. *The Crucified Jesus Is No Stranger*. New York: Paulist, 1977.

———. *The Fire and the Rose Are One*. New York: Seabury, 1980.

Moosbrugger, Mathias. *Die Rehabilitierung des Opfers: Zum Dialog zwischen René Girard und Raymund Schwager um die Angemessenheit der Rede vom Opfer im christlichen Kontext*. Innsbruck: Tyrolia, 2014.

Moyise, Steve. "Quotations." In *New Interpreter's Dictionary of the Bible*, 4:709–10. Nashville, TN: Abingdon, 2009.

Newman, John Henry. *Fifteen Sermons Preached before the University of Oxford*. Notre Dame, IN: University of Notre Dame Press, 1997.

Nietzsche, Friedrich. *Basic Writings of Nietzsche*. Edited by Walter Kaufmann. New York: Modern Library, 1992.

———. *The Portable Nietzsche*. Translated by Walter Kaufmann. New York: Penguin, 1968.

———. *Sämtliche Werke. Kritische Studienausgabe in 15 Bänden*. Edited by Giorgio Colli and Mazzino Montinari. Berlin: Walter de Gruyter, 1967–77.

———. *Twilight of the Idols and The Anti-Christ*. Translated by R. J. Hollingdale. New York: Penguin Classics, 1990.

Nongbri, Brent. *Before Religion: A History of a Modern Concept*. New Haven, CT: Yale University Press, 2013.

North, Robert. "Violence and the Bible: The Girard Connection." *Catholic Biblical Quarterly* 47 (1985): 1–27.

O'Connor, Flannery. "A Good Man Is Hard to Find." In *The Complete Stories*, 117–33. New York: Farrar, Straus and Giroux, 1973.

O'Meara, Thomas. "Toward a Subjective Theology of Revelation." *Theological Studies* 36, no. 3 (1975): 401–27.

Ong, Walter. *Orality and Literacy: The Technologizing of the Word*. New York: Routledge, 1982.

———. *The Presence of the Word: Some Prolegomena for Cultural and Religious History*. New Haven, CT: Yale University Press, 1967.

———. *Ramus, Method, and the Decay of Dialogue*. Cambridge, MA: Harvard University Press, 1958.

O'Regan, Cyril. "Girard and the Spaces of Apocalyptic." *Modern Theology* 28, no. 1 (2012): 112–40.

Ormerod, Neil. "Doran's *The Trinity in History*: The Girardian Connection." *Method: Journal of Lonergan Studies* 4, no. 1 (2013): 47–60.

———. *Meaning, Method, and Revelation: The Meaning and Function of Revelation in Bernard Lonergan's Method in Theology*. Lanham, MD: University Press of America, 2000.

Palaver, Wolfgang. "A Letter from the President." *The Bulletin of the Colloquium on Violence & Religion* 38 (May 2011): 4–7.

———. *René Girard's Mimetic Theory*. Translated by Gabriel Borrud. East Lansing: Michigan State University Press, 2013.

Pannenberg, Wolfhart. *Revelation as History*. Translated by David Granskou. New York: Macmillan, 1960.

Pascal, Blaise. *Pensées/The Provincial Letters*. Translated by W. F. Trotter. New York: Modern Library, 1941.

———. *Pensées*. Translated by A. J. Krailsheimer. New York: Penguin, 1995.

Pecknold, Chad. *Christianity and Politics: A Brief Guide to the History*. Eugene, OR: Cascade, 2010.

Peterson, Erik. "Monotheism as a Political Problem." In *Theological Tractates*, translated by Michael J. Hollerich, 68–105. Stanford, CA: Stanford University Press, 2011.

Pfau, Thomas. *Minding the Modern: Human Agency, Intellectual Tradition, and Responsible Knowledge*. Notre Dame, IN: University of Notre Dame Press, 2013.

Pié-Ninot, Salvador. "Church I: Fundamental Ecclesiology," and "Church IV: Via Empirica." In *Dictionary of Fundamental Theology*, edited by René Latourelle and Rino Fisichella, 143–44; 170–73. New York: Crossroad, 1994.

Pinker, Steven. *The Better Angels of Our Nature: Why Violence Has Declined*. New York: Viking, 2011.

Pope Benedict XVI. "Regensburg Lecture." http://www.vatican.va/holy_father /benedict_xvi/speeches/2006/september/documents/hf_ben-xvi_spe _20060912_university-regensburg_en.html.

Pope Francis. *The Church of Mercy: A Vision for the Church*. Chicago: Loyola, 2014.

———. *Evangelii gaudium*. http://w2.vatican.va/content/francesco/en/apost _exhortations/documents/papa-francesco_esortazione-ap_20131124 _evangelii-gaudium.html.

Pottmeyer, Hermann Joseph. "Die Frage nach der wahren Kirche." In *Handbuch der Fundamentaltheologie. 3 Traktat: Kirche*, 212–41. Freiburg: Herder, 1985.

Rahner, Karl. "The Concept of Mystery in Catholic Theology." In *Theological Investigations*, 4:36–73. New York: Crossroad, 1973.

———. "Mysticism." In *Encyclopedia of Theology: The Concise "Sacramentum Mundi,"* 1010. New York: Seabury, 1975.

Rahner, Karl, and Herbert Vorgrimler, eds. "Fundamentaltheologie." In *Kleines Theologisches Wörterbuch*, 10th ed., 131–33. Freiburg: Herder, 1976.

Ranieri, John. *Disturbing Revelation: Leo Strauss, Eric Voegelin, and the Bible*. Columbia: University of Missouri, 2009.

Regensburger, Dietmar. "Bibliography of Literature on the Mimetic Theory of René Girard." https://www.uibk.ac.at/theol/cover/girard/pdf/bibliography_vol.xxxv.pdf.

Rosenberg, Randy. "The Catholic Imagination and Modernity: William Cavanaugh's Theopolitical Imagination and Charles Taylor's Modern Social Imagination." *Heythrop Journal* 48 (2007): 911–31.

Rush, Ormond. *The Eyes of Faith: The Sense of the Faithful and the Church's Reception of Revelation*. Washington, DC: Catholic University of America Press, 2009.

———. "*Sensus fidei*: Faith 'Making Sense' of Revelation." *Theological Studies* 62 (2001): 231–61.

Sabatier, Auguste. *Outlines of a Philosophy of Religion Based on Psychology and History*. London: Hodder and Stoughton, 1897.

Schmidt, Klaus. "Zuerst kam der Tempel, dann die Stadt. Vorläufiger Bericht zu den Grabungen am Göbekli Tepe und am Gürcütepe 1995–1999." *Istanbuler Mitteilungen* 50 (2000): 5–41.

Schneiders, Sandra. *The Revelatory Text: Interpreting the New Testament as Sacred Scripture*. New York: HarperCollins, 1991.

Schwager, Raymund. *Jesus in the Drama of Salvation: Toward a Biblical Doctrine of Redemption*. Translated by James Williams and Paul Haddon. New York: Herder and Herder, 1999.

———. *Must There Be Scapegoats? Violence and Redemption in the Bible*. Translated by Maria Assad. New York: Crossroad, 1987.

Schweiker, William. "Sacrifice, Interpretation, and the Sacred: The Import of Gadamer and Girard for Religious Studies." *Journal of the American Academy of Religion* 55, no. 4 (1987): 791–810.

Scubla, Lucien. "The Christianity of René Girard and the Nature of Religion." In *Violence and Truth*, edited by Paul Dumouchel, 160–78. Stanford, CA: Stanford University Press, 1988.

Serres, Michel. *Atlas*. Paris: Julliard, 1994.

Siebers, Tobin. "Language, Violence, and the Sacred: A Polemical Survey of Critical Theories." In *To Honor René Girard: Presented on the Occasion of His Sixtieth Birthday by Colleagues, Students, and Friends*, edited by Alphonse Juilland, 203–19. Saratoga, CA: Anma Libri, 1986.

Sillitoe, Paul, and Mako John Kuwimb. "Rebutting Jared Diamond's Savage Portrait: What Tribal Societies Can Tell Us about Justice and Liberty," April 28, 2010. Accessed October 18, 2011. http://www.imediaethics.org/rebutting-jared-diamonds-savage-portrait/.

Simmons, Bill. "Interview with Alex Gibney." ESPN Radio, September 27, 2011. Accessed October 23, 2011. http://espn.go.com/espnradio/play?id=7025837.

Smart, Ninian. "René Girard: Violence and the Sacred." *Religious Studies Review* 63 (1980): 173–77.

Smith, George H. *Why Atheism?* Amherst, NY: Prometheus, 2000.

Smith, Wilfred Cantwell. *The Meaning and End of Religion*. Minneapolis: Fortress, 1991 [1962].

Steve Bartman: Catching Hell. Directed by Alex Gibney. ESPN Films, 2011.

Strauss, Leo. *Natural Right and History*. Chicago: University of Chicago Press, 1953.

Swartley, William, ed. *Violence Renounced: René Girard's Biblical Studies and Peacemaking*. Telford: Pandora, 2000.

Sullivan, Francis. "Church V: Notes of the Church." In *Dictionary of Fundamental Theology*, edited by René Latourelle and Rino Fisichella, 28–35. New York: Crossroad, 1994.

Taylor, Charles. *A Catholic Modernity? Charles Taylor's Marianist Award Lecture*. Edited by James L. Heft, 13–37. Oxford: Oxford University Press, 1999.

———. *The Ethics of Authenticity*. Cambridge, MA: Harvard University Press, 1991.

———. *Modern Social Imaginaries*. Durham, NC: Duke University Press, 2004.

———. *A Secular Age*. Cambridge, MA: Belknap, 2007.

———. *Sources of the Self: The Making of the Modern Identity*. Cambridge, MA: Harvard University Press, 1989.

Toulmin, Stephen. *Cosmopolis: The Hidden Agenda of Modernity*. Chicago: University of Chicago Press, 1990.

Tracy, David. *The Analogical Imagination: Christian Theology in the Culture of Pluralism*. New York: Crossroad, 1981.

Valadier, Paul. "Bouc émissaire et revelation chrétienne selon René Girard." *Études* 357 (1982): 251–60.

Viviano, Benedict. "The Gospel according to Matthew." In *The New Jerusalem Biblical Commentary*, edited by Raymond E. Brown, Joseph A. Fitzmyer, and Roland E. Murphy, 630–74. Englewood Cliffs, NJ: Prentice Hall, 1990.

Voegelin, Eric. *Modernity without Restraint*. Edited by Manfred Henningson. Vol. 5 of *The Collected Works of Eric Voegelin*. Columbia: University of Missouri Press, 2000.

Volf, Miroslav. *Exclusion and Embrace: A Theological Exploration of Identity, Otherness, and Reconciliation*. Nashville, TN: Abingdon, 1996.

Wallace, Mark I. "Postmodern Biblicism: The Challenge of René Girard for Contemporary Theology." *Modern Theology* 5, no. 4 (1989): 309–25.

Weber, Max. *The Protestant Ethic and the Spirit of Capitalism*. Translated by Talcott Parsons. New York: Scribner, 1958.

White, Hayden. "Ethnological 'Lie' and Mythical 'Truth.'" *Diacritics* 8, no. 1 (1978): 2–9.

Wikipedia contributors. "The Curse of the Billy Goat." *Wikipedia*. http://en.wikipedia.org/wiki/Curse_of_the_Billy_Goat.

———. "Regensburg Lecture." *Wikipedia*. Accessed July 25, 2012. http://en.wikipedia.org/wiki/Regensburg_lecture.

Williams, Bernard. *Truth and Truthfulness*. Princeton, NJ: Princeton University Press, 2002.

Williams, James. *Girardians: The Colloquium on Violence and Religion, 1990–2010*. Münster: Lit Verlag, 2012.

Williams, Rowan. *Wrestling with Angels: Conversations in Modern Theology*. Edited by Mike Higton. Grand Rapids, MI: Eerdmans, 2007.

Wink, Walter. *Engaging the Powers: Discernment and Resistance in a World of Domination*. Minneapolis: Fortress, 1992.

Wright, N. T. *Jesus and the Victory of God*. Minneapolis: Augsburg Fortress, 1996.

INDEX

Grant Kaplan is associate professor of theological studies at Saint Louis University.

CPSIA information can be obtained
at www.ICGtesting.com
Printed in the USA
LVOW12*0802170816

500490LV00004B/5/P